CLINICAL PRACTICE GUIDELINES WE CAN TRUST

Committee on Standards for Developing
Trustworthy Clinical Practice Guidelines

Board on Health Care Services

Robin Graham, Michelle Mancher, Dianne Miller Wolman,
Sheldon Greenfield, and Earl Steinberg, *Editors*

INSTITUTE OF MEDICINE
OF THE NATIONAL ACADEMIES

THE NATIONAL ACADEMIES PRESS
Washington, D.C.
www.nap.edu

THE NATIONAL ACADEMIES PRESS 500 Fifth Street, N.W. Washington, DC 20001

NOTICE: The project that is the subject of this report was approved by the Governing Board of the National Research Council, whose members are drawn from the councils of the National Academy of Sciences, the National Academy of Engineering, and the Institute of Medicine. The members of the committee responsible for the report were chosen for their special competences and with regard for appropriate balance.

This study was supported by Contract No. HHSP23320042509XI between the National Academy of Sciences and the Department of Health and Human Services. Any opinions, findings, conclusions, or recommendations expressed in this publication are those of the author(s) and do not necessarily reflect the view of the organizations or agencies that provided support for this project.

Library of Congress Cataloging-in-Publication Data

Institute of Medicine (U.S.). Committee on Standards for Developing Trustworthy Clinical Practice Guidelines.
  Clinical practice guidelines we can trust / Committee on Standards for Developing Trustworthy Clinical Practice Guidelines, Board on Health Care Services, Institute of Medicine of the National Academies ; Robin Graham ... [et al.], editors.
    p. ; cm.
  Includes bibliographical references.
  ISBN 978-0-309-16422-1 (pbk.) — ISBN 978-0-309-16423-8 (pdf)
  1. Medicine—Practice—Standards—United States. 2. Total quality management—United States. I. Graham, Robin, 1952- II. Title.
  [DNLM: 1. Practice Guidelines as Topic—standards—United States. 2. Total Quality Management—standards—United States. W 84.4 AA1]
  R728.I47 2011
  610.68—dc23
                            2011017454

Additional copies of this report are available from the National Academies Press, 500 Fifth Street, N.W., Lockbox 285, Washington, DC 20055; (800) 624-6242 or (202) 334-3313 (in the Washington metropolitan area); Internet, http://www.nap.edu.

For more information about the Institute of Medicine, visit the IOM home page at: **www. iom.edu.**

The serpent has been a symbol of long life, healing, and knowledge among almost all cultures and religions since the beginning of recorded history. The serpent adopted as a logotype by the Institute of Medicine is a relief carving from ancient Greece, now held by the Staatliche Museen in Berlin.

Cover credit: Photograph by Mai Le.

Suggested citation: IOM (Institute of Medicine). 2011. *Clinical Practice Guidelines We Can Trust*. Washington, DC: The National Academies Press.

"Knowing is not enough; we must apply.
Willing is not enough; we must do."
—Goethe

INSTITUTE OF MEDICINE
OF THE NATIONAL ACADEMIES

Advising the Nation. Improving Health.

THE NATIONAL ACADEMIES
Advisers to the Nation on Science, Engineering, and Medicine

The **National Academy of Sciences** is a private, nonprofit, self-perpetuating society of distinguished scholars engaged in scientific and engineering research, dedicated to the furtherance of science and technology and to their use for the general welfare. Upon the authority of the charter granted to it by the Congress in 1863, the Academy has a mandate that requires it to advise the federal government on scientific and technical matters. Dr. Ralph J. Cicerone is president of the National Academy of Sciences.

The **National Academy of Engineering** was established in 1964, under the charter of the National Academy of Sciences, as a parallel organization of outstanding engineers. It is autonomous in its administration and in the selection of its members, sharing with the National Academy of Sciences the responsibility for advising the federal government. The National Academy of Engineering also sponsors engineering programs aimed at meeting national needs, encourages education and research, and recognizes the superior achievements of engineers. Dr. Charles M. Vest is president of the National Academy of Engineering.

The **Institute of Medicine** was established in 1970 by the National Academy of Sciences to secure the services of eminent members of appropriate professions in the examination of policy matters pertaining to the health of the public. The Institute acts under the responsibility given to the National Academy of Sciences by its congressional charter to be an adviser to the federal government and, upon its own initiative, to identify issues of medical care, research, and education. Dr. Harvey V. Fineberg is president of the Institute of Medicine.

The **National Research Council** was organized by the National Academy of Sciences in 1916 to associate the broad community of science and technology with the Academy's purposes of furthering knowledge and advising the federal government. Functioning in accordance with general policies determined by the Academy, the Council has become the principal operating agency of both the National Academy of Sciences and the National Academy of Engineering in providing services to the government, the public, and the scientific and engineering communities. The Council is administered jointly by both Academies and the Institute of Medicine. Dr. Ralph J. Cicerone and Dr. Charles M. Vest are chair and vice chair, respectively, of the National Research Council.

www.national-academies.org

COMMITTEE ON STANDARDS FOR DEVELOPING TRUSTWORTHY CLINICAL PRACTICE GUIDELINES

MARITA G. TITLER, Professor and Associate Dean, Office of Practice and Clinical Scholarship, University of Michigan School of Nursing, Ann Arbor, MI

Study Staff

ROBIN GRAHAM, Senior Program Officer, Study Director
DIANNE MILLER WOLMAN, Senior Program Officer (through December 2010)
MICHELLE MANCHER, Research Associate
ALLISON McFALL, Senior Program Assistant (through August 2010)
JILLIAN LAFFREY, Senior Program Assistant (starting July 2010)
ROGER HERDMAN, Director, Board on Health Care Services

Consultants

DAVID ATKINS, Director, Quality Enhancement Research Initiative, Veterans Health Administration
RONEN AVRAHAM, Thomas Shelton Maxey Professor of Law, University of Texas School of Law
JONATHAN D. DARER, Medical Director of Clinical Transformation, Innovation, Geisinger Health System
MARTIN ECCLES, Professor of Clinical Effectiveness and The William Leech Professor of Primary Care Research, Institute of Health and Society, Newcastle University
JEREMY GRIMSHAW, Director, Clinical Epidemiology Program, Ottawa Hospital Research Institute
J.B. JONES, Research Investigator I, Geisinger Center for Health
MORI KRANTZ, Associate Professor, Cardiology, University of Colorado, Denver Health Medical Center
WILLIAM SAGE, Vice Provost for Health Affairs and James R. Dougherty Chair for Faculty Excellence in Law, University of Texas–Austin
ANNE SALES, Adjunct Professor, Department of Family Medicine, Faculty of Medicine and Dentistry, University of Alberta
HOLGER SCHÜNEMANN, Chair, Department of Clinical Epidemiology & Biostatistics, McMaster University
PAUL SHEKELLE, Medical Center Director, Quality Assessment and Improvement Program, RAND Health
DEAN SITTIG, Professor, School of Biomedical Informatics, UT–Memorial Hermann Center for Healthcare Quality & Safety, University of Texas Health Science Center at Houston
LEIF SOLBERG, Director for Care Improvement Research, HealthPartners Research Foundation
STEVE WOOLF, Director, VCU Center on Human Needs, Professor of Family Medicine, Virginia Commonwealth University

Reviewers

This report has been reviewed in draft form by individuals chosen for their diverse perspectives and technical expertise, in accordance with procedures approved by the National Research Council's Report Review Committee. The purpose of this independent review is to provide candid and critical comments that will assist the institution in making its published report as sound as possible and to ensure that the report meets institutional standards for objectivity, evidence, and responsiveness to the study charge. The review comments and draft manuscript remain confidential to protect the integrity of the deliberative process. We wish to thank the following individuals for their review of this report:

JESSE A. BERLIN, Vice President, Epidemiology, Johnson & Johnson Pharmaceutical Research and Development
RICHARD BERMAN, President and CEO, LICAS
JAKO BURGERS, Senior Researcher, IQ healthcare, Radboud University, Nijmegen Medical Centre
MARJORIE FUNK, Professor, Yale School of Nursing
ALAN M. GARBER, Henry J. Kaiser, Jr. Professor and Professor of Medicine, Director, Center for Health Policy, Director, Center for Primary Care and Outcomes Research, Stanford University
MARGUERITE A. KOSTER, Practice Leader, Technology Assessment and Guidelines Unit, Kaiser Permanente Southern California

GREG PAWLSON, Executive Vice President, National Committee for Quality Assurance

DAVID RANSOHOFF, Professor of Medicine, Clinical Professor of Epidemiology, Director, Clinical Research Curriculum (K30), University of North Carolina School of Medicine

CAROL SAKALA, Director of Programs, Childbirth Connection

VINCENZA SNOW, Medical Director, Vaccines, Specialty Care Medical Affairs, Pfizer, Inc.

SHOSHANNA SOFAER, Professor, and Robert P. Luciano Chair of Health Care Policy, Baruch College, The City University of New York

MARY E. TINETTI, Department of Internal Medicine/ Geriatrics, Yale University School of Medicine

KATRIN UHLIG, Division of Nephrology, Tufts Medical Center

JAMES WEINSTEIN, Director, The Dartmouth Institute for Health Policy and Clinical Practice; President, The Dartmouth-Hitchcock Clinic; Peggy Y. Thomson Professor in the Evaluative Clinical Sciences

Although the reviewers listed above have provided many constructive comments and suggestions, they were not asked to endorse the conclusions or recommendations nor did they see the final draft of the report before its release. The review of this report was overseen by **ENRIQUETA C. BOND** of the Burroughs Wellcome Fund, and **MARK R. CULLEN** of Stanford University. Appointed by the National Research Council and the Institute of Medicine, they were responsible for making certain that an independent examination of this report was carried out in accordance with institutional procedures and that all review comments were carefully considered. Responsibility for the final content of this report rests entirely with the authoring committee and the institution.

Foreword

Many factors enter into healthcare decisions. What alternatives are available? What does the evidence suggest about their potential benefits and harms? How firm is the evidence? Is there reason to adjust expectations based on a particular patient's age, gender, race, comorbidities, or other attributes? How might different patient preferences affect the best choice for a particular patient? Are there any social, economic, or other practical considerations that could affect the results of a particular care option?

Clinical Practice Guidelines (CPGs) are intended to provide a systematic aid to making such complex medical decisions. When rigorously developed using a transparent process that combines scientific evidence, clinician experiential knowledge, and patient values, CPGs have the potential to improve many clinician and patient healthcare decisions, and enhance healthcare quality and outcomes.

The present state of CPG development has yet to fully meet this promise. At the request of the U.S. Congress, the Institute of Medicine (IOM) undertook this study to develop a set of standards for developing rigorous, trustworthy clinical practice guidelines. The proposed standards cover a number of elements essential to developing sound practice guidelines, including transparency; conflict of interest; guideline development group composition; CPG–SR intersection; establishing evidence foundations for and strength of recommendations; articulation of recommendations; external review; and updating. This report and the eight proposed standards it contains are intended to reinforce the work of numerous researchers, developers and users of guidelines. This report clarifies where evidence and expert consensus buttress best CPG development practices, and where there is still much to learn. We hope and expect these standards to be pilot-tested, assessed for reliability and validity, evaluated for effectiveness, and to evolve as science and experience dictate.

I want to thank the excellent committee who conducted this work, ably led by Sheldon Greenfield, chair, and Earl Steinberg, vice chair. The committee was assisted by dedicated IOM staff led by Robin Graham. A companion report will set out standards for conducting systematic reviews of comparative effectiveness research. I hope that these reports together will advance the state of the art of systematic review and clinical practice guideline development, and contribute to a more transparent, scientifically rigorous, and patient-centered healthcare system in the United States.

Harvey V. Fineberg, M.D., Ph.D.
President, Institute of Medicine
February 2011

Preface

In the early 1990s, the Institute of Medicine (IOM) issued several reports on clinical practice guidelines (CPGs). In the ensuing years, CPGs and guideline development groups have proliferated enormously to the point that the Agency for Healthcare Research and Quality's National Guideline Clearinghouse contains nearly 2,700 CPGs. Parallel growth in CPGs has occurred in other countries; the Guidelines International Network's database currently lists more than 3,700 CPGs.

Although the numbers of CPGs and CPG developers have increased substantially, our understanding of the impact of CPGs on clinical practice and patient outcomes is limited. However, research has shown that CPGs have the potential to reduce inappropriate practice variation, enhance translation of research into practice, and improve healthcare quality and safety. CPGs also have had an important influence on development of physician and hospital performance measures. The data gathered from use of such measures have provided consumers with information on the quality of different healthcare providers and, in some instances, provided physicians and hospitals with an economic incentive to improve quality of care.

At the same time, there has been considerable concern expressed by physicians, consumer groups, and other stakeholders about the quality of the processes supporting development of CPGs, and the resulting questionable validity of many CPGs and CPG-based clinical performance measures. Specifically, this concern extends from limitations in the scientific evidence base on which CPGs rely; a lack of transparency of development groups' methodologies; conflict of interest among guideline development group members and funders; and questions regarding how to reconcile conflicting guidelines. In light of these challenges, and in response to the growing demand for insight into the quality of care being delivered in conjunction with rising healthcare costs and the strong indications of the need to improve clinical decision making and healthcare quality, a provision was included in the *Medicare Improvements for Patients and Providers Act of 2008*. It directed the IOM to form two separate, but related, committees to develop standards for systematic reviews (SRs) of comparative effectiveness research and for CPGs. If standards for development of valid SRs and CPGs were available, then clinicians and the public should have greater trust in standards-based CPGs and clinical performance measures founded on them. Standards for development of trustworthy CPGs additionally could foster the easier translation of guidelines into electronic forms of clinical decision support.

When the CPG committee was formed, we regarded the charge as more or less updating the state of the art based on accumulated experience and advances in thinking. As we delved into our work, however, we recognized that the rapid growth of CPG development efforts had resulted in substantial variation in CPG development processes. If CPGs were to have their intended impacts, there was a pressing need for standards regarding many dimensions of guideline development, including the potential for conflict of interest; the importance of transparency of the guideline development process; the appropriate type and level of patient and public input into the CPG development process; the need for clarity regarding the reasoning supporting each CPG recommendation; the approaches used to rate the quality of evidence underlying and strength of each CPG recommendation; the need to ensure that CPGs take account of patients with coexisting conditions; and the relationship between individuals who develop a guideline and those who perform SRs on topics relevant to the CPG. The committee found no existing set of standards that addressed all of the above elements or offered prospective guidance for developing high-quality, trustworthy CPGs. Thus, the committee proposes its own standards.

The diversity of talents and experiences of the committee members made our task more complicated and challenging than we had anticipated, but ultimately resulted in a highly thoughtful, rich report. Academicians from a variety of disciplines, experts from various types of stakeholder entities, and a diverse array of individuals involved in guideline development and implementation participated in our deliberations and contributed to this report. More than 2,500 publications were reviewed by staff and committee members; a public forum was conducted for organizations that develop and want to use CPGs; and several papers were commissioned to enable the committee to gain as much perspective as possible. The extraordinary efforts of Robin Graham, Study Director, and Michelle Mancher and Dianne Wolman made the task possible.

The two of us express our great appreciation to the committee members and staff for their commitment, effort, dedication, and wisdom. The spirited discussions during meetings and the frequent communications between meetings all contributed to this report. We hope the committee's findings and proposed standards and recommendations will foster trustworthy CPGs that increase quality of care and improve patient outcomes.

> Sheldon Greenfield, *Chair*
> Earl Phillip Steinberg, *Vice Chair*
> Committee on Standards for Developing
> Trustworthy Clinical Practice Guidelines

Acknowledgments

The committee and staff are indebted to a number of individuals and organizations for their contributions to this report. The following individuals testified before the committee during public meetings or workshops:

Workshop Participants
William G. Adams, American Academy of Pediatrics
David Atkins, Veterans Administration
Michael Bettmann, American College of Radiology
Zobeida Bonilla, Our Bodies Ourselves
Kent Bottles, Institute for Clinical Systems Improvement
Cynthia Boyd, Physician Expert in Multimorbidity, Johns Hopkins Department of Medicine
Arleen Brown, Physician Expert in Health Disparities, UCLA Internal Medicine
Vivian Coates, National Guideline Clearinghouse/ECRI Institute
Joyce Dubow, AARP
Laura Fochtmann, American Psychiatric Association
Ted Ganiats, American Academy of Family Physicians
Alice Jacobs, American College of Cardiology and American Heart Association
Louis B. Jacques, Centers for Medicare & Medicaid Services
Richard Kahn, Former Chief Scientific and Medical Officer of the American Diabetes Association

Karen Kelly-Thomas, National Association of Pediatric Nurse
     Practitioners
Marguerite Koster, Kaiser Permanente Southern California
Sandra Zelman Lewis, American College of Chest Physicians
Joan McClure, National Comprehensive Cancer Network
Elizabeth Mort, Quality and Safety, Massachusetts General
     Hospital, Massachusetts General Physicians Organization
Jim Schibanoff, Milliman Care Guidelines
Nita L. Siebel, National Cancer Institute
Denise Simons-Morton, National Heart, Lung, and Blood Institute
Vincenza Snow, American College of Physicians
Katrin Uhlig, Tufts Medical Center, Boston

Public Forum Testifiers
Ethan Basch, American Society of Clinical Oncology
Christopher Bever, American Academy of Neurology
Terrie Cowley, The TMJ Association
Steven Findlay, Consumers Union
Merrill Goozner, Health Tech Review/GoozNews.com
David Paul Harries, International Spine Intervention Society
Belinda Ireland, BJC HealthCare
Norman Kahn, Council of Medical Specialty Societies
Lisa Mojer-Torres, Chair, Citizens' Advisory Council for the
     Division of Addiction Services, State of New Jersey
Katherine Nordal, American Psychological Association
Jennifer Padberg, Infectious Diseases Society of America (IDSA)
William Rich, American Academy of Ophthalmology
Richard Rosenfeld, American Academy of Otolaryngology–Head
     and Neck Surgery
Kathleen Sazama, Society for the Advancement of Blood
     Management (SABM)
Aryeh Shander, Society for the Advancement of Blood
     Management (SABM)
Christopher Wolfkiel, American College of Occupational and
     Environmental Medicine (ACOEM)
Diana Zuckerman, National Research Center for Women & Families

We also extend special thanks to the following individuals who
were essential sources of information, generously giving their time
and knowledge to further the committee's efforts:

Josh Adler, Vice President, Business Development, Archimedes, Inc.

Ned Calogne, Chief Medical Officer, Colorado Department of Public Health and Environment

Paul Chrisp, Associate Director, Accreditation, NHS Evidence, NICE

David Eddy, Founder, Archimedes, Inc.

Jeremy Grimshaw, Director, Clinical Epidemiology Program, Ottawa Hospital Research Institute

Richard Grol, Chair, Department of Quality of Care, Radboud University Nijmegen; Director, Centre for Quality of Care Research (WOK)

Russell Harris, Professor of Medicine, Adjunct Professor of Epidemiology, Division of General Medicine, University of North Carolina at Chapel Hill

Greg Pawlson, Executive Vice President, NCQA

David Ransohoff, Professor of Medicine, Clinical Professor of Epidemiology, Director, Clinical Research Curriculum, University of North Carolina School of Medicine

Holger Schünemann, Chair, Department of Clinical Epidemiology & Biostatistics, McMaster University

Funding for this study was provided by the Agency for Healthcare Research and Quality (AHRQ). The committee appreciates the opportunity and support extended by AHRQ for the development of this report.

Finally, many within the IOM were helpful to the study staff. We especially would like to thank Jillian Laffrey, a new member of our staff, for her great ingenuity and dedication, and the staff of the Systematic Reviews report for their insight and cooperation: Lea Binder, Jill Eden, Mai Le, and Laura Levit. Additionally, the staff would like to thank Clyde Behney, Greta Gorman, Cheryl Levey, William McLeod, Abbey Meltzer, Vilija Teel, and Lauren Tobias.

Contents

APPENDIXES

Boxes, Figures, and Tables

Summary

Clinicians can no longer stay abreast of the rapidly expanding knowledge bases related to health. The number of randomized controlled trials published in MEDLINE (a medical literature database) grew from 5,000 per year in 1978–1985 to 25,000 per year in 1994–2001. Furthermore, contentions that much of the literature may be biased and not applicable to important subsets of target populations have caused its quality to be suspect. Overall, clinicians increasingly are barraged with a vast volume of evidence of uncertain value. Hence, critically appraised and synthesized scientific evidence has become fundamental to clinical practice. At the same time, and particularly under conditions of uncertainty regarding optimal decisions, clinician experiential knowledge and skill (the "art of medicine") and patient values and preferences remain essential contributors to quality healthcare practice, in a complex interplay with science.

Clinical practice guidelines (CPGs) embody and support the interrelationships among these critical contributors to clinical decision making. Rather than dictating a one-size-fits-all approach to patient care, CPGs are able to enhance clinician and patient decision making by clearly describing and appraising the scientific evidence and reasoning (the likely benefits and harms) behind clinical recommendations, making them relevant to the individual patient encounter.

Although it remains important for CPGs to be evaluated fully for their effectiveness in improving health, when rigorously developed, they have the power to translate the complexity of scientific research findings into recommendations for clinical practice and potentially enhance healthcare quality and outcomes. However, the current state of CPG development has yet to meet this potential.

CPG DEVELOPMENT CHALLENGES

Clinical practice guidelines are ubiquitous in our healthcare system. The Guidelines International Network database currently lists more than 3,700 guidelines from 39 countries. Its U.S. counterpart, the National Guideline Clearinghouse (NGC), accepted 722 guidelines to its database in 2008 alone, so that its total collection is nearly 2,700. CPG developers and users are characterized by varied organizations such as clinical specialty societies, disease advocacy groups, federal and local agencies, health plans, and commercial companies. However, CPGs suffer from shortcomings in the guideline development process, often compounding limitations inherent in their scientific evidentiary bases. Certain factors commonly undermine the quality and trustworthiness of CPGs. These include variable quality of individual scientific studies; limitations in systematic reviews (SRs) upon which CPGs are based; lack of transparency of development groups' methodologies (particularly with respect to evidence quality and strength of recommendation appraisals); failure to convene multi-stakeholder, multi-disciplinary guideline development groups, and corresponding non-reconciliation of conflicting guidelines; unmanaged conflicts of interest (COI); and overall failure to use rigorous methodologies in CPG development. Furthermore, evidence supporting clinical decision making and CPG development relevant to subpopulations, such as patients with comorbidities, the socially and economically disadvantaged, and those with rare conditions, is usually absent.

More generally, the quality of CPG development processes and guideline developer adherence to quality standards have remained unsatisfactory and unreliable for decades. Non-standardized development results in substantial variation in clinical recommendations. At the same time, CPGs produced within a structured environment, in which a systematic procedure or "Guidelines for Guidelines" are available to direct production are more likely to be of higher quality. Furthermore, documentation of guideline development is enhanced by developer use of appraisal instruments or tools for systematically assessing and reporting the quality of guideline development processes. While uniformly endorsed standards for clinical practice guidelines development do not yet exist, there appears to be widespread agreement regarding elements basic to quality CPG development.

The concept that quality standards should inform CPG development is a pervasive concern globally, underscored by increasing calls for international standards to hasten rigorous CPG development and appraisal. Although a number and variety of guideline development appraisal tools (e.g., The Appraisal of Guidelines for Research and Evaluation [AGREE] Tool), which point to standards, are available, they inadequately reflect the full range of quality CPG development. They commonly focus on development process and form, with only a small number attending to the quality of evidence and the strength of recommendations. Furthermore, COI, the role of judgment in the derivation of recommendations, prioritization of the recommendations, development group composition, and how to assure patient-centeredness all lack sufficient attention in current standards for CPG development. These appraisal tools also are not designed for prospective application to guideline development. There are no agreed-on standards for prospective enhancement of high-quality, trustworthy clinical practice guidelines.

COMMITTEE CHARGE

In 2008, the Institute of Medicine (IOM) report *Knowing What Works in Health Care* recommended that the U.S. Secretary of Health and Human Services create a public–private program to develop (or endorse) and promote a common set of standards addressing the structure, process, reporting, and final products of systematic reviews of comparative effectiveness research and evidence-based clinical practice guidelines. Congress, through the *Medicare Improvements for Patients and Providers Act of 2008*, subsequently called on the Secretary to contract with the IOM, through the Agency for Healthcare Research and Quality (AHRQ), to undertake two studies: (1) to "identify the methodological standard for conducting systematic reviews of clinical effectiveness research on health and health care in order to ensure that organizations conducting such reviews have information on methods that are objective, scientifically valid, and consistent," and (2) to focus on "the best methods used in developing clinical practice guidelines in order to ensure that organizations developing such guidelines have information on approaches that are objective, scientifically valid, and consistent."

The IOM formed two committees, the Committee on Standards for Systematic Reviews of Comparative Effectiveness Research and the Committee on Standards for Developing Trustworthy Clinical

Practice Guidelines, to meet the above requests. The two committees worked independently, but in coordination with each other, because the topics were related. While the SR committee attended exclusively to methods for SR development, from formulation of the research question to derivation of the final report, the CPG committee worked from the premise that SRs reflecting the methodological standard, as defined by the SR committee, are instrumental to a trustworthy guideline development process.

The CPG committee defined "standard" as a process, action, or procedure for developing CPGs that is deemed essential to producing scientifically valid, transparent, and reproducible results. The committee examined existing standards for guidelines development, assessing whether any would ensure development of trustworthy clinical practice guidelines. Special attention was given to standards incorporating systems for appraising quality of evidence and strength of recommendations. The committee also considered methods for modifying CPGs for patients with multiple conditions; ways to reduce the number of overlapping guidelines and harmonize CPGs on the same topic; strategies to promote and evaluate adoption of development standards and trustworthy CPGs; means to distinguish trustworthy CPGs; and procedures for identifying guideline recommendations potentially appropriate for measuring the quality of healthcare systems or clinicians.

CLINICAL PRACTICE GUIDELINES: A NEW DEFINITION

The literature assessing the best methods for guideline development has evolved dramatically in the 20 years since the IOM's first report on the subject, *Clinical Practice Guidelines: Directions for a New Program*, which defined CPGs as "systematically developed statements to assist practitioner and patient decisions about appropriate health care for specific clinical circumstances." The committee saw the need to update this definition, in accordance with the AHRQ contract, and to better reflect current consensus on what constitutes a CPG, including aspects of guideline development that the committee believes are defining characteristics. The new definition is as follows: **Clinical practice guidelines are statements that include recommendations intended to optimize patient care that are informed by a systematic review of evidence and an assessment of the benefits and harms of alternative care options.**

To be *trustworthy*, guidelines should

- be based on a systematic review of the existing evidence;
- be developed by a knowledgeable, multidisciplinary panel of experts and representatives from key affected groups;
- consider important patient subgroups and patient preferences, as appropriate;
- be based on an explicit and transparent process that minimizes distortions, biases, and conflicts of interest;
- provide a clear explanation of the logical relationships between alternative care options and health outcomes, and provide ratings of both the quality of evidence and the strength of the recommendations; and
- be reconsidered and revised as appropriate when important new evidence warrants modifications of recommendations.

The new definition provides a clear distinction between the term "CPG" and other forms of clinical guidance derived from widely disparate development processes (e.g., consensus statements, expert advice, and appropriate use criteria). Furthermore, it underscores systematic review and both benefits and harms assessment as essential characteristics of CPGs. Although the committee recognizes that other forms of clinical guidance may have value, addressing those other forms was beyond the scope of this report. Furthermore, the committee is aware that, for many clinical domains, high-quality evidence is lacking or even nonexistent. However, even given such constraints, guideline developers may still produce trustworthy CPGs if their development reflects those committee standards detailed below.

STANDARDS FOR TRUSTWORTHY CLINICAL PRACTICE GUIDELINES

As enumerated below, the committee's proposed standards reflect the latest literature, expert consensus, and public comment, and the committee hopes they represent an important advance in the newest and best practice standards for CPG development. The committee expects its standards to be assessed for reliability and validity (including applicability), and to evolve as the science and experience demand. The committee has given increased attention to aspects of COI, such as details of guideline development group exclusions; aspects of guideline group composition, including training of patient and consumer representatives in evidence appraisal; the specific nature of working relationships between systematic review teams and CPG developers; critical steps in establishing evidence foundations for clinical recommendations and rating recom-

mendations' strength; external review of the CPG, including specified mechanisms for ensuring public stakeholder comment; and
elements essential to CPG updating, including ongoing monitoring
and review of the CPG-relevant scientific literature and factors indi-
cating the need for updates. The eight standards extend across the
development process from conception to completion to revision.
The standards should provide sufficient flexibility to be applicable
to all guideline development groups (whether evidence in a particular clinical area is lacking or abundant), unlike many development
methodologies, which are specific to a particular guideline development entity and clinical problem. The committee's eight proposed
standards follow.

STANDARDS FOR DEVELOPING TRUSTWORTHY CLINICAL PRACTICE GUIDELINES (CPGS)

1. **Establishing Transparency**
   1.1 **The processes by which a CPG is developed and funded
      should be detailed explicitly and publicly accessible.**
2. **Management of Conflict of Interest (COI)**
   2.1 **Prior to selection of the guideline development group
      (GDG), individuals being considered for membership
      should declare all interests and activities potentially re-
      sulting in COI with development group activity, by writ-
      ten disclosure to those convening the GDG:**
      - **Disclosure should reflect all current and planned
        commercial (including services from which a clini-
        cian derives a substantial proportion of income), non-
        commercial, intellectual, institutional, and patient–
        public activities pertinent to the potential scope of
        the CPG.**
   2.2 **Disclosure of COIs within GDG:**
      - **All COI of each GDG member should be reported and
        discussed by the prospective development group prior
        to the onset of his or her work.**
      - **Each panel member should explain how his or her
        COI could influence the CPG development process or
        specific recommendations.**
   2.3 **Divestment**
      - **Members of the GDG should divest themselves of
        financial investments they or their family members
        have in, and not participate in marketing activities or
        advisory boards of, entities whose interests could be
        affected by CPG recommendations.**

2.4 Exclusions
- Whenever possible GDG members should not have COI.
- In some circumstances, a GDG may not be able to perform its work without members who have COIs, such as relevant clinical specialists who receive a substantial portion of their incomes from services pertinent to the CPG.
- Members with COIs should represent not more than a minority of the GDG.
- The chair or cochairs should not be a person(s) with COI.
- Funders should have no role in CPG development.

3. Guideline Development Group Composition
   3.1 The GDG should be multidisciplinary and balanced, comprising a variety of methodological experts and clinicians, and populations expected to be affected by the CPG.
   3.2 Patient and public involvement should be facilitated by including (at least at the time of clinical question formulation and draft CPG review) a current or former patient, and a patient advocate or patient/consumer organization representative in the GDG.
   3.3 Strategies to increase effective participation of patient and consumer representatives, including training in appraisal of evidence, should be adopted by GDGs.

4. Clinical Practice Guideline–Systematic Review Intersection
   4.1 Clinical practice guideline developers should use systematic reviews that meet standards set by the Institute of Medicine's Committee on Standards for Systematic Reviews of Comparative Effectiveness Research.
   4.2 When systematic reviews are conducted specifically to inform particular guidelines, the GDG and systematic review team should interact regarding the scope, approach, and output of both processes.

5. Establishing Evidence Foundations for and Rating Strength of Recommendations
   5.1 For each recommendation, the following should be provided:
   - An explanation of the reasoning underlying the recommendation, including
     o a clear description of potential benefits and harms;
     o a summary of relevant available evidence (and evidentiary gaps), description of the quality (including applicability), quantity (including com-

pleteness), and consistency of the aggregate available evidence;

o   an explanation of the part played by values, opinion, theory, and clinical experience in deriving the recommendation.
- A rating of the level of confidence in (certainty regarding) the evidence underpinning the recommendation
- A rating of the strength of the recommendation in light of the preceding bullets
- A description and explanation of any differences of opinion regarding the recommendation

6. Articulation of Recommendations

6.1 Recommendations should be articulated in a standardized form detailing precisely what the recommended action is, and under what circumstances it should be performed.

6.2 Strong recommendations should be worded so that compliance with the recommendation(s) can be evaluated.

7. External Review

7.1 External reviewers should comprise a full spectrum of relevant stakeholders, including scientific and clinical experts, organizations (e.g., health care, specialty societies), agencies (e.g., federal government), patients, and representatives of the public.

7.2 The authorship of external reviews submitted by individuals and/or organizations should be kept confidential unless that protection has been waived by the reviewer(s).

7.3 The GDG should consider all external reviewer comments and keep a written record of the rationale for modifying or not modifying a CPG in response to reviewers' comments.

7.4 A draft of the CPG at the external review stage or immediately following it (i.e., prior to the final draft) should be made available to the general public for comment. Reasonable notice of impending publication should be provided to interested public stakeholders.

8. Updating

8.1 The CPG publication date, date of pertinent systematic evidence review, and proposed date for future CPG review should be documented in the CPG.

8.2 Literature should be monitored regularly following CPG publication to identify the emergence of new, potentially relevant evidence and to evaluate the continued validity of the CPG.

8.3 CPGs should be updated when new evidence suggests the need for modification of clinically important recommendations. For example, a CPG should be updated if new evidence shows that a recommended intervention causes previously unknown substantial harm; that a new intervention is significantly superior to a previously recommended intervention from an efficacy or harms perspective; or that a recommendation can be applied to new populations.

The committee derived several recommendations directly relevant to the ultimate effectiveness of the eight standards in increasing the quality and trustworthiness of CPGs and enhancing healthcare quality and patient outcomes.

RECOMMENDATIONS FOR IDENTIFYING AND EVALUATING TRUSTWORTHY CLINICAL PRACTICE GUIDELINES

The committee views all eight proposed standards as essential elements in the development of trustworthy guidelines. Thus, the committee recommends the following:

To be trustworthy, a clinical practice guideline should comply with proposed standards 1–8.

Optimally, CPG developers should adhere to these proposed standards and CPG users should adopt CPGs compliant with these proposed standards.

Some guideline developers will readily adapt their development process to embrace these eight standards; however, not all developers will be able to do so, and a process of evolutionary adoption over time may be more practical. Although certain standards, such as those directed to patient and public involvement in the CPG development process and external review, may appear particularly resource intensive, strategies to increase effective public participation can minimize this burden.

The committee understands that the uniqueness of guideline development contexts may seemingly preclude certain developers from fully adhering to the standards the committee has proposed. For example, certain clinical areas (e.g., rare malignant tumors) are characterized by an exceptional dearth of scientific literature and an urgent need to deliver patient care. The committee recognizes that developers in this instance may conclude they are unable to comply with Standard 4: "Clinical practice guideline developers should use systematic reviews that meet standards set by the IOM's Committee on Standards for Systematic Reviews of Comparative Effectiveness Research." However, SRs that conclude there are no high-quality randomized controlled trials or observational studies on a particular clinical question would still fulfill Standard 4. In all cases, whether evidence is limited or abundant, guideline development groups should comply with the complementary Standard 5: "Establishing evidence foundations for and rating strength of recommendations" by providing a summary of relevant available evidence (and evidentiary gaps), descriptions of the quality (including applicability), quantity (including completeness), and consistency of the aggregate available evidence; an explanation of the part played by values, opinion, theory, or clinical experience in deriving recommendations; a judgment regarding the level of confidence in (certainty regarding) the evidence underpinning the recommendations; and a rating of the strength of recommendations.

For certain clinical areas, such as rare diseases, there may be no disease group or clinical specialty society with resources to develop trustworthy CPGs. In these cases, outside funding assistance could spur the development of needed guidelines. The committee urges organizations desiring to produce such guidelines to coordinate their efforts and pool resources with related organizations. This could also strengthen their efforts to seek support from foundations, government agencies, and other sources without conflict. The Department of Health and Human Services (HHS) should promote the identification of best practices in CPG development, guided by the committee's proposed standards, and should assist in training individuals in specific technical skills needed in the CPG process, particularly patient and consumer representatives.

Furthermore, to encourage the promulgation and adoption of standards, the committee recommends HHS create a mechanism to identify trustworthy guidelines. Such identification will serve three purposes, as follows:

- Promote wider adoption of the IOM standards by developers because there will be an advantage attached to CPGs publicly identified as trustworthy.
- Provide CPG users with an easy guide to identify trustworthy ones.
- Promote adoption of trustworthy CPGs.

The committee recommends

The Secretary of HHS should establish a public–private mechanism to examine, at the request of developer organizations, the procedures they use to produce their clinical practice guidelines and to certify whether these organizations' CPG development procedures comply with standards for trustworthy CPGs.

Although AHRQ is not directly involved in CPG development, it does play a vital role in the dissemination and evaluation of guidelines and creation of guideline development methodologies. The NGC is a highly useful guideline dissemination tool. AHRQ should continue to operate this service, and expand its capacities to provide syntheses of recommendations by clinical topic and conduct research on best guideline development practices. As a central repository for all CPGs, the committee does not believe the NGC should be restricted to listing only those CPGs identified as trustworthy. However, the NGC's contribution may be of questionable value when listing guidelines providing too little information for an informed reader to judge quality and trustworthiness. To be a constructive resource, the NGC should eliminate CPGs for which trustworthiness cannot be determined, and identify the trustworthiness of those retained. Further, the committee recommends that AHRQ pilot-test and assess the reliability and validity of the IOM's proposed standards, and evaluate their effects on healthcare quality and patient outcomes. The committee expects its standards to evolve as science and experience regarding CPG development demand.

The committee recommends

The Agency for Healthcare Research and Quality (AHRQ) should do the following:

- **Require the National Guideline Clearinghouse (NGC) to provide a clear indication of the extent to which clinical practice guidelines (CPGs) submitted to it adhere to standards for trustworthiness.**
- **Conduct research on the causes of inconsistent CPGs, and strategies to encourage their harmonization.**
- **Assess the strengths and weaknesses of proposed IOM standards by pilot-test; estimate the validity and reliability of proposed standards; evaluate the effectiveness of interventions to encourage standards' implementation; and**

evaluate the effects of standards on CPG development, healthcare quality, and patient outcomes.

RECOMMENDATIONS FOR INDIVIDUAL AND ORGANIZATIONAL INTERVENTIONS FOR CPG IMPLEMENTATION

Promoting uptake and use of CPGs at the point of care represents a final translation hurdle to move scientific findings into practice. An important guiding principle for promoting adoption of CPGs is that attributes of the CPG (e.g., ease of use, strength of the evidence) as perceived by users and stakeholders are neither stable features nor sure determinants of adoption. Rather it is the interaction among characteristics of the CPG (e.g., specificity, clarity), the intended users (physicians, nurses, pharmacists), and a particular context of practice (e.g., inpatient, ambulatory, long-term care) that determines rate and extent of adoption. Active dissemination and adoption strategies used by implementers to promote use of trustworthy CPGs include academic detailing; audit and feedback and public reporting of performance; opinion leaders; clinical reminders and quick reference guides; payment mechanisms; and shared decision-making aides.

Organizations and health systems can also provide necessary resources, workflow modifications, and infrastructures for CPG implementation by all relevant users, and engage clinician stakeholders in the implementation process. Fundamentally, for trustworthy guidelines to affect quality of care and patient outcomes they must be implemented; hence, the committee offers the following recommendation:

Effective multifaceted implementation strategies targeting all relevant populations affected by CPGs, should be employed by implementers to promote adherence to trustworthy CPGs.

Increased adoption of electronic health records and computer-aided clinical decision support (CDS) will offer unique opportunities to rapidly move clinical knowledge from the scientific literature to the patient encounter. To achieve this goal, guideline developers should structure CPGs to facilitate ready implementation of electronic clinical decision support by health systems (e.g., clinical practices, payers, delivery systems, hospitals). Furthermore, CPG developers should specify definitive and important gaps in scientific evidence for practice recommendations, including those relevant to the target population, to facilitate understanding of potential limitations of clinical decision support. Formal organizational relationships among CPG developers, implementers, and CDS designers are encouraged to align requirements for CDS with the needs and standards of CPG developers. The committee recommends guideline developers and implementers take the following actions to advance this aim:

Guideline developers should structure the format, vocabulary, and content of CPGs (e.g., specific statements of evidence, the target population) to facilitate ready implementation of computer-aided CDS by end-users.

CPG developers, CPG implementers, and CDS designers should collaborate in an effort to align their needs with one another.

CONCLUSION

Clinical decisions are made under uncertainty. Yet, as medical, biomedical, and health services research advance, translation of scientific evidence increasingly reduces uncertainty in clinical practice. However, requisite to this promise are clinician and patient access to trustworthy clinical practice guidelines informed by high-quality evidence and a guideline development process reflective of best practices. The committee believes the eight standards proposed herein, when embraced by guideline developers, have the capacity to increase quality and trustworthiness of CPGs and ultimately enhance healthcare quality and patient outcomes.

1

Introduction

Abstract: This chapter describes the legislative mandate and scope of work for the current study, as well as previous Institute of Medicine reports on Clinical Practice Guideline (CPG) development and related topics. It also briefly touches on the current state of CPGs and common challenges faced by many CPG developers and users, which will be further explored in Chapters 2 and 3. An updated definition of CPG is provided along with an argument to differentiate high-quality, evidence-based CPGs from other forms of clinical guidance. The new definition reads: **Clinical Practice Guidelines are statements that include recommendations intended to optimize patient care that are informed by a systematic review of evidence and an assessment of the benefits and harms of alternative care options.** *Following the definition, the committee identifies essential attributes for a CPG to be considered trustworthy. Finally, the committee's methodology for deriving its eight standards for trustworthy CPGs, enumerated in Chapters 4 and 5, is described.*

Nationally and around the world, health professionals increasingly understand that health care must be based on a combination of scientific evidence, knowledge gained from clinical experience, and patient value judgments and preferences. Clinical Practice Guidelines

(CPGs) ideally reflect this understanding when they are developed via a transparent process by a group of multidisciplinary experts (including patient representatives) screened for minimal potential bias and conflicts of interest, and supported by a systematic review of the evidence. Rather than dictating a one-size-fits-all approach to patient care, CPGs should aid clinician and patient decision making by clearly describing and appraising the evidence and reasoning regarding the likely benefits and harms related to specific clinical recommendations. This chapter provides background on the history of Institute of Medicine (IOM) involvement in issues related to CPG development, a discussion of the scope of work for this study, and a new definition for trustworthy CPGs.

BUILDING ON PREVIOUS IOM STUDIES

The IOM's involvement in the clinical practice guideline arena began with the *Omnibus Budget Reconciliation Act of 1989*,[1] which created the Agency for Health Care Policy and Research (AHCPR), now known as the Agency for Healthcare Research and Quality (AHRQ), to focus on outcomes and effectiveness research. The agency was created in part due to frustrations with "ceaselessly escalating healthcare costs, wide variations in medical practice patterns, evidence that some health services are of little or no value, and claims that various kinds of financial, educational, and organizational incentives can reduce inappropriate utilization" (IOM, 1990, p. 2). A relatively small portion of the agency's budget was dedicated to creation and update of guidelines through a public–private enterprise. The agency contracted with the IOM for expert advice on launching this function, and in 1990, the IOM's Committee to Advise the Public Health Service on Clinical Practice Guidelines issued its report, *Clinical Practice Guidelines: Directions for a New Program*. In 1990, the IOM defined CPGs as "systematically developed statements to assist practitioner and patient decisions about appropriate health care for specific clinical circumstances" (IOM, 1990, p. 8). The first IOM guideline committee recommended that CPGs include the following:

- A statement about the strength of the scientific evidence and expert judgment

---

[1] *Omnibus Budget Reconciliation Act of 1989*, Public Law 101-239, 101st Cong. (December 19, 1989).

- An explanation of the rationale for any deviations from the scientific evidence
- Key stakeholders or their representatives as participants in the development process, either through membership on the development panel, formal testimony, or other forms of participation
- Consideration of implementation and evaluation issues from the beginning of the development process

In 1990, before completion of the first report to AHCPR, the IOM formed a second expert committee to assess processes of guideline development and use, and recommended an improved conceptual and practical framework for future CPGs. Its report, *Guidelines for Clinical Practice: From Development to Use*, published in 1992, expanded on the 1990 report, adopted the eight guideline attributes proposed in 1990 (Box 1-1), and stressed the importance of both CPG content and the development process in guideline credibility and utility. The study also identified four problems with guideline efforts at that time:

1. Multiple organizations developing guidelines was an inefficient use of resources, resulting in varying methods of development and uneven quality. Also, selection of guideline topics was not coordinated.
2. The guideline development process often lacked methodological quality controls. Guideline users and review criteria designers had no means for assessing the quality of methods and products of various developers.
3. Most guidelines failed to meet the needs of multiple stakeholders, such as quality assurance, cost control, comparison with alternative practices, and medical liability reduction. Because evidence and rationale for guidelines typically were not offered, the educational value of the guidelines was limited.
4. Finally, because only a limited evaluation of the impact of clinical practice guidelines had been conducted, their effectiveness in improving quality of care was indeterminate (IOM, 1992).

During this period, concerns regarding the selection of guideline topics by AHCPR caused Congress to direct AHCPR to report on methods for setting priorities for guideline topics. This resulted in the IOM report, *Setting Priorities for Clinical Practice Guidelines* (IOM,

BOX 1-1
Recommended Attributes of CPGs

Validity: Practice guidelines are valid if, when followed, they lead to the health and cost outcomes projected for them, with other things being equal. A prospective assessment of validity will consider the projected health outcomes and costs of alternative courses of action, the relationship between the evidence and recommendations, the substance and quality of the scientific and clinical evidence cited, and the means used to evaluate the evidence.

Reliability/Reproducibility: Practice guidelines are reliable and reproducible: (1) if—given the same evidence and methods for guidelines development—another set of experts would produce essentially the same statements; and (2) if—given the same circumstances—the guidelines are interpreted and applied consistently by practitioners or other appropriate parties. A prospective assessment of reliability may consider the results of independent external reviews and pretests of guidelines.

Clinical Applicability: Practice guidelines should be as inclusive of appropriately defined patient populations as scientific and clinical evidence and expert judgment permit, and they should explicitly state the populations to which statements apply.

Clinical Flexibility: Practice guidelines should identify the specifically known or generally expected exceptions to their recommendations.

Clarity: Practice guidelines should use unambiguous language, define terms precisely, and use logical, easy-to-follow modes of presentation.

Multidisciplinary Process: Practice guidelines should be developed by a process that includes participation by representatives of key affected groups. Participation may include serving on panels that develop guidelines, providing evidence and viewpoints to the panels, and reviewing draft guidelines.

Scheduled Review: Practice guidelines should include statements about when they should be reviewed to determine whether revisions are warranted, given new clinical evidence or changing professional consensus.

Documentation: The procedures followed in developing guidelines, the participants involved, the evidence used, the assumptions and rationales accepted, and the analytic methods employed should be meticulously documented and described.

SOURCE: IOM (1990).

1995), which recommended principles and methods for prioritizing guideline topics. Although many of that report's recommendations became moot when AHCPR discontinued its guideline development function, one conclusion of the report remains relevant: the agency should serve as a clearinghouse and disseminate guidelines developed by others.

In 2008, the current status of clinical practice guidelines was discussed in the IOM report, *Knowing What Works in Health Care: A Roadmap for the Nation* (IOM, 2008). The committee identified many of the quality problems cited by earlier committees, and in remediation of those long-standing problems, recommended a public–private "program" to create standards for guideline development and a process of documentation of adherence to standards.

Development standards that the committee identified included

- objectivity in both the development process and the conclusions, resulting from a balanced panel;
- transparency of the deliberative process in all aspects, including conflicts of interest among panelists or the sponsoring organization, the methods of data gathering and evidence assessment, and evaluation of strength of recommendations;
- efficiency and timeliness when considering clinicians' need for timely advice and minimization of duplication and resource wastage by guideline developers;
- external review by outside experts of draft guidelines and independent party oversight of developer responses to reviewer comments;
- continuous monitoring of relevant literature so that guidelines are reevaluated when important new evidence is produced and their currency is ensured; and
- reduction of overlaps and gaps through voluntary efforts to increase consensus among various organizations developing guidelines on the same topics and to address topics that need guidelines (IOM, 2008).

Furthermore, *Knowing What Works in Health Care* (IOM, 2008) and the 2009 IOM report, *Conflict of Interest in Medical Research, Education, and Practice* (IOM, 2009), address conflicts of interest specific to guideline development. That issue will be discussed thoroughly in Chapter 4.

CURRENT STATE OF CLINICAL PRACTICE GUIDELINES

The development and application of CPGs have evolved dramatically in the 20 years since the IOM first became involved in this area. Specialty societies, disease advocacy groups, the federally supported U.S. Preventive Services Task Force, health plans, commercial companies, and other organizations in the United States and across the globe have produced thousands of guidelines of widely varying quality (Coates, 2010). This current IOM study was initiated in response to concerns about the state-of-the-art of the quality of CPGs.

Many current clinical practice guidelines suffer from limitations in the scientific evidence base and shortcomings in the guideline development process (IOM, 2008; Shaneyfelt and Centor, 2009). First, the evidence base is limited by an absence or paucity of studies on relevant topics, as well as variable quality of individual scientific studies and systematic reviews of the efficacy and effectiveness of medical and surgical procedures, treatments, drugs, and devices. Consequently, CPG recommendations often rely on low quality evidence or expert opinion. For example, in a study of practice bulletins from the American College of Obstetricians and Gynecologists, just 29 percent of recommendations were supported by "good and consistent scientific evidence" (Chauhan et al., 2006, p. 94).

Furthermore, evidence for clinical decision making regarding patients with rare conditions or subpopulations, such as patients with comorbidities and the socially and economically disadvantaged, is often nonexistent or inaccurate. Consequently, many guidelines either do not address or apply to a significant number of patients (Boyd, 2010). Also, few CPGs address many significant clinical conditions and decisions; consequently, tension persists between the need for guidance in a particular clinical area and the lack of an evidence base to allow the development of high-quality guidelines (IOM, 2008).

The quality of many CPGs is further diminished by the process used to develop some CPGs, including CPG development panel formation without sufficient attention to conflicts of interest (either financial or intellectual) or to balancing bias and including all relevant topical and methodological disciplines and stakeholders; poor coordination with systematic review groups, which does not permit tailoring of reviews to the specific CPG topic; and a lack of transparency concerning the derivation of recommendations (Coates, 2010; Jacobs, 2010; Koster, 2010). GDGs may cherry pick studies that support their positions, even when high quality SRs are available. Or, different reviewers of high-quality individual studies and systematic reviews on the same topic may reach inconsistent conclusions because of conflicting interests or research methodologies (Shrier et al., 2008). Ultimately, these evidence and process deficiencies have led to a plethora of often-conflicting recommendations produced by multiple organizations, and little means for potential CPG users to evaluate CPG quality and identify the most trustworthy CPGs (Coates, 2010).

Knowledge of which guidelines are based on high-quality scientific evidence and employ desired standards of development is important for clinicians and other guideline users. *Knowing What Works in Health Care* recommended further focus on these issues (IOM, 2008). This study builds on that earlier report.

STUDY SCOPE

Study Objectives

The U.S. healthcare environment has evolved dramatically since the IOM's early guideline reports. This committee was challenged to determine how that evolution has affected and should affect the CPG development process, exploring which prior recommendations are no longer relevant, where progress has been made, and what new problems have arisen.

Legislative Mandate

The U.S. Congress, through the *Medicare Improvements for Patients and Providers Act (MIPPA) of 2008*,[2] took steps to implement two recommendations of IOM's *Knowing What Works in Health Care* (2008). It called on the Secretary of Health and Human Services (HHS) to contract with the IOM to "develop evidence-based, methodological standards for systematic reviews" (IOM, 2008, p. 108) and to develop standards for clinical practice guidelines. Specifically, Congress requested the IOM to undertake two studies: one "to identify the methodological standards for conducting systematic review of clinical effectiveness research on health and health care in order to ensure that organizations conducting such reviews have information on methods that are objective, scientifically valid, and consistent" and the other to focus on "the best methods used in developing clinical practice guidelines in order to ensure that organizations

---

[2]*Medicare Improvements for Patients and Providers Act*, Public Law 110-275, 110th Cong. (July 15, 2008).

developing such guidelines have information on approaches that are objective, scientifically valid, and consistent."[3]

Request from the Department of Health and Human Services

The Secretary of HHS, through AHRQ, contracted with the IOM in July 2009 to conduct these studies. The IOM formed two committees with expertise across a broad range of relevant domains. The committees worked independently, but in coordination, to enhance the relevance of each study to the other and to minimize duplication. The Committee on Standards for Developing Trustworthy Clinical Practice Guidelines produced the report that follows, and the Committee on Standards for Systematic Reviews of Comparative Effectiveness Research produced a companion report.

IOM Committee Charge

Given the MIPPA legislative charge to the IOM mentioned previously, the IOM formed the Committee on Standards for Developing Trustworthy Clinical Practice Guidelines to concentrate on processes for the development of unbiased, scientifically valid, and trustworthy clinical practice guidelines. The committee examined existing standards for guideline development, assessing which might be suitable for adoption or adaptation in the United States. It considered methods for modifying CPGs for patients with multiple conditions, ways to reduce the number of overlapping guidelines and harmonize CPGs on the same topic, methods to distinguish and promote adoption of quality CPGs, and procedures for identifying strong recommendations that could become the basis for measures of quality of care. Throughout the study process, the committee was mindful of the great number and variety of guideline developers and users, and systematically elicited their input.

Relation to Committee on Standards for Systematic Reviews of Comparative Effectiveness Research

High-quality, effective guidelines depend on high-quality, comparative effectiveness research and systematic reviews (SRs) of

---

[3]*Medicare Improvements for Patients and Providers Act*, Public Law 110-275, 110th Cong. (July 15, 2008).

that evidence. A systematic review is a scientific investigation that focuses on a specific question and uses explicit, preplanned scientific methods to identify, select, assess, and summarize the findings of individual, relevant studies. It may or may not include a quantitative synthesis of the results from separate studies (meta-analysis). For SRs to support development of a CPG, the SRs need to address clinical questions critical to formulation of a recommendation about a particular clinical practice in a certain circumstance. Guideline Development Groups (GDGs) and SR teams may be highly interrelated, where a GDG might conduct its own SR, or an SR member might serve on a GDG panel. However, for the purpose of dividing the two MIPPA studies, all activities related to selecting, assessing and summarizing findings of individual studies fittingly are covered by the SR report.

As a result of the substantive association of the two mandated MIPPA studies, the IOM took the unusual step of ensuring close collaboration of the two committees. In addition to two study staffs working cooperatively, the IOM created an informal Coordinating Group, consisting of the chairs, vice chairs, and another member from each committee. The Coordinating Group met in person four times during the study course and held conference calls to share insight on interrelated issues and build on the progress of both committees. In the end, however, each committee authored its own report and recommendations.

Research Methods

Essential to the IOM committee formation process is the recruitment of relevant subject–matter experts and individuals with relevant experience, as well as inclusion of a diversity of opinion and sociodemographics. These tenets are consistent with guidance found within the standard-setting literature (Norcini and Shea, 1997). Once formed, the committee complied with established standards by requiring review of the relevant published (including grey) literature, solicitation of expert advice, and public comment through the activities described below.

Literature Searches

The committee conducted an initial literature search in late 2009 of the following databases: MEDLINE, Embase, PsychInfo, Global Health, Web of Science, and several grey literature sources. Computerized literature searches were updated routinely and the table of contents alerts from more than 20 journals were monitored throughout the committee's term. Searches focused on articles with "Clinical Practice Guideline" or "Practice Guideline" in the topic heading, and any of the following terms in the title or abstract: consensus development, decision-making, development, evaluation, implementation, comorbidities, heterogeneity, policy, law, legal, implications, tool, taxonomy, reimbursement, measurement, performance, performance measures, consumer, public, grading, rating, issues, concerns, methods, quality, electronic medical record, computer decisions support system. The committee reviewed abstracts and complete texts for more than 2,500 peer-reviewed, published articles. For a complete description of the committee's literature search, see Appendix E.

Gathering Data from the Web

Data from the National Guideline Clearinghouse and the Guidelines International Network, collected from the web, formed foundations for some committee analyses and provided considerable background on the current status of guidelines. The web also contributed information on other major activities in the CPG world.

Public Forum, January 11, 2010

Sixteen individuals and organizations responded to the committee's broadly disseminated invitation to present public testimony at its second meeting. Respondents were asked to offer advice regarding the key issues the committee should address in deriving standards for clinical practice guideline development. Some speakers made statements on behalf of organizations; others made personal statements or offered expert counsel. These statements and testimonials, as well as speaker responses to committee queries, were valuable contributions to committee understanding of the CPG status quo, its limitations, and improvement options.

Workshop Panels

The committee asked representative organizations and individuals to address questions of interest across a series of public panel presentations and discussions. Panelists responded to the following questions: (1) What do you believe are the biggest challenges that clinical practice guidelines developers face today? (2) What are the biggest challenges that CPG users face? (3) What topics and/

or processes do you think the committee should consider in deriving quality standards for clinical practice guidelines? Twenty-four individuals participated and presented valuable information to the committee based on their experiences in developing and applying CPGs.

Public Comments

In addition to the January experience, members of the public communicated with the committee through its public website, staff, and direct contact with committee members. Those contributions enriched committee understanding. All submitted materials have been placed in the project's Public Access File, which is accessed through the National Academy of Sciences website.

Commissioned Papers

Staff commissioned several papers from technical experts to complement the committee's expertise across the following topics:

- "The State-of-the-Art of CPG Development and Best Practices," by Paul Shekelle, Steve Woolf, Martin Eccles, Jeremy Grimshaw, and Holger Schünemann
- "Legal and Administrative Alternatives for Enhancing CPG Quality and Adherence," by Ronen Avraham and William Sage
- "The Implementation and Evaluation of CPGs in the Present," by Anne Sales, David Atkins, Mori Krantz, and Leif Solberg
- "The Implementation and Evaluation of CPGs in an Electronic Future," by Walter Stewart, J. B. Jones, Jon Darer, and Dean F. Sittig

These papers contributed to committee discussion and the evidentiary underpinnings of its report, although the perspectives and any implicit recommendations within each are solely those of the authors.

PURPOSE AND UPDATED DEFINITION OF CLINICAL PRACTICE GUIDELINES

Clinical Practice Guidelines are statements that include recommendations intended to optimize patient care. They are informed by a systematic review of evidence and an assessment of the ben-

efits and harms of alternative care options. To be *trustworthy*, guidelines should

- be based on a systematic review of the existing evidence;
- be developed by a knowledgeable, multidisciplinary panel of experts and representatives from key affected groups;
- consider important patient subgroups and patient preferences, as appropriate;
- be based on an explicit and transparent process that minimizes distortions, biases, and conflicts of interest;
- provide a clear explanation of the logical relationships between alternative care options and health outcomes, and provide ratings of both the quality of evidence and the strength of recommendations; and
- be reconsidered and revised as appropriate when important new evidence warrants modifications of recommendations.

The new definition provides clarification of the term "CPG," which in the past was commonly used to describe clinical guidance derived from widely different development processes and statements taking various forms, including consensus statements, practice bulletins, expert advice, quality measures, and evidence-based recommendations. This study emphasizes characteristics that distinguish among methodologically rigorous, transparent, evidence-based guidelines (CPGs) and other forms of clinical guidance. Although the committee recognizes that other forms of clinical guidance may have value, addressing them was beyond the scope of this report. Furthermore, the committee is aware that for many clinical domains, there is little or no high-quality evidence; however, guideline developers may still produce trustworthy CPGs if they follow a rigorous and transparent process, as will be detailed. This study recommends standards for development of trustworthy guidelines in Chapters 4 and 5, and methods for identifying those guidelines in Chapter 7.

Trustworthy CPGs have the potential to reduce inappropriate practice variation, enhance translation of research into practice, and improve healthcare quality and safety. Patient and public involvement and trust in guideline development and their engagement in CPG implementation will enhance adoption of guidelines by all stakeholders. Optimally, CPGs may

- guide clinician and patient decision making based on evidence regarding the care outcomes that particular practices are expected to produce;

- provide a basis for measuring, evaluating, and improving provider performance and quality of care;
- support appropriate resolution of malpractice claims by considering guideline recommendations as a standard of care;
- contribute to the development of clinical decision support systems and other decision aids;
- assist in educating patients, caregivers, and the media regarding best healthcare practices; and
- aid policy makers in the allocation of healthcare resources.

Many of these activities are supported by CPGs, but they are not always informed by rigorous assessment of the science. Guidelines based on systematic literature review, consideration of the benefits and harms associated with particular recommendations, and unambiguous translation of this appraisal for clinicians and patients could enhance the above activities.

ORGANIZATION OF REPORT

Six chapters follow this introductory chapter. Chapter 2 presents background and an overview of CPGs, including a historical perspective on evidence-based medicine and the evolution of and a description of major participants in CPG development.

A critical appraisal of the current status of CPGs follows in Chapter 3, including assessment of the limitations that exist in the scientific evidence base and the CPG development process.

Chapters 4 and 5 discuss current best practices in the guideline development process and emphasize critical elements in the creation of trustworthy CPGs, including methods for systematic appraisal of the guideline development process. These chapters include proposed standards for guideline development.

Chapter 6 examines strategies for enhancing the likelihood of guideline adoption, and applying health information technology to promote guideline implementation. Additionally, it considers the legal implications of guidelines. This chapter includes recommendations for guideline implementation interventions.

Chapter 7 discusses national policy issues related to CPGs. The committee makes a recommendation for how to identify high-quality CPGs because even with quality standards, practitioners, patients, and other potential users can have difficulties recognizing which guidelines are unbiased, scientifically valid, and trustworthy. The chapter also includes recommendations concerning guideline harmonization, assessing the reliability and validity of proposed standards, and process and impact evaluation.

REFERENCES

Boyd, C. 2010. *CPGs for people with multimorbidities*. Paper presented at IOM Committee on Standards for Developing Trustworthy Clinical Practice Guidelines meeting, November 11, 2010, Washington, DC.

Chauhan, S. P., V. Berghella, M. Sanderson, E. F. Magann, and J. C. Morrison. 2006. American College of Obstetricians and Gynecologists practice bulletins: An overview. *American Journal of Obstetrics and Gynecology* 194(6):1564–1572.

Coates, V. 2010. *National Guidelines Clearinghouse NGC/ECRI Institute*. Paper presented at the IOM Committee on Standards for Developing Trustworthy Clinical Practice Guidelines meeting, January 11, 2010, Washington, DC.

IOM (Institute of Medicine). 1990. *Clinical practice guidelines: Directions for a new program*. Edited by M. J. Field and K. N. Lohr. Washington, DC: National Academy Press.

IOM. 1992. *Guidelines for clinical practice: From development to use*. Edited by M. J. Field and K. N. Lohr. Washington, DC: National Academy Press.

IOM. 1995. *Setting priorities for clinical practice guidelines*. Edited by M. J. Field. Washington, DC: National Academy Press.

IOM. 2008. *Knowing what works in health care: A roadmap for the nation*. Edited by J. Eden, B. Wheatley, B. McNeil, and H. Sox. Washington, DC: The National Academies Press.

IOM. 2009. *Conflict of interest in medical research, education, and practice*. Edited by B. Lo and M. J. Field. Washington, DC: The National Academies Press.

Jacobs, A. 2010. *American College of Cardiology and American Heart Association*. Presented at the IOM Committee on Standards for Developing Trustworthy Clinical Practice Guidelines meeting, January 11, 2010, Washington, DC.

Koster, M. A. 2010. *Technology assessment and guidelines unit: Kaiser Permanente Southern California*. Paper presented at IOM Committee on Standards for Developing Trustworthy Clinical Practice Guidelines meeting, January 11, 2010, Washington, DC.

Norcini, J. J., and J. A. Shea. 1997. The credibility and comparability of standards. *Applied Measurement in Education* 10(1):39–59.

Shaneyfelt, T. M., and R. M. Centor. 2009. Reassessment of clinical practice guidelines: Go gently into that good night. *JAMA* 301(8):868–869.

Shrier, I., J.-F. Boivin, R. Platt, R. Steele, J. Brophy, F. Carnevale, M. Eisenberg, A. Furlan, R. Kakuma, M. Macdonald, L. Pilote, and M. Rossignol. 2008. The interpretation of systematic reviews with meta-analyses: An objective or subjective process? *BMC Medical Informatics and Decision Making* 8(1):19.

2

Background and Key Stakeholders in Guidelines Development and Use

Abstract: Before specific consideration of standards for trustworthy clinical practice guidelines (CPGs), the committee examined the history of evidence-based medicine and guideline development. This chapter provides a brief review of modern applications of scientific evidence in the development of clinical care and evolution of CPGs in the United States and internationally, as well as a review of the major guideline developers and users today. The chapter is by no means an exhaustive history of guideline development or a complete list of current stakeholders; instead it aims to present the reader with a general overview of the guideline landscape.

BACKGROUND

"Clinical practice guidelines are now ubiquitous," observed Weisz and colleagues in 2007 (p. 691). The Guidelines International Network database currently lists more than 3,700 guidelines from 39 countries. Its U.S.-based counterpart, the National Guideline Clearinghouse (NGC), accepted 722 guidelines to its database in 2008 alone, bringing its total collection to nearly 2,700.[1] Furthermore, numerous other clinical guidance statements (e.g., the Centers for Disease Control and Prevention [CDC] rapid response recommen-

---

[1]Personal communication, M. Nix, 2010. Project officer for National Guideline Clearinghouse.

dations) and tools (e.g., computerized physician order entry systems) are created to aid clinical care decisions each year. As stated in Chapter 1, clinical practice guideline (CPG) development has evolved dramatically in the 20 years since the Institute of Medicine (IOM) first became involved in this area. This chapter provides a brief review of modern applications of scientific evidence in the development of clinical care and evolution of CPGs. It then offers an overview of many participants in current CPG development and use, providing selected examples.

Healthcare Decision Making Prior to Evidence-Based Medicine (EBM)

Before the end of the 20th century, clinical decisions were based largely on experience and skill (the "art" of medicine); medical teaching and practice were dominated by knowledge delivered by medical leaders (Davidoff, 1999; Eddy, 2005; Evidence-Based Medicine Working Group et al., 1992). Although some form of evidence has long contributed to clinical practice, there was no generally accepted, formal way of ensuring a scientific, critical approach to clinical decision making (Daly, 2005). The 1992 Evidence-Based Medicine Working Group, primarily McMaster University professors, who created a training program to teach EBM to internal medicine residents, described the historical paradigm of medical decision in the following sentences:

- "Unsystematic observations from clinical experience are a valid way of building and maintaining one's knowledge about patient prognosis, the value of diagnostic tests, and the efficacy of treatment.
- The study and understanding of basic mechanisms of disease and pathophysiologic principles are a sufficient guide for clinical practice.
- A combination of thorough traditional medical training and common sense is sufficient to allow one to evaluate new tests and treatments.
- Content expertise and clinical experience are a sufficient base from which to generate valid guidelines for clinical practice." (Evidence-Based Medicine Working Group et al., 1992, p. 2421)

The modern commitment to EBM dates to the 1970s, when a growing body of health services research refuted long-held assumptions about the quality of medical care practiced by U.S. physicians. In 1973, John Wennberg documented wide variations in practice patterns among local provider communities (hospital market areas) with seemingly similar patient populations (Wennberg and Gittelsohn, 1973). Then, the RAND Health Services Utilization Study showed that three common procedures (coronary angiography, carotid endarterectomy, and upper gastrointestinal tract endoscopy) were applied inappropriately at a rate of 17, 32, and 17 percent, respectively (Chassin et al., 1987; Davidoff, 1999). Around the same time, a major study in the *New England Journal of Medicine* (NEJM) concluded that indications for permanent pacemakers were inadequate or undocumented for 20 percent (77 of 382) of implant cases (Greenspan et al., 1988). To many health policy leaders, the RAND, NEJM, and other complementary investigational findings demonstrated that large proportions of procedures performed by physicians were deemed inappropriate even by experts in associated fields, and that one quarter to one third of all medical care may be unnecessary (Eddy, 2005; Woolf, 1990). In 1990, Steven Woolf wrote in reaction to the above findings that "the perception is that at least some of the variation reflects excessive (or inadequate) use of procedures by physicians in certain areas" (Woolf, 1990, p. 1812).

The Expansion of the Evidence Base

The first randomized controlled trial (RCT) in the health sciences was published in 1948 and demonstrated the efficacy of streptomycin in the treatment of tuberculosis. Since the 1970s there has been an exponential increase in RCTs and in observational research. From 1978 to 2001, 8.1 million journal articles were indexed in MEDLINE, with nearly half occurring from 1994 to 2001. The proportion of MEDLINE RCT articles also grew, from 1.9 percent or 5,174 per year from 1978 to 1985, to 6.2 percent or 24,724 per year from 1994 to 2001 (Druss and Marcus, 2005). Health sciences literature growth was concentrated in clinical research, with an increase in the percentage of studies with human subjects, and Medical Subject Headings (MeSH) in MEDLINE that shifted from basic science to clinical care and public health (Druss and Marcus, 2005). The introduction in the mid-1990s of the *ACP (American College of Physicians) Journal Club* and the journal *Evidence-Based Medicine*, which contain quality-evaluated article abstracts selected from hundreds of primary publications, illustrated the dramatic increase in the evidence base and its intended use among practicing physicians (Daly, 2005).

Exploitation of observational research methods as supplements to the RCT has long held traction among EBM's top proponents. Observational in this context refers exclusively to "quantitative, epidemiological methods and not qualitative, sociological methods. The principal observational epidemiological methods are non-randomized trials, cohort studies (prospective and retrospective), and case control methods," wrote Black in 1996 (p. 1215). Experimentation may be inadequate as an evidentiary base for clinical practice due to questionable external validity. More recently, Berwick and others have asserted that healthcare has much to gain if the view of EBM is broadened to include sources of observational data such as registries and electronic health records (Berwick, 2005). Overall, study designs and methods of analysis in support of EBM have become increasingly more sophisticated, and now include decision analysis, systematic review of the literature (including meta-analysis), and cost-effectiveness analysis (IOM, 2001).

This increase in knowledge was accompanied by a broad pattern of decentralization, both in sources of funding and authorship. The largest source of nongovernmental funding, by far, was industry in order to support Food and Drug Administration (FDA) approvals of drugs and devices (Druss and Marcus, 2005).

Clinical Epidemiology and Evidence-Based Medicine

Clinical epidemiology and evidence-based medicine emerged as solutions to failings of the traditional approach to medical decision making. Alvan Feinstein and David Sackett were the first to introduce clinical epidemiology as a distinct clinical discipline at Yale University (1968) and McMaster University (1970) respectively. In the late 20th century, the field of clinical epidemiology, defined by Sackett as "the application, by a physician who provides direct patient care, of epidemiologic and biostatistical methods to the study of diagnostic and therapeutic processes in order to effect an improvement in health" (Sackett, 2002, p. 1162), not only survived, but thrived, and its leaders were placed in highly influential positions in departments of medicine, journal editorships, and professional societies (Berwick, 2005).

Major figures in the rise of EBM included Archie Cochrane, Iain Chalmers, Murray Enkin, and Mark Keirse. Cochrane, a British epidemiologist, promoted the RCT as the best means of assessing medical technologies and practices, as early as the 1950s and 1960s. His work later gave rise to the Cochrane Collaboration (IOM, 2001). Chalmers, Enkin and colleagues, created the Oxford Database of

Perinatal trials, which compiled, first in hard copy (1988) and then in an electronic version (1990), all clinical trials data pertaining to effective care in pregnancy and childbirth (Chalmers, 1988, 1990). In addition, Chalmers, Enkin, and colleagues published *Effective Care in Pregnancy and Childbirth,* an overview of best pregnancy and childbirth evidence with a compendium of systematic reviews, and corresponding summary guide of the results. This work inspired the establishment of the Cochrane Collaboration, described later in this chapter (Chalmers et al., 1989; Enkin et al., 1989). These leaders, as well as others, fostered a new generation of scholars in healthcare, who focused their careers on clinical practice research (Berwick, 2005). "As a result, over the last several decades, the standards for evidence have become more stringent, and the tools for its assembly and analysis have become more powerful and widely available," according to Davidoff (1999) (IOM, 2001, p. 147).

The term "evidence-based medicine," coined in 1990, is defined by Daly as "the application of scientific method in determining the optimal management of the individual patient" (Daly, 2005, p. 89). In 1992 the EBM Working Group described the emergent paradigm of Evidence-Based Clinical Decision Making:

- While clinical experience and skill are important, systematic attempts to record observations in a reproducible and unbiased fashion markedly increase the confidence one can have in knowledge about patient prognosis, the value of diagnostic tests, and the efficacy of treatment.
- In the absence of systematic observation, one must be cautious in the interpretation of information derived from clinical experience and intuition, for it may at times be misleading.
- The study and understanding of basic mechanisms of disease are necessary but insufficient guides for clinical practice.
- Understanding certain rules of evidence is necessary to correctly interpret literature on causation, prognosis, diagnostic tests, and treatment strategy. (Evidence-Based Medicine Working Group et al., 1992, p. 2421)

Additionally, the EBM Working Group asserted that clinicians must accept uncertainty and the notion that clinical decisions are often made with scant knowledge of their true impact. The EBM paradigm assigns reduced weight to authority of experts, instead valuing physician understanding of underlying rigorous, high quality scientific evidence in patient care provision (Evidence-Based

Medicine Working Group et al., 1992). Importantly, more recent definitions also emphasize that clinical expertise and patient preferences remain vital to clinical decision making, and clarify that scientific evidence refers not only to RCT findings, but to those arising from research designs such as nonrandomized cohort trials and case control studies (IOM, 2001). The development of CPGs, detailed in the next section, is an important extension of EBM (Luce et al., 2010).

Evolution of Clinical Practice Guideline Development

Clinical practice guidelines (CPGs) have enjoyed a presence in medical practice since the early 20th century; many sources cite the American Academy of Pediatrics' *Redbook of Infectious Diseases* (1938) as one of the first CPGs produced in the United States (IOM, 2008). Most early guidelines were developed by expert panels or individuals who had gained authority status within specific medical specialties. As research evidence in support of, and methodologies for implementing, EBM had yet to be developed, these CPGs rarely were informed by systematic interpretation of the scientific evidence (IOM, 2008).

By the 1990s, the evolution in research methods and expansion of the scientific evidence base detailed above increased both the need for and ability of CPGs to reflect the latest EBM trend. Physicians could no longer keep up with the growing knowledge base: An internist would have to read 33 articles 365 days a year to stay up to date (Sackett, 2002). Furthermore, the validity of much of the growing body of evidence was suspect. "These two situations combined to place clinicians at increasing risk of 'drowning in doubtful data,' " Sackett wrote in 2002 (p. 1164). Critically appraised, synthesized information such as systematic reviews and CPGs became necessary tools for clinicians desiring to practice EBM (IOM, 2008). The IOM entered the conversation during this time with the two previously mentioned (in Chapter 1) reports, *Clinical Practice Guidelines: Directions for a New Program* (1990) and *Guidelines for Clinical Practice: From Development to Use* (1992) (IOM, 1990, 1992), which were requested by Congress to help inform a new government entity, then called the Agency for Healthcare Policy and Research (AHCPR), tasked with CPG development. David Eddy, an early pioneer in guideline development methods, influenced the work of AHCPR, Blue Cross-Blue Shield Association's TEC program, as well as others. His book, *A Manual for Assessing Health Practices and Designing Practice Policies: The Explicit Approach*, established a foundation for patient-centered outcomes based guideline development in the United States (Eddy, 1992).

Early groups applying systematic evidence reviews to CPG recommendations were the Canadian Task Force on the Periodic Health Examination (1976), the U.S. Preventive Services Task Force (USPSTF) (1984), and the American College of Physicians Clinical Efficacy Assessment Project (1980) (IOM, 2008). The involvement of specialty societies in practice guidelines development increased dramatically throughout the 1980s and 1990s. In 1990 Steven Woolf stated that, "Societies with previously limited activity have now revised their internal organizational structure, have established new committees to develop guidelines, and have adopted formal procedures to guide their efforts" (Woolf, 1990, p. 1814). By 1989, more than 35 medical societies and physician organizations had developed at least one CPG. Umbrella organizations such as the American Medical Association (AMA) and the Council of Medical Specialty Societies also became active participants in the guideline development movement, mostly in the role of coordinators and guideline development process "standardizers" (Woolf, 1990).

While U.S. federal agencies such as the USPSTF and the National Institutes of Health's (NIH's) Consensus Development Program had been making practice recommendations, federal efforts increased dramatically in 1989, when Congress passed a series of bills that increased funding for "effectiveness research" and called for creation of a formal public health service agency with responsibility for development and dissemination of CPGs (Woolf, 1990). Organized medicine, including the AMA and many medical specialty societies, embraced the legislation and employment of guidelines as alternatives to proposed stricter expenditure targets, endorsed by the George H. W. Bush Administration and certain congressional leaders, for curbing increases in healthcare spending (Woolf, 1990). The newly created AHCPR developed approximately 20 guidelines across a wide spectrum of clinical areas over the next several years (Lohr et al., 1998). The AHCPR's direct involvement in CPG development was short lived, however, due to political opposition in 1995 from back surgeons who disagreed with the agency's guidelines for the treatment of lower back pain (IOM, 2009). Following congressional threats to withdraw its funding, the agency, renamed the Agency for Healthcare Research and Quality (AHRQ), limited its responsibilities to financial support of Evidence-based Practice Centers' (EPCs') production of systematic reviews. In 2008, AHRQ's 14 EPCs produced systematic reviews that government agencies (e.g., the NIH and USPSTF), professional societies, and other organizations could access in their development of CPGs. AHRQ remains involved in guideline dissemination via the National Guideline Clearinghouse, a web-based collection of CPGs from around the world. These activities are discussed in the upcoming section.

CURRENT MAJOR STAKEHOLDERS IN GUIDELINES DEVELOPMENT AND USE

As the preceding background section indicates, numerous stakeholders are involved in the development and use of CPGs. The next two sections discuss examples from stakeholder classes: government agencies, clinical specialty societies, disease-specific societies, and other private and international organizations that develop guidelines and are key players. The examples illustrate the variety of organizations involved with CPGs, and are not intended to be all-inclusive. Also, the examples focus on organizations' CPG-related activities and do not provide a full description of each organization as a whole.

Guideline Developers

Government Agencies

A few national agencies have contributed significantly to guideline development, both financially and intellectually (NGC, 2010d). The USPSTF has been a CPG developer since the 1980s. It is noted for its early use of transparent standards and inclusion of multidisciplinary experts in the development process. This body was created by the U.S. Public Health Service in 1984 and has been supported by AHRQ staff and funding since 1998. The USPSTF is composed mainly of individuals from primary care specialties, such as internists, pediatricians, nurses, family physicians, methodologists, and some subspecialists. Its preventive care guidelines include topics for screening, counseling, immunizations, and preventive medications and services (AHRQ, 2010a). Because of its prevention focus, its perspective reflects that of primary care for asymptomatic people (Atkins, 2010). The USPSTF relies on systematic reviews (SRs) of relevant literature conducted by AHRQ staff, AHRQ's EPCs, or outside experts (AHRQ, 2010b). It has 60 CPGs in the NGC (NGC, 2010b).

The USPSTF updates its CPGs at least every 5 years (AHRQ, 2010b). To promote adoption of its guidelines, the USPSTF has developed relationships with a group of partners, including primary care associations and specialty societies; policy, quality improvement, and population groups (e.g., AARP); and selected federal agencies. These organizations serve as technical experts, peer reviewers, and disseminators (AHRQ, 2010a).

The NIH also has been involved heavily with guidelines and related endeavors through some of its institutes and programs, as part of its mission to translate basic research into medical practice (Simons-Morton, 2010). For example, the National Heart, Lung, and Blood Institute has 12 guidelines listed in the NGC as of October 2009 (NGC, 2010b) and posts 7 CPGs covering 5 health conditions on its website (NHLBI, 2009). It lists four new guidelines and one guideline update in development.

The previously mentioned Consensus Development Program of NIH issues three to five major evidence-based consensus statements annually, extending from highly structured conferences on controversial clinical topics of use to the broad medical community and general public (NIH, 2009). Many aspects of this consensus development process are similar to that used in development of high-quality CPGs: use of an unbiased, independent, expert panel including research investigators, health professionals, methodologists, and representatives of the public without conflicts of interest; a systematic review conducted by AHRQ; and opportunities for public input. Although the statement is not updated after issuance, after 5 years it is considered "historical" and the assumption is that much of the content is of questionable validity. Although the consensus statement may prompt reassessment of medical practice, it differs from a CPG in that it merely synthesizes the latest information, often from current and ongoing medical research; it does not recommend specific clinical actions in particular circumstances. The existence of a current Consensus Statement could be important to the evidence base of a CPG. In fact, the NIH currently posts three such statements in the NGC (NGC, 2010b).

The CDC is a major issuer of guidelines. The CDC Prevention Guidelines database includes more than 400 guidelines for the prevention and control of public health threats such as AIDS, cholera, disasters, dengue fever, suicide, vaccine-preventable diseases, lung cancer, sexually transmitted diseases, birth defects, and malaria. About two thirds of the documents in the database were originally published in the CDC's *Morbidity and Mortality Weekly Report*. The others were published as CDC monographs, as books or book chapters, as brochures, or as articles in peer-reviewed journals (CDC, 2007). The CDC currently lists 82 CPGs in the NGC (NGC, 2010b). These guidelines are generally based on a systematic review of the literature and written in consultation with experts in the germane field. The CDC also produces many recommendations in response to rapidly evolving public health concerns, such as the influenza epidemic. Given the urgent nature of these issues, these recommendations are rarely based on a systematic review of the evidence[2] (Briss, 2010).

The Department of Defense (DoD) and the Veterans Administration (VA) develop guidelines for their unique populations, and undertake efforts to implement them within their health systems and cost constraints, while also employing CPGs derived by others (Atkins, 2010). The VA and DoD list 25 CPGs in the NGC, predominantly directed to primary care conditions. The VA uses guidelines to improve quality of care and minimize unjustified variation in practice across geographic areas. Sometimes the VA embeds CPGs in its electronic health record and uses the CPGs to develop clinical performance measures (Atkins, 2010).

In addition to federal agencies, some states, such as Massachusetts, Washington, and New York, have taken responsibility for developing guidelines for their Medicaid and other state programs (NGC, 2010b).

Clinical Specialty Societies

Many medical societies and organizations of other healthcare professionals have taken responsibility for CPG development in responding to members' requests for guidance on best treatment practices and as an opportunity to provide continuing education. Some societies, such as the American College of Cardiology, or ACC (see discussion below on the American Heart Association, or AHA), are characterized by long histories of CPG development, have established development procedures, and have devoted significant financial resources to underwrite comprehensive SRs, carefully craft guidelines, and promote their implementation. The American Thoracic Society and American College of Physicians are similarly dedicated to development of high-quality guidelines and have recently updated their conflict-of-interest and rating of evidence and recommendation policies respectively, to reflect the latest consensus on that topic (Guyatt et al., 2010; Qaseem et al., 2010). Other societies have more limited resources for guideline development, less experience, and produce fewer CPGs. Most societies work independently on guidelines, although they may address the same conditions and

---

[2]Personal communication, P. A. Briss, Chief of the Community Guide Branch, Centers for Disease Control and Prevention, June 5, 2010.

develop related CPGs. For example, an AHA guideline may have a recommendation for blood pressure treatment in persons with diabetes, as do the American College of Physicians and the American Diabetes Association (Kahn, 2010).

Some societies have collaborated in the development of CPGs, integrating contributions of multiple specialties in the treatment of particular medical conditions. For example, many of the American Society for Clinical Oncology (ASCO) guidelines were developed in partnership with other specialty societies, such as the American Society of Hematology and the College of American Pathologists. ASCO has at least 17 guidelines in the NGC (NGC, 2010b).

Non-physician clinical societies such as occupational and physical therapists and many nursing specialties develop CPGs as well. For example, in 1997 the American Association of Neuroscience Nurses (AANN) created a series of educational tools to aid in patient care, called the *AANN Reference Series for Clinical Practice*; the series' name changed in 2007 to the *AANN Clinical Practice Guideline Series* to reflect the evidence-based nature of the guides. The AANN currently has 10 guidelines downloadable on its website and 5 CPG summaries in the NGC (AANN, 2010; NGC, 2010b).

Disease- or Population-Specific Organizations

Individual disease- or population-specific organizations, some from beyond U.S. borders and some in conjunction with other professional or disease-specific societies, sponsored 202 guidelines in the NGC as of March 2009 (IOM, 2009). The breadth of focus of disease-specific societies as well as their resources and capacity for CPG production vary widely.

For example, the Alzheimer's Association has produced three guidelines currently listed in NGC, including one entitled *Dementia Care Practice Recommendations for Assisted Living Residences and Nursing Homes: Phase 3 End-of-Life Care* (NGC, 2010a). This guideline is based on a literature review sponsored by the association and conducted by a consultant, a background paper written by association staff, and a 1-day meeting of representatives from 30 national provider, professional, and consumer advocacy organizations. The guideline's recommendations reflect expert consensus and are directed at professionals rather than patients and informal caregivers.[3]

---

[3]Personal communication, K. Maslow, 2010. Former director of policy development, Alzheimer's Association, August 27, 2010.

AHA has had a unique relationship with a specialty society, the ACC since 1981 (Jacobs, 2010). Through this partnership the AHA/ACC developed their first joint CPG in 1984. Twenty-two jointly sponsored CPGs are currently available; five new CPGs are in production and five earlier ones are being revised or updated. The guidelines focus on diagnostic procedures, therapeutic interventions, and management therapies for cardiovascular disease. For some of these guidelines, the collaboration has expanded to include other groups, such as the Heart Rhythm Society, European Society of Cardiology (ESC), Society of Cardiovascular Angiography and Interventions, Society of Thoracic Surgeons, and others. The AHA/ACC also gathers guidelines' endorsements from related organizations to enhance implementation (Jacobs, 2010).

The AHA/ACC guideline development effort is detailed and comprehensive, each requiring an average of more than 2 years to produce and publish; 22 current guidelines include more than 3,000 recommendations, and final products run more than 350 pages. To inform this process, the AHA has published a manual of methodologies and policies. Also, as part of their quality improvement and guideline implementation efforts, the AHA and ACC develop individual physician performance measures based on guideline recommendations (AHA, 2010b).

The American Geriatrics Society has developed three guidelines since 2003, most recently in 2009 on prevention of falls in older persons (an update from 2001). The multidisciplinary panel that developed this update was led jointly by representatives of the American Geriatrics Society and the British Geriatrics Society. Panel participants included members of the American Academy of Orthopedic Surgeons, American Board of Internal Medicine, American College of Emergency Physicians, American Geriatrics Society, American Medical Association, American Occupational Therapy Association, American Physical Therapy Association, American Society of Consultant Pharmacists, British Geriatrics Society, John A. Hartford Foundation Institute for Geriatric Nursing at New York University, and National Association for Home Care and Hospice (AGS, 2010).

Other Private Organizations

Other private organizations, such as large healthcare organizations, academic medical centers, quality improvement organizations, and commercial companies, also develop CPGs. They draw, in part, on existing CPGs from respected specialty societies and related rigorous SRs, but involve their own expert staff and physicians in evidence review and recommendations derivation befitting their patient and clinician contexts.

For example, Kaiser Permanente staffs a centralized, internal organizational structure dedicated to CPG development. It was originally developed by David Eddy with an explicit standard-ized methodology, critical appraisal and grading of evidence, and a guideline quality committee of methodologists. It maintains a core set of 19 CPGs related to preventive care and chronic condi-tions, 8 of which are currently listed in the NGC (Koster, 2010). The Institute for Clinical Systems Improvement (ICSI) produces many CPGs through collaboration in Minnesota of 10,000 predominantly primary care doctors, most hospitals, not-for-profit health plans, and some employers and patients. The NGC includes summaries of 41 ICSI guidelines (Bottles, 2010). (ICSI's CPG efforts are further detailed in Chapter 6.)

Limited public information about CPGs is produced commer-cially. The following description is based on information available on the web and a presentation by, and committee discussion with, the editor-in-chief of Milliman's guidelines. McKesson, a large cor-poration providing services to healthcare providers and insurers, produces clinical practice guidelines in its Interqual Division. These are the two main purveyors of commercial guidelines.

These proprietary guidelines reportedly concentrate on quality of care, efficient resource expenditure, and reduction in inappro-priate care variations. Guidelines are founded on evidence when available and expert opinion when not. What distinguishes these guidelines from most publicly available CPGs is promotion of use through accompanying software that integrates behavior change into real-time management reports usage reviews, workflow and resource controls, and decision tools devoted to quality improve-ment and cost efficiency. Often providers' own data as well as larger databases can be integrated for feedback and benchmarking. Both companies provide training and support of clients and are available for additional consulting. The guideline companies support research staffs to continuously mine the literature and consultants to review and revise draft guidelines and provide expert advice and consensus on recommendations when evidence is lacking[4] (McKesson Health Solutions LLC, 2004; Milliman Care Guidelines, 2009; Milliman Inc., 2009; Schibanoff, 2010).

---

[4]Personal communication, H. E. Blumen, 2010, Milliman care guidelines, August 15, 2009.

International Organizations

Organizations in several countries outside the United States also produce CPGs. Foreign organizations have contributed 895 (36 percent) of the CPGs in the U.S. NGC. Such guidelines may be developed by foreign medical societies, disease organizations, or government-related bodies. Although the attentions of this committee did not extend internationally, several organizations merit highlighting because of the important roles they play.

For example, the National Institute for Health and Clinical Excellence (NICE) is an independent organization that advises the UK National Health Service (NHS) on promoting health and preventing and treating illness (NICE, 2010). It conducts or contracts for technology assessments of new treatments and devices as well as systematic reviews and comparative effectiveness studies used to produce clinical guidance. In addition, NICE supports CPG development through accredited organizations. It accredits organizations that comply with explicit, transparent NICE standards and produce high-quality clinical guidance (see further discussion in Chapter 7). Although the guidelines and accreditation work is designed for use in England by the NHS, these processes potentially could be employed in other countries. NICE staff offer consulting services internationally to assist in adoption of NICE standards and CPG development methodologies, particularly those related to integration of scientific evidence and social values in health care policy and clinical decision making. NICE also issues a suite of products for each review and guideline it produces, including shorter NICE guidelines, full guidelines with systematic reviews, consumer summaries, and implementation assistance (NHS, 2010).

The World Health Organization (WHO) develops a large number of health-related recommendations for a diverse group of target audiences, including the general public, healthcare professionals, health facility managers (e.g., hospital administrators) or regions (e.g., districts), and public policy makers. These recommendations address a wide range of clinical, public health, and health policy topics related to achieving WHO health goals (Oxman et al., 2007). In 2006, the WHO Advisory Committee on Health Research published a series of 16 papers advising WHO guideline developers on how to ensure that their healthcare recommendations are informed by best available research evidence (Schünemann et al., 2006).

Other international developers of CPGs include the European Society of Cardiology and the Kidney Disease Improving Global Outcomes (KDIGO). The ESC Committee for Practice Guidelines was established in 1994 to address new health-related policies in clinical practice, prevention, quality assurance, research programs, and health economics in cardiovascular diseases. Its committee is composed of 8 to 10 members who are elected for 2 years. It developed 4 guidelines in 2009, and 36 since 2001 (ESC, 2010). KDIGO, an international guideline development organization, was established in 2003 to promote the "coordination, collaboration and integration of initiatives to develop and implement clinical practice guidelines" (Eknoyan et al., 2004, p. 1310). It is currently managed by the U.S.-based National Kidney Foundation and is supported by national kidney disease guideline development initiatives around the world (KDIGO, 2008).

Other Stakeholders Related to Guideline Dissemination or Use

In addition to the organizations cited above that develop CPGs, numerous government, private, and international groups participate in activities vital to guideline dissemination or use. As with the above examples, the organizations below are meant to illustrate the various stakeholders and not be a complete representation. The discussion here, as well, is limited to their CPG-related activities.

Federal Agencies

As noted previously, AHRQ no longer develops guidelines, but helps other organizations to develop guidelines. Two previously mentioned major functions supported by AHRQ will be discussed below: the support of EPCs and the NGC.

AHRQ's network of EPCs has expertise in conducting methodologically rigorous, independent SRs and technology assessments of scientific evidence, and research to advance SR methodologies. Reports from these centers encompass comprehensive literature reviews and research syntheses (possibly comprising meta-analyses or cost analyses) on priority health topics conducted by experts with a range of relevant skills. Reports include documentation of process and undergo peer review and public comment before they are made final. These reports are available to all public and private CPG developers (AHRQ, 2008). Further, medical specialty societies such as the American College of Physicians (ACP), the Renal Physicians Association (RPA) and many other guideline developers utilize the EPC's topic nomination system to encourage the production of high quality SRs in clinical areas relevant to their guidelines (Matchar et al., 2005).

AHRQ, in conjunction with the American Medical Association and America's Health Insurance Plans, through a contract with ECRI

Institute, created the NGC in 1997 to ensure no-charge availability of CPGs to clinicians, health plans, providers, purchasers, and the general public. The NGC supports dissemination, adoption, and use of CPGs through an online database of summaries of CPGs that satisfy certain minimal quality criteria (see Box 2-1 for a list of current criteria). The criteria were established to promote inclusiveness so potential adopters were granted access to a large proportion of available guidelines (Coates, 2010).

**BOX 2-1
Criteria for Inclusion in
The National Guideline Clearinghouse (NGC)**

1. The clinical practice guideline (CPG) contains systematically developed statements that include recommendations, strategies, or information that helps physicians and/or other healthcare practitioners and patients to make decisions about appropriate health care for specific clinical circumstances.

2. The CPG was produced under the auspices of medical specialty associations; relevant professional societies; public or private organizations; government agencies at the federal, state, or local levels; or healthcare organizations or plans. A CPG developed by an individual not officially sponsored by one of the above organizations does not meet the inclusion criteria for NGC.

3. Corroborating documentation can be produced and verified to prove that a systematic literature search and review of existing scientific evidence published in peer-reviewed journals were performed during the guideline development. A guideline is not excluded from NGC if corroborating documentation can be produced and verified, detailing specific gaps in scientific evidence for some guideline recommendations.[a]

4. The full-text guideline is available on request in print or electronic format (free or for a fee) in English. The guideline is current and the most recent version produced. Documented evidence can be produced or verified to prove the guideline was developed, reviewed, or revised within the past 5 years.

---

[a] AHRQ reports the quality of supporting evidence bases for CPGs in the NGC vary substantially. Personal communication, M. Nix, 2010. Project officer for National Guideline Clearinghouse.
SOURCE: NGC (2010c).

NGC and ECRI staff scrutinize CPGs submitted by developers. If CPGs meet basic criteria, ECRI summarizes them, and posts them on a live, interactive website, www.guideline.gov. Since this website was opened in 1999, ECRI has summarized and posted nearly 8,000 CPGs from more than 300 U.S. and international government agencies, specialty societies, and other nonprofit organizations. Currently, NGC provides more than 2,500 summaries with links to full guideline texts, as well as personal digital assistant downloads of summaries; 25 Guideline Syntheses contrasting CPGs on similar topics; an annotated guidelines bibliography; and a weekly e-mail newsletter update on recent additions (Coates, 2010). To remain in the NGC, a CPG must be updated at least every 5 years; 1,331 CPGs have been withdrawn from the NGC, mainly because they did not satisfy this criterion.

The FDA is involved in developing evidence-based[5] recommendations for drug use through its role in approving drug labeling. For example, the FDA now requires pharmaceutical firms to implement Risk Evaluation and Mitigation Strategies, which detail how the benefits of a drug or biological product outweigh its risks (FDA, 2009).

The federal Centers for Medicare & Medicaid Services (CMS) is a particularly important user of guidelines. Because CMS spent billions of dollars on healthcare services for an estimated 118.6 million Medicare, Medicaid, and Children's Health Insurance Program beneficiaries (including some dual eligibles) in 2009, Medicare and Medicaid policies have a significant impact on patient care and healthcare providers' and insurers' revenue (HHS, 2010). CMS employs guidelines in several ways:

- A guideline from the USPSTF or a Technology Assessment conducted through AHRQ's EPC Program could support an expansion or reduction of Medicare coverage to include, for example, a screening test for beneficiaries. Under the *Patient Protection and Affordable Care Act*, Medicare (and commercial insurers) will be required to include coverage of preventive services that receive a highly rated recommendation from a CPG of the USPSTF.[6]
- Medicare's quality improvement program, contracted through Quality Improvement Organizations in each state,

---

[5]Evidence-based in this case does not denote that a systematic review of the evidence was conducted.

[6]*The Patient Protection and Affordable Care Act*, Public Law 111-148, 111th Cong. (March 23, 2010).

can concentrate collaboration with hospitals, physicians, and other providers on guideline-recommended actions and apply guidelines-driven quality measures to track improvements in practice and outcomes over time.

- CMS requires participating hospitals, home health agencies, dialysis facilities, and nursing homes to report quality measures, frequently based on CPGs. Full reimbursement or an incentive payment is linked to this reporting for selected providers. A voluntary Physician Quality Reporting Initiative provides incentives to physicians and group practices reporting measures. The agency then posts these measures and other quality data on its website, www.medicare.gov/nhcompare/, to encourage beneficiaries and other consumers to make careful provider choices (Jacques, 2010).
- Medicare additionally has supported experimentation with Pay-for-Performance schemes that are based on quality measures derived in part from well-accepted CPGs (Jacques, 2010).

International Organizations

Along with organizations in many countries around the world developing CPGs, there are support organizations with functions of interest to U.S. developers too. For example, Guidelines International Network (GIN), a Scottish-based, not-for-profit, international association of 50 individuals and 91 organizations representing 39 countries, was founded in 2002 to promote development and use of CPGs, in part by collecting published CPGs (Guidelines International Network, 2010a). In addition to compiling a publicly accessible library of more than 3,700 guidelines and 3,000 related documents (guideline clearing reports, methodologies, implementation tools and systematic reviews) from members (Guidelines International Network, 2010c), the organization holds annual conferences to encourage collaboration among guideline-producing organizations and experts and enhance dissemination of guidelines-related research. GIN also has a Patient and Public Involvement Working Group (G-I-N PUBLIC) of consumers, developers, and researchers that supports effective patient and public involvement in guideline development and implementation, and has recently approved a request to establish a G-I-N affiliated U.S. interest group to foster the development and use of high-quality CPGs in the United States (Guidelines International Network, 2010b).

Another international group, the Cochrane Collaboration, is dedicated to improving healthcare decisions through development of systematic reviews of healthcare outcomes evidence. The SRs are conducted by a network of 10,000 individuals around the globe, predominantly volunteers. CPG developers in the United States often include these SRs in their evidence bases. The Collaboration has a small staff and is supported by donations, including extensive contribution of in-kind services from individuals and institutions and support form governments in many countries, and subscriptions to the Cochrane Library; commercial funds for SRs are prohibited. In addition to producing reviews and related abstracts and derivative products, the Collaboration has created a library of SRs and their scientific evidence foundations (The Cochrane Collaboration, 2010a). The Collaboration also has developed extensive guidance, a reviewers' handbook, and training programs on how to conduct rigorous SRs (The Cochrane Collaboration, 2010b).

Funders of CPGs

Funders of CPG development play a critical role in the process; however, the committee found no systematic sources of information regarding CPG funders or their levels of financial support. Although CPGs developed by federal agencies would likely be funded from federal tax dollars, the amount spent on that function in the various agencies is unknown. A reasonable assumption is that commercial guidelines are funded, at least in part, through their sale and sales of related support products and services. Many guidelines developed by medical societies and other private organizations are self-funded, through membership dues, donations, or other means. CPGs funded by medical societies dependent on membership dues may be cause for concern regarding conflict of interest if their recommendations would likely affect their members' income.

Guidelines listed in the NGC may report support from government, a parent professional organization, private foundations or individual donors, sales of guidelines, payers, or major health systems. Funding from medical imaging, device, or pharmaceutical industries associated with a guideline topic may also be suspect due to Conflict of Interest (COI), yet it may be difficult to discern that financial presence. A guideline might report to the NGC that it was fully funded by its sponsoring organization, but that body might or might not receive significant portions of revenue from industry. For example, the Alzheimer's Association's listing in the NGC for its guideline, *Dementia Care Practice Recommendations for Assisted Living Residences and Nursing Homes: Phase 3 End-of-Life Care,* a 2007 submission (NGC, 2010a), indicates that it was funded by the Association. That, in turn, is supported by national corporations (including pharmaceutical firms), foundations, and private donations (Alzheimer's Association, 2010).

In another case, funding for the AHA's 2008 CPG on adults with congenital heart disease came totally from AHA and ACC Foundations (AHA, 2010a). AHA's funding primarily arises from individual donations (46 percent) and corporate funds (28 percent), with less than 4 percent from the medical device and drug industries; according to AHA policy, CPG development receives no direct industry support (AHA, 2010a).

This chapter has briefly detailed the history of evidence-based medicine and the variety of organizations historically and currently involved with CPG development. The next chapter examines the ongoing challenges undermining the trustworthiness and impact of CPGs and potential ways to overcome them.

REFERENCES

AANN (American Association of Neuroscience Nurses). 2010. *AANN clinical practice guideline series.* http://www.aann.org/ (accessed September 9, 2010).

AGS (American Geriatric Society). 2010. *Prevention of falls in older persons: AGS/BGS clinical practice guideline.* http://www.medcats.com/FALLS/frameset.htm (accessed September 16, 2010).

AHA (American Heart Association). 2010a. *2008–2009 national center support from pharmaceutical companies and device manufacturers and AHA total corporate support.* http://americanheart.org/downloadable/heart/1265232869160126512805051 2008-2009%20Pharma%20Device%20and%20CorporateFunding%2011110.pdf (accessed March 7, 2010).

AHA. 2010b. *Performance measures.* http://www.americanheart.org/presenter. jhtml?identifier=3012904 (accessed March 7, 2010).

AHRQ (Agency for Healthcare Research and Quality). 2008. *Evidence-based Practice Centers: Synthesizing scientific evidence to improve quality and effectiveness in health care.* http://www.ahrq.gov/clinic/epc/ (accessed March 2, 2010).

AHRQ. 2010a. *About USPSTF.* http://www.ahrq.gov/clinic/uspstfab.htm (accessed March 2, 2010).

AHRQ. 2010b. *Frequently asked questions.* http://info.ahrq.gov/cgi-bin/ahrq.cfg/php/ enduser/std_alp.php?p_sid=sf*ffSVj&p_lva=&p_li=&p_new_search=1&p_ accessibility=0&p_redirect=&p_srch=1&p_sort_by=&p_gridsort=&p_row_ cnt=45%2C45&p_prods=&p_cats=16%2C5&p_pv=&p_cv=2.5&p_search_ text=&p_nav=head&p_trunc=0&p_page_head=1&p_page=1 (accessed March 2, 2010).

Alzheimer's Association. 2010. *Current partners and sponsors.* http://www.alz.org/ join_the_cause_19090.asp (accessed March 7, 2010).

Atkins, D. 2010. *Veterans Administration.* Paper presented at the IOM Committee on Standards for Developing Trustworthy Clinical Practice Guidelines meeting, January 11, 2010, Washington, DC.

Berwick, D. M. 2005. Broadening the view of evidence-based medicine. *Quality and Safety in Health Care* 14(5):315–316.

Black, N. 1996. Why we need observational studies to evaluate the effectiveness of health care. *BMJ* 312(7040):1215–1218.

Bottles, K. 2010. *Institute for clinical systems improvement (ICSI).* Paper presented at the IOM Committee on Standards for Developing Trustworthy Clinical Practice Guidelines meeting, January 11, 2010, Washington, DC.

CDC (Centers for Disease Control and Prevention). 2007. *CDC Wonder: CDC prevention guidelines.* http://wonder.cdc.gov/wonder/prevguid/library/library.asp (accessed September 9, 2010).

Chalmers, I. 1988. *Oxford database of perinatal trials.* Oxford; New York: Oxford University Press.

Chalmers, I. 1990. *Oxford database of perinatal trials.* Place Published: Oxford University Press (accessed September 25, 2009).

Chalmers, I., M. Enkin, and M. J. N. C. Keirse. 1989. *Effective care in pregnancy and childbirth, Oxford medical publications.* Oxford; New York: Oxford University Press.

Chassin, M. R., J. Kosecoff, R. E. Park, C. M. Winslow, K. L. Kahn, N. J. Merrick, J. Keesey, A. Fink, D. H. Solomon, and R. H. Brook. 1987. Does inappropriate use explain geographic variations in the use of health care services? A study of three procedures. *JAMA* 258(18):2533–2537.

Coates, V. 2010. *National Guidelines Clearinghouse NGC/ECRI Institute.* Presented at the IOM Committee on Standards for Developing Trustworthy Clinical Practice Guidelines meeting, January 11, 2010, Washington, DC.

The Cochrane Collaboration. 2010a. *Cochrane reviews.* http://www.cochrane.org/cochrane-reviews#reviews (accessed March 7, 2010).

The Cochrane Collaboration. 2010b. *Training.* http://www.cochrane.org/training (accessed March 7, 2010).

Daly, J. 2005. *Evidence-based medicine and the search for a science of clinical care, California/Milbank books on health and the public.* Berkeley, CA: University of California Press.

Davidoff, F. 1999. In the teeth of the evidence: The curious case of evidence-based medicine. *Mount Sinai Journal of Medicine* 66(2):75–83.

Druss, B. G., and S. C. Marcus. 2005. Growth and decentralization of the medical literature: Implications for evidence-based medicine. *Journal of the Medical Library Association* 93(4):499–501.

Eddy, D.M. 1992. *A manual for assessing health practices and designing practice policies: The explicit approach.* Philadelphia, PA: American College of Physicians.

Eddy, D. M. 2005. Evidence-based medicine: A unified approach. *Health Affairs* 24(1):9–17.

Eknoyan, G., N. Lameire, R. Barsoum, K.-U. Eckardt, A. Levin, N. Levin, F. Locatelli, A. MacLeod, R. Vanholder, R. Walker, and H. Wang. 2004. The burden of kidney disease: Improving global outcomes. *Kidney International* 66(4):1310–1314.

Enkin, M., M. J. N. C. Keirse, I. Chalmers, and E. Enkin. 1989. *A guide to effective care in pregnancy and childbirth, Oxford medical publications.* Oxford [England]; New York: Oxford University Press.

ESC (European Society of Cardiology). 2010. *Committee for Practice Guidelines (CPG) 2010–2012.* http://www.escardio.org/about/who/committees/programmes/Pages/practice-guidelines.aspx (accessed September 16, 2010).

Evidence-Based Medicine Working Group, G. Guyatt, J. Cairns, D. Churchill, D. Cook, B. Haynes, J. Hirsh, J. Irvine, M. Levine, M. Levine, J. Nishikawa, D. Sackett, P. Brill-Edwards, H. Gerstein, J. Gibson, R. Jaeschke, A. Kerigan, A. Neville, A. Panju, A. Detsky, M. Enkin, P. Frid, M. Gerrity, A. Laupacis, V. Lawrence, J. Menard, V. Moyer, C. Mulrow, P. Links, A. Oxman, J. Sinclair, and P. Tugwell. 1992. Evidence-based medicine: A new approach to teaching the practice of medicine. *JAMA* 268(17):2420–2425.

FDA (Food and Drug Administration). 2009. *FDA issues draft guidance on risk evaluation and mitigation strategies.* http://www.fda.gov/NewsEvents/Newsroom/PressAnnouncements/2009/ucm184399.htm (accessed October 7, 2010).

Greenspan, A. M., H. R. Kay, B. C. Berger, R. M. Greenberg, A. J. Greenspon, and M. J. S. Gaughan. 1988. Incidence of unwarranted implantation of permanent cardiac pacemakers in a large medical population. *New England Journal of Medicine* 318(3):158–163.

Guidelines International Network. 2010a. *About G-I-N: Introduction.* http://www.g-i-n.net/about-g-i-n (accessed March 7, 2010).

Guidelines International Network. 2010b. *Homepage.* http://www.g-i-n.net/ (accessed March 7, 2010).

Guidelines International Network. 2010c. *International Guidelines Library.* http://www.g-i-n.net/library/international-guidelines-library (accessed March 7, 2010).

Guyatt, G., E. A. Akl, J. Hirsh, C. Kearon, M. Crowther, D. Gutterman, S. Z. Lewis, I. Nathanson, R. Jaeschke, and H. Schünemann. 2010. The vexing problem of guidelines and conflict of interest: A potential solution. *Annals of Internal Medicine* 152(11):738–741.

HHS (Department of Health and Human Services). 2010. *Data compendium: Overview.* http://www.cms.gov/DataCompendium/ (accessed July 15, 2010).

IOM (Institute of Medicine). 1990. *Clinical practice guidelines: Directions for a new program.* Edited by M. J. Field and K. N. Lohr. Washington, DC: National Academy Press.

IOM. 1992. *Guidelines for clinical practice: From development to use.* Edited by M. J. Field and K. N. Lohr. Washington, DC: National Academy Press.

IOM. 2001. *Crossing the quality chasm: A new health system for the 21st century.* Washington, DC: National Academy Press.

IOM. 2008. *Knowing what works in health care: A roadmap for the nation.* Edited by J. Eden. Washington, DC: The National Academies Press.

IOM. 2009. *Conflict of interest in medical research, education, and practice.* Edited by B. Lo and M. J. Field. Washington, DC: The National Academies Press.

Jacobs, A. 2010. *American College of Cardiology and American Heart Association.* Paper presented at the IOM Committee on Standards for Developing Trustworthy Clinical Practice Guidelines meeting, January 11, 2010, Washington, DC.

Jacques, L. B. 2010. *Centers for Medicare & Medicaid Services (CMS).* Paper presented at the IOM Committee on Standards for Developing Trustworthy Clinical Practice Guidelines meeting, January 11, 2010, Washington, DC.

Kahn, R. 2010. *Former chief of scientific and medical officer of the American Diabetes Association.* Presented at the IOM Committee on Standards for Developing Trustworthy Clinical Practice Guidelines meeting, January 11, 2010, Washington, DC.

KDIGO. 2008. *Kidney Disease: Improving Global Outcomes (KDIGO): About Us.* http://www.kdigo.org/about_us.php#history (accessed January 21, 2011).

Koster, M. A. 2010. *Technology assessment and guidelines unit: Kaiser Permanente Southern California.* Paper presented at the IOM Committee on Standards for Developing Trustworthy Clinical Practice Guidelines meeting, January 11, 2010, Washington, DC.

Lohr, K. N., K. Eleazer, and J. Mauskopf. 1998. Health policy issues and applications for evidence-based medicine and clinical practice guidelines. *Health Policy* 46(1):1–19.

Luce, B. R., M. Drummond, B. Jonsson, P. J. Neumann, J. S. Schwartz, U. Siebert, and S. D. Sullivan. 2010. EBM, HTA, and CER: Clearing the confusion. *Milbank Quarterly* 88(2):256–276.

Matchar, D. B., E. V. Westermann-Clark, D. C. McCrory, M. Patwardhan, G. Samsa, S. Kulasingam, E. Myers, A. Sarria-Santamera, A. Lee, R. Gray, and K. Liu. 2005. Dissemination of Evidence-based Practice Center reports. *Annals of Internal Medicine* 142(2):1120–1125.

McKesson Health Solutions LLC. 2004. *InterQual clinical decision support tools: Super solutions for improving quality and managing resources.* http://www.mckesson.com/static_files/McKesson.com/MHS/Documents/iqbroc_payor.pdf (accessed July 18, 2010).

Milliman Care Guidelines. 2009. *Milliman Care Guidelines® innovations spur eight-fold growth in hospital client base.* http://www.careguidelines.com/company/press/pr_111209.shtml (accessed November 12, 2009).

Milliman Inc. 2009. *Milliman Care Guidelines.* http://www.milliman.com/expertise/healthcare/products-tools/milliman-care-guidelines/ (accessed June 9, 2009).

NGC (National Guideline Clearinghouse). 2010a. *Brief summary: Dementia care practice recommendations for assisted living residences and nursing homes: Phase 3 end-of-life care: National Guideline Clearinghouse.* http://www.guideline.gov/summary/summary.aspx?doc_id=13541&nbr=006925&string=alzheimer's (accessed March 7, 2010).

NGC. 2010b. *Guidelines by organization: National Guideline Clearinghouse.* http://ngc.gov/browse/by-organization.aspx?alpha=C (accessed September 9, 2010).

NGC. 2010c. *Inclusion criteria: National Guideline Clearinghouse.* http://ngc.gov/submit/inclusion.aspx (accessed April 5, 2010).

NGC. 2010d. *NGC browse—organizations.* http://ngc.gov/browse/browseorgsbyLtr.aspx (accessed July 15, 2010).

NHLBI (National Heart, Lung, and Blood Institute). 2009. *Current clinical practice guidelines and reports.* http://www.nhlbi.nih.gov/guidelines/current.htm (accessed December 29, 2009).

NHS Evidence (National Health Service Evidence). 2010. *Guidance producer subject to accreditation: British Transplantation Society.* National Institute for Health and Clinical Excellence. http://www.evidence.nhs.uk/Accreditation/Documents/Brit%20Transpl%20Soc_final%20accreditation%20report_1.6.pdf

NICE (National Institute for Health and Clinical Excellence). 2010. *Homepage.* http://www.nice.org.uk/ (accessed March 7, 2010).

NIH (National Institutes of Health). 2009. *NIH Consensus Development Program, frequently asked questions.* http://consensus.nih.gov/FAQS.htm, http://consensus.nih.gov/ABOUTCDP.htm (accessed December 29, 2009).

Oxman, A. D., J. N. Lavis, and A. Fretheim. 2007. Use of evidence in WHO recommendations. *The Lancet* 369(9576):1883–1889.

Qaseem, A., V. Snow, D. K. Owens, and P. Shekelle. 2010. The development of clinical practice guidelines and guidance statements of the American College of Physicians: Summary of methods. *Annals of Internal Medicine* 153(3):194–199.

Sackett, D. L. 2002. Clinical epidemiology: What, who, and whither. *Journal of Clinical Epidemiology* 55(12):1161–1166.

Schibanoff, J. 2010. *Milliman Care Guidelines.* Paper presented at the IOM Committee on Standards for Developing Trustworthy Clinical Practice Guidelines meeting, January 11, 2010, Washington, DC.

Schünemann, H. J., A. Fretheim, and A. D. Oxman. 2006. Improving the use of research evidence in guideline development: Guidelines for guidelines. *Health Research Policy and Systems* 4:13.

Simons-Morton, D. 2010. *National Heart, Lung, and Blood Institute.* Paper presented at the IOM Committee on Standards for Developing Trustworthy Clinical Practice Guidelines meeting, January 11, 2010, Washington, DC.

Weisz, G., A. Cambrosio, P. Keating, L. Knaapen, T. Schlich, and V. J. Tournay. 2007. The emergence of clinical practice guidelines. *Milbank Quarterly* 85(4):691–727.

Wennberg, J., and Gittelsohn. 1973. Small area variations in health care delivery. *Science* 182(117):1102–1108.

Woolf, S. H. 1990. Practice guidelines: A new reality in medicine: Recent developments. *Archives of Internal Medicine* 150(9):1811–1818.

3

Trustworthy Clinical Practice Guidelines: Challenges and Potential

Abstract: *This chapter examines ongoing challenges surrounding the current clinical practice guideline (CPG) development process that diminish the quality and trustworthiness of guidelines for clinicians and the public. These challenges include limitations in the scientific evidence on which CPGs are based, lack of transparency of development groups' methodologies, questions about how to reconcile conflicting guidelines, and conflicts of interests among guideline development group members and funders. The committee explored the literature devoted to empirical assessments of guideline development methodologies, and an array of guideline quality appraisal instruments. Although guideline quality has improved over the past several decades, improvement has been too slow, and the quality of many guidelines remains subpar. Furthermore, past and current quality appraisal instruments do not sufficiently address all components of the guideline development process, particularly the rating of evidence quality and recommendation strength, nor are they intended for prospective application to development of high-quality, trustworthy guidelines.*

INTRODUCTION

Efforts to promote high-quality development of clinical practice guidelines (CPGs) have met challenges and controversy. The following section describes issues undermining the trustworthiness and impact of CPGs (illustrated in the case studies presented in Boxes 3-1, 3-2, and 3-3), including many associated with the guideline development process. These issues include limitations in the scientific evidence on which CPGs are based; lack of transparency of development groups' methodologies, especially in deriving recommendations and determining their strength; conflicting guidelines; and challenges of conflict of interest (COI). Additional factors threatening CPG trustworthiness and influence are reflected in tensions among guideline developers and users with respect to balancing desires for evidence-based recommendations with clinician desires for guidance on clinical situations in which great uncertainty exists. Resource limitations in guideline development and updating present further challenges to the promise of high-quality, effective guidelines. Overall, though researchers have reported empirical evidence of modest gains in guidelines' quality, there is substantial room for improvement (Shaneyfelt and Centor, 2009). The committee did not identify comprehensive and adequate standards for development of unbiased, scientifically valid, and trustworthy CPGs. Hence, the committee formulated and proposed new standards for developing trustworthy CPGs, as explained in the following two chapters.

DEVELOPMENT OF EVIDENCE-BASED CPGs

Concerns Regarding Bias, Generalizability, and Specificity

Appreciation for evidence-based medicine has grown over the past several decades, due in part to increased interest in and funding for clinical practice research, and improvements in associated research methodologies. However, many CPG experts and practicing clinicians increasingly regard the scientific evidence base with suspicion for a variety of reasons, including gaps in evidence, poor-quality research and systematic reviews, biased guideline developers, and the dominance of industry-funded research and guideline development. A 2005 study found that industry sponsored approximately 75 percent of clinical trials published in *The Lancet, New England Journal of Medicine*, and *Journal of the American Medical Association* (The House of Commons Health Committee, 2005). Two-thirds of this industry-sponsored published research is directly conducted by profit-making research companies and one third by academic medical centers. Furthermore, even high-quality commercial clinical investigations (e.g., those included in Cochrane Reviews) are

5.3 times more likely to endorse their sponsors' products than non-commercially funded studies of identical products (Als-Nielsen et al., 2003). Much of this industry-sponsored research is conducted for Food and Drug Administration approval of medications. Approval requires careful evaluation and demonstrated efficacy for given indications. However, there are important limitations on the meaning of such approval for clinical practice. Because preapproval studies designed by a drug's manufacturer often follow patients for relatively brief periods of time, involve comparatively small numbers of younger and healthier patients than the drug's target population, may rely on comparison with placebo only, and often use surrogate endpoints, the value of these studies for the development of useful CPGs can be severely limited (Avorn, 2005).

Guideline developers and users emphasize that guideline recommendations should be based on only the most methodologically rigorous evidence, whether in the form of randomized controlled trials (RCTs) or observational research, where current guidelines often fall short (Coates, 2010; Koster, 2010). However, even when studies are considered to have high internal validity, they may not be generalizable to or valid for the patient population of guideline relevance. Randomized trials commonly have an underrepresentation of important subgroups, including those with comorbidities, older persons, racial and ethnic minorities, and low-income, less educated, or low-literacy patients. Many RCTs and observational studies fail to include such "typical patients" in their samples; even when they do, there may not be sufficient numbers of such patients to assess them separately or the subgroups may not be properly analyzed for differences in outcomes. Investigators often require that patients have new disease onset, have no or few comorbid conditions, and/or be relatively young and sociodemographically limited (Brown, 2010). A 2007 evaluation of the quality of evidence underlying therapeutic recommendations for cardiovascular risk management found that only 28 percent of 369 recommendations (in 9 national guidelines) were supported by high-quality evidence. The most frequent reason for downgrading quality of RCT-based evidence was concern about extrapolating from highly selected RCT populations to the general population (McAlister et al., 2007). Failure to include major population subgroups in the evidence base thwarts our ability to develop clinically relevant, valid guidelines (Boyd, 2010). A 2005 study found that seven of nine guidelines studied did not modify or discuss the applicability of recommendations for older patients with multiple morbidities (Boyd et al., 2005).

Lack of Transparency in Recommendations' Derivation

A second criticism of the current state of CPG development is lack of transparency in deriving and rating the strength of recommendations. Representatives from Kaiser Permanente and Partners Healthcare in Massachusetts, who evaluate and use guidelines in patient care, noted that the major weaknesses of CPGs were wide variation in transparency in guideline development processes and products and omission of description of processes for consensus-based recommendations (particularly when evidence is absent or poor). The 2006 investigation by Connecticut's attorney general into the Infectious Diseases Society of America's Lyme Disease Guidelines (Box 3-1) is illustrative. Although commentaries have described this case as a "politicization of professional practice guidelines" (Kraemer and Gostin, 2009, p. 665), with the attorney general "[substituting] his judgment for that of medical professionals" (Ferrette, 2008, p. 2), this case highlights the need for standardization and transparency in all aspects of systemic data collection and review, committee administration, and guideline development, so that these issues do not detract from the science. GDGs must be aware of the many, varied observers who will consider their development processes, particularly when their recommendations are likely to be controversial.

Although certain empirical evidence indicates guideline developers mostly have adopted the practice of rating the strength of evidence and recommendations (of those in the National Guideline Clearinghouse, or NGC, 158, or 77 percent, of 204 use some sort of rating scheme), roughly 70 percent (142 of 204 developers) do not identify the origins of their rating schemes, and appear to be using ones unique to their organizations (Coates, 2010). Although many GDGs claim that their recommendations are informed by a systematic review of the evidence, few include the details of their evidence reviews in their guidelines, leaving many users skeptical of their claims. Furthermore, a large percentage of guidelines submitted to the NGC also are "vague" and "ambiguous" and lacking in "explicit recommendations" (Coates, 2010). Even given a diversity of backgrounds and perspectives (i.e., guideline methodologists from medical specialty societies, practicing clinicians, payers, and representatives from integrated health systems), the committee found broad consensus among stakeholders urging guideline developers to articulate clearly the full evidentiary rationale in support of recommendations, as well as methods for deriving recommendation strength (Bottles, 2010; Coates, 2010; Jacques, 2010; Koster, 2010).

BOX 3-1
Infectious Diseases Society of
America Lyme Disease Guidelines (2006)

In a fall 2006 practice guideline, the Infectious Diseases Society of America (IDSA) addressed the controversial diagnosis of chronic Lyme disease: "There is no convincing biologic evidence for the existence of symptomatic chronic *B. burgdorferi* infection among patients after receipt of recommended treatment regimens for Lyme disease. Antibiotic therapy has not proven to be useful and is not recommended for patients with chronic ($\geq$ 6 months) symptoms after recommended treatment regimens for Lyme disease (E-1)." Here, E denotes a recommendation strongly against an action and 1 refers to evidence from one or more properly randomized, controlled trials (Wormser et al., 2006, p. 1094).

Concerned the new IDSA guidelines would impact insurance reimbursements, advocacy groups immediately objected, citing concerns about the IDSA guideline development group's bias and an incomplete review of the data (Johnson and Stricker, 2009). In November 2006, Connecticut Attorney General Richard Blumenthal, himself personally active in support of Lyme disease advocates (McSweegan, 2008), conducted an antitrust investigation against the IDSA, alleging that the broad ramifications of its guidelines require it to use a fair, open development process free from conflicts of interest (Johnson and Stricker, 2009).

At the culmination of its investigation, the Connecticut Attorney General's Office (AGO) questioned the objectivity of the process by which the guideline review committee was selected, the lack of opportunity for interested third parties to provide input, and conflicts of interest of committee members—despite disclosure in the guideline document (Connecticut Attorney General's Office, 2008). In addition, the AGO expressed concern that several IDSA Committee members had concomitantly served on another panel, for the American Academy of Neurology, which discussed and issued a related "Practice Parameter" about chronic Lyme disease in 2007 (Halperin et al., 2007). Refuting these claims, the IDSA maintained that committee members were chosen based on clinical and scientific expertise and that the guideline represented a thorough, peer-reviewed analysis of all available literature and resources (IDSA, 2008; Klein, 2008). Although the guideline does not describe processes for committee selection and guideline development, the document did grade both the strength of its recommendations and evidence quality using a standard scale.

Following nearly 18 months of investigation and $250,000 in legal fees (Klein, 2008), the IDSA entered into a non-punitive agreement with the Attorney General's Office, voluntarily committing to a one-time structured review of their 2006 guidelines to, according to IDSA President Dr. Donald Poretz, "put to rest any questions about them" (IDSA, 2008, online). In Summer 2009, the new Committee, with the oversight of a jointly-appointed ombudsman, met to gather additional evidence for their guideline review, and shortly thereafter unanimously agreed to uphold its 2006 guideline recommendations (IDSA, 2010).

Conflicting Guidelines

To many CPG users, one of the most pressing problems in the current CPG landscape is existence of conflicting guidelines within many disease categories. The Centers for Medicare & Medicaid Coverage and Analysis Group director told the committee, "We are also challenged with dueling guidelines across specialties. What do you do when you have the interventional radiologist versus the surgeon versus medical management?" (Jacques, 2010). For example, in 2008 the U.S. Preventive Services Task Force (USPSTF) and a panel of the American Cancer Society (ACS/MSTF/ACR) published guidelines on colorectal cancer screening objectives and modalities for its detection, with divergent recommendations (described in Box 3-2) within 6 months of one another. This example illustrates how the composition and interests of a GDG may impact its decision mak-

---

BOX 3-2
Colorectal Cancer Screening Guidelines (2008)

In 2008, independent colorectal cancer screening guidelines were published by the U.S. Preventive Services Task Force (USPSTF) and a joint panel of the American Cancer Society, the U.S. Multi-Society Task Force on Colorectal Cancer, and the American College of Radiology (ACS-MSTF-ACR). Although published within 6 months of each other, the two guidelines offer divergent recommendations about the goals of screening as well as the use of specific diagnostic modalities (Goldberg, 2008; Pignone and Sox, 2008). The ACS-MSTF-ACR joint guideline's support for newer technologies such as stool DNA and CT colonoscopy (CAT Scan), as well as its prioritization of "structural" diagnostic modalities such as colonoscopy, contrast with the USPSTF's statement, which did not recommend their use, resulting in confusion among physicians and patients (Goldberg, 2008).

Differences in development methodologies and committee composition likely contribute to the divergence (Imperiale and Ransohoff, 2010; Pignone and Sox, 2008). To inform its work, the USPSTF drew on findings of a commissioned systematic review and benefit/risk simulation modeling (Pignone and Sox, 2008). The USPSTF methods were predefined, rigorous, and quantitative and they separated the systematic review process from that of guideline development (Imperiale and Ransohoff, 2010). However, Pignone and Sox (2008, p. 680) describe "some surprising choices" and missing analyses (e.g., cost/Quality Adjusted Life Years [QALY]) in the data modeling. Of the USPSTF's processes, ACS panelist Tim Byers noted in *The Cancer Letter:* "Even though they say this is a systematic review and it's quantitative and it's all very orderly, some of those key aspects are judgment calls" (Goldberg, 2008, p. 3). In the joint ACS-MSTF-ACR guideline, the panel only briefly describes its evidence review method and offers no

ing. The ACS/MSTF/ACR guideline development group, composed primarily of gastroenterologists and radiologists placed higher priority on newer tests that were most often utilized by the specialties represented on the panel; while the USPSTF, composed exclusively of generalists and methodologists, recommended otherwise. Consequently, some outside observers worry that the recommendations of these groups are predictable, based on the committee members' interests, rather than the evidence. No system is currently accepted for achieving consensus among conflicting sets of guidance. Conflicting guidelines most often result when evidence is weak; developers differ in their approach to evidence reviews (systematic vs. nonsystematic), evidence synthesis or interpretation; and/or developers have varying assumptions about intervention benefits and harms. Conflict of interest (discussed more fully below) may also

insight into its consensus-building process. Imperiale and Ransohoff (2010) report that "the process of evidence review was not clearly separated from the process of guidelines-making" and that "no pre-stated process [was] used to translate evidence into recommendations, nor was the strength of recommendations graded" (Imperiale and Ransohoff, 2010, p. 5). The joint ACS-MSTF-ACR guideline document codifies two guiding principles that informed their recommendations: (1) the importance of one-time test sensitivity (e.g., a requirement that a test achieve > 50 percent sensitivity with a single use), given poor adherence to lower sensitivity program approaches, and (2) the primacy of colon cancer prevention in screening efforts (Levin et al., 2008). Commentaries on the guideline raise concerns about oversimplifications inherent in these decisions (Imperiale and Ransohoff, 2010) and note that this is the only guideline in which the American Cancer Society has adopted and expressed such guiding principles (Goldberg, 2008).

The USPSTF panel was composed of generalist physicians and methodologists (Imperiale and Ransohoff, 2010); the ACS-MSTF-ACR committee consisted of medical specialists and experts in the fields of radiology, gastroenterology, and oncology (Bottles, 2010; Goldberg, 2008). Bernard Levin, a member of the joint panel, remarked in *The Cancer Letter*, "It is extremely hard to bring disparate professional groups together, to have them operate totally out of objectivity, not because they are bad people, but because they see the world through different lenses. Everyone, in some respects, has their vested interests" (Bottles, 2010; Goldberg, 2008, p. 3; Jacques, 2010). Such sentiments have been echoed in multiple commentaries relating to clinical practice guidelines, with authors recognizing that bias extends beyond financial interests to include intellectual and emotional interests as well (Lederer, 2007). As of March 2010, no updates had been made to the guidelines of either organization.

play a role, and value judgments inevitably influence translation of scientific evidence to clinical recommendations (IOM, 2009). The NGC has identified at least 25 different conditions in which conflicting guidelines exist (Coates, 2010).

Conflict of Interest

Conflict of interest among guideline developers continues to be a worrisome area for guideline users. Public forum testimony

---

BOX 3-3
National Kidney Foundation's Kidney Disease and Outcomes Quality Initiative Anemia Management Guidelines (2006)

As one of Medicare's largest pharmaceutical expenses—costing $1.8 billion in 2007 (USRDS, 2009)—erythropoietin has attracted widespread attention (Steinbrook, 2007). Recombinant erythropoietin stimulates receptors in the bone marrow, resulting in increased red blood cell production and a "natural" treatment for anemia (low blood hemoglobin), a common consequence of chronic kidney disease (CKD) (NKF, 2006).

In 2006, when the National Kidney Foundation (NKF) published a new series of Kidney Disease Outcomes Quality Initiative (KDOQI) guidelines, the ideal hemoglobin target for CKD was unclear. The prior KDOQI guidelines, published in 2001, had recommended a range of 11–12 g/dL, striking a balance between the improved quality of life and medical benefits resulting from correction of very low hemoglobin levels and the uncertain value of raising hemoglobin levels more significantly (NKF, 2001). The 16-person 2006 KDOQI Anemia Work Group, citing "insufficient evidence" to produce a guideline, instead issued a clinical practice recommendation about the upper limit of its hemoglobin range: "In the opinion of the Work Group, there is insufficient evidence to recommend routinely maintaining [hemoglobin] levels at 13 g/dL or greater in (Erythropoiesis Stimulating Agents) ESA-treated patients" (NKF, 2006, p. S33). As Coyne (2007b, p. 11) wrote, in the 2006 KDOQI guidelines, "the upper hemoglobin limit was increased to 13 g/dL, despite the lack of sufficient evidence that a hemoglobin target of 12 to 13 g/dL is as safe or results in a significant increase in the quality of life compared with 11 to 12 g/dL."

According to the Work Group, the widened target (now 11–13 g/dL) would be more practical for physicians and patients, although the Work Group cautioned against the medical risks of routinely exceeding the recommended upper bound (NKF, 2006). The guideline document further described a need for additional data and references two recently completed, applicable randomized controlled trials (RCTs) that had data not yet used in guideline development because they had not yet been published (NKF, 2006).

A 2006 Cochrane review—published after the guidelines, but based on the same literature available to the KDOQI panel—found no all-cause

to the committee indicated that COI is particularly concerning to many types of stakeholders. One example that captured media and public attention is the direct financial or research ties that development panelists had with the drug manufacturer that funded the National Kidney Foundation's Kidney Disease and Outcomes Quality Initiative anemia management guidelines (depicted in Box 3-3). Recent research findings provide further evidence of the pervasiveness of COI in guideline development. Choudhry et al. (2002) surveyed 100 individual authors across 37 guidelines, and found that

mortality benefit to raising hemoglobin levels to $\geq$ 13.3 g/dL, compared with 12 g/dL (Strippoli et al., 2006). Within the year, data from two large-scale RCTs and a meta-analysis demonstrated no cardiovascular benefit and an increased risk of adverse events and all-cause mortality associated with maintenance of CKD patients at levels between 12 and 16 g/dL (Drueke et al., 2006; Phrommintikul et al., 2007; Singh et al., 2006). Seeing the discrepancy between these data and the recently released KDOQI guidelines, several critics questioned the timing of the new KDOQI guideline release, the "rules of evidence" used by the KDOQI Work Group, and the significant industry sponsorship and conflicts of interest of Work Group members (Coyne, 2007a,b; Ingelfinger, 2007; Steinbrook, 2006).

Specifically, Coyne (2007a) questioned the KDOQI Anemia Work Group's decision to release the updated guidelines in early 2006, in the absence of new definitive data, especially when two highly applicable, large-scale RCTs were known to be shortly available. In addition, in an editorial accompanying the publication of the two RCTs in the *New England Journal of Medicine*, Remuzzi and Ingelfinger (2006, p. 2144) noted that the NKF–KDOQI guidelines were "not based on persuasive randomized, controlled trials," and other authors questioned the decision of the Work Group to not review unpublished data and abstracts in the review process (Coyne, 2007a; IOM, 2008). Coyne (2007a) also raised significant concerns about conflicts of interest among the NKF's KDOQI Anemia Work Group because the guidelines were published bearing the logo of Amgen (a major U.S. manufacturer of erythropoietin and the KDOQI's "founding and principal sponsor") on the front cover. The majority of panelists had direct financial or research-based ties with erythropoietin manufacturers or marketers (Steinbrook, 2006), and the *Wall Street Journal* reported significant financial support for the committee work by Amgen (Armstrong, 2006).

In a defense of the guideline development process, Van Wyck et al. (2007, p. 8) emphasized the "scientific and methodological rigor" of the guideline development, including standardization of evidentiary review, an intensive internal and public two-stage review process, and full conflict-of-interest disclosure and formal restrictions on members' contacts with sponsors during guideline development.

In light of the new evidence, the KDOQI guidelines were reissued in 2007, recommending an upper bound hemoglobin target of 13 g/dL (Levin and Rocco, 2007).

87 percent had a financial relationship with industry and 59 percent had financial relationships with companies whose products were considered in a guideline (of the 59 percent, 64 percent received speaking honorariums and 38 percent were company employees or consultants). The majority of respondents reported no discussion or disclosure of financial relationships with industry among panel participants during the guideline development process (Choudhry et al., 2002). A 2008 analysis of NGC guideline summaries found that 47 percent indicated "Not stated" in responding to a financial disclosure/conflict of interest query.[1] The proportion of summaries, including information on financial relationships or COI, increased from just over 20 percent to approximately 50 percent from 1999 to 2006 (Tregear, 2007). Chapter 4 discusses strategies for managing COI by organizations such as the American College of Cardiology and American Heart Association (ACC/AHA), American Thoracic Society, USPSTF, and the American College of Physicians and recommends a practice standard.

Funding and Resource Limitations

Funding and resource limitations remain top concerns for many CPG developers, as reported to the committee. According to an international survey of guideline developers from 2003, the average budget for a single guideline developed in the United States was $200,000, not including any additional dissemination costs, which could reach $200,000 per guideline (Burgers et al., 2003a). Guideline developers experience many resource and time constraints, and many entities cannot afford to undertake in-depth evidence syntheses. Additionally, obtaining non-conflicted sources of funding for development and updating of CPGs remains a major challenge. The value of autonomy from industry funding, limited funding available for staff and other support, and limited public grant opportunities are prevailing challenges (Coates, 2010; Fochtmann, 2010).

Contrasting Viewpoints on Scope and Purpose

Guideline developers' and users' views on purpose and scope of guidelines may create tensions on the best way to approach development. Certain developers advocate restricting guideline development and recommendations to clinical domains associated with

---

[1]Personal communication, M. Nix, 2010. Project officer for National Guideline Clearinghouse.

strong evidence, which would result in far fewer guidelines (Lewis, 2010). By contrast, many medical specialty society members and payers seek guidance, particularly in contentious clinical areas, even when evidence is scarce (Milliman Inc., 2009). Some guideline developers have attempted to accommodate both needs by distinguishing CPG recommendations based on high-quality evidence from statements about practice based on expert opinion. However, this approach often has led to confusion among users who are unaware of the varying systems for evidence rating, and some developers continue to struggle with how to differentiate low- to mid-level evidence-based recommendations from those of high quality without compromising guideline usability.

A second tension reflects debate about whether guidelines should detail recommendations for the full continuum of care for a condition(s), or focus on a few key recommendations that are well supported by evidence, easy to implement, and perhaps can be translated into quality measures. Guidelines traditionally have followed the former model, with developers often taking pride in the level of detail and work associated with their products. However, time and resource constraints are significant factors because comprehensive documents take years to complete and costs are high (Lewis, 2010).

EMPIRICAL ASSESSMENT OF GUIDELINE
DEVELOPMENT METHODOLOGY

A literature devoted to assessing methodological quality of CPG development reveals uneven progress over the past 25 years. A 1999 study by Shaneyfelt and colleagues evaluated 279 CPGs from 69 developers, published from 1985 to 1997. The authors found the methodological quality of guidelines improved from 1985 to 1997, as the overall percentage of quality indicators (located in Appendix C) satisfied by all developers increased from 36.9 to 50.4 percent. The greatest advance occurred in development and format (41.5 percent satisfied quality criteria before 1990, 55.9 percent after 1995), and there was little change in evaluation of evidence (34.6–36.1 percent from before 1990 to after 1995). Modest improvements were found in formulation of recommendations (42.8–48.4 percent). A relatively low percentage of guideline developers (less than 10 and 20 percent, respectively) described formal methods of combining scientific evidence and expert opinion and specified how evidence was identified. Moreover, at least one quarter failed to cite any literature basis. Finally, while 89.6 percent specified patient or practice characteristics justifying acceptance or rejection of recommendations, only 21.5 percent detailed the precise role of patient preferences in decision making, and only 6 percent of guidelines described values applied by developers in formulating recommendations (Shaneyfelt et al., 1999).

Similarly, Grilli and colleagues (2000) examined methodological quality of 431 guidelines developed by medical specialty societies between 1988 and 1998. Overall, most guidelines did not meet their three assessment criteria: 67 percent reported no description of stakeholders, 88 percent did not report search strategies for published studies, and 82 percent did not explicitly rate strength of recommendations. All 3 criteria were met in only 22 guidelines, or 5 percent. However, guidelines improved over time with regard to providing search information (from 2 to 18 percent) and explicit grading of evidence (from 6 to 27 percent). The authors concluded that despite evidence of moderate progress, the quality of practice guidelines developed by specialty societies remained unsatisfactory (Grilli et al., 2000).

A 2003 study by Hansenfeld and Shekelle compared methodological quality of 17 guidelines published by the Agency for Health Care Policy and Research (AHCPR) to subsequent non-AHCPR guidelines published in the same topical areas. The authors state, "In contrast to the findings of Shaneyfelt et al. and Grilli et al. that the methodological quality of guidelines has been improving over time, we found that newer guidelines in the same topic areas as the AHCPR guidelines were sharply and disturbingly poorer in methodological quality than the AHCPR guidelines" (Hasenfeld and Shekelle, 2003, p. 433). Using the Appraisal of Guidelines Research & Evaluation (AGREE) instrument (found in Appendix C), the authors found that, overall, AHCPR guidelines met the most standards, scoring 80 percent or more on 24 of 30 criteria. Non-AHCPR guidelines (updates and adapted AHCPR guidelines) scored 80 percent on 14 and 11 of 30 criteria, respectively. All 17 AHCPR guidelines used both multidisciplinary panels and systematic reviews of the literature; by comparison, guidelines updated and adapted by non-AHCPR entities used multidisciplinary panels and systemic reviews 40 and 60 percent of the time, respectively. However, the AHCPR guidelines had lower scores on several criteria: none of the AHCPR guidelines applied and described formal methods of combining evidence or expert opinion (though non-AHCPR guidelines fared only slightly better at 3 percent), only 2 (12 percent) AHCPR guidelines specified expiration dates compared with 12 (40 percent) non-AHCPR guidelines, and finally, 1 (6 percent) AHCPR guideline discussed the role of value judgments in formulating recommendations while 6 (20 percent) of the non-AHCPR guidelines did so (Hasenfeld and Shekelle, 2003).

A 2009 study examining 12 years of Canadian guideline development, dissemination, and evaluation drew similar conclusions of uneven progress. After evaluating 730 guidelines from 1994 to 1999 and 630 from 2000 to 2005, Kryworuchko and colleagues (2009) concluded that over time, developers were more likely to use and publish computerized literature search strategies, and reach consensus via open discussion. Unfortunately, developers were less likely to support guidelines with literature reviews. Kryworuchko et al. concluded that "Guidelines produced more recently in Canada are less likely to be based on a review of the evidence and only half discuss levels of evidence underlying recommendations" (Kryworuchko et al., 2009, p. 1).

Finally, in a 2009 follow-up article to Shaneyfelt and colleagues' 1999 study, Shaneyfelt and Centor lamented the current state of guideline development, specifically the overreliance on expert opinion and inadequate management of COI, with some examples drawn from recent ACC/AHA guidelines (Shaneyfelt and Centor, 2009). Some of Shaneyfelt's and Centor's conclusions were refuted by past chairs of the ACC/AHA Task Force on Practice Guidelines, who defended the methodological quality of the Task Force's guidelines and their development policies (Antman and Gibbons, 2009).

STANDARDIZING GUIDELINE DEVELOPMENT QUALITY APPRAISAL

Some studies have demonstrated that clinical practice guidelines can improve care processes and patient outcomes (Fervers et al., 2005; Ray-Coquard et al., 1997; Smith and Hillner, 2001). When rigorously developed, CPGs have the power to translate the complexity of scientific research findings and other evidence into recommendations for clinical care action (Shiffman et al., 2003). However, CPG development is fraught with challenges. Certain characteristics of guidelines can play a vital part in guideline effectiveness (Grol et al., 2005). CPG guidelines of high methodological rigor can enhance healthcare quality (Grimshaw et al., 2004), and low-quality guidelines may degrade it (Shekelle et al., 2000). Although experimental demonstrations are not available to suggest that provision of formal development guidance leads to improved quality of care, observational evidence indicates that CPGs produced within a structured environment, in which a systematic procedure or "Guidelines for Guidelines" are available to direct production are more likely to be of higher quality (Burgers et al., 2003b; Schünemann et al., 2006). More specifically, non-standardized development results in substantial troubling variation in clinical recommendations (Beck et al., 2000; Schünemann et al., 2006). Furthermore, guideline development methodology has been shown to be enhanced by appraisal instruments; this has been explained in part by their service as "aide-memoire(s)" for guideline developers (Cluzeau and Littlejohns, 1999).

Hence, the accepted notion is that standards regarding quality should guide CPG development (Feder et al., 1999; Shaneyfelt et al., 1999). Calls are increasing for international standards to hasten rigorous CPG development and appraisal (Grilli et al., 2000; Grol et al., 2003; Shaneyfelt et al., 1999; Shaneyfelt and Centor, 2009). The definition of quality guidelines put forth by the AGREE Collaboration is as follows: "the confidence that the potential biases inherent in guideline development have been addressed adequately and that the recommendations are both internally and externally valid (i.e., supported by evidence and applicable to target populations), and are feasible for practice" (AGREE, 2001, p. 2). This definition has been commonly adopted in the scientific literature (Burgers et al., 2003b; Grol et al., 2003). Although uniformly endorsed standards for quality CPG development do not yet exist, there is widespread agreement regarding basic elements of guidelines quality (Schünemann et al., 2006; Shaneyfelt et al., 1999; Turner et al., 2008; Vlayen et al., 2005). This agreement is reflected across multiple, varied sources, including detailed procedures for guideline development or "handbooks" produced by governments (AHRQ, 2008; New Zealand Guidelines Group, 2001; NICE, 2009; SIGN, 2008); professional organizations such as ACC/AHA, American College of Chest Physicians, and American Thoracic Society (ACCF and AHA, 2008; Baumann et al., 2007; Schünemann et al., 2009); and individual leaders in the field (Rosenfeld and Shiffman, 2009).

Overall, development handbooks address the following central elements of the guideline development process: establishment of a multidisciplinary guideline development group, consumer involvement, identification of clinical questions or problems, systematic searches and appraisal of research evidence, procedures for drafting recommendations, external consultation, and ongoing review and update (Turner et al., 2008).

Moreover, a number of taxonomies have been devised for the purposes of guideline methodology quality appraisal and/or improved reporting of guideline development processes (AGREE, 2003; Brouwers et al., 2010; Cluzeau et al., 1999; IOM, 1992; Shaneyfelt et al., 1999; Shiffman et al., 2003). The IOM published the first CPG appraisal instrument (found in Appendix C) in its 1992 report

Guidelines for Clinical Practice: From Development to Use. In a 2005 systematic review of CPG appraisal instruments, Vlayen and colleagues reported that since 1995, 22 appraisal tools have been designed in 8 countries: 6 in the United States, 5 in Canada, 4 in the United Kingdom, 2 each in Australia and Italy, and 1 each in France, Germany, and Spain. Eleven of these instruments are based on the original IOM tool, while several others arose from Hayward et al. (1993) or Cluzeau (1999) (both described in Appendix C) (Cluzeau et al., 1999; Hayward et al., 1993). The tools vary in number (3–52) of guideline attributes considered, availability and form (qualitative or numeric) of scoring systems, and whether they have been subject to validation.

The majority of CPG appraisal tools have been published in peer-reviewed journals (Vlayen et al., 2005). In essence, they share many commonalities captured within the generic AGREE instrument (and the updated AGREE II [2010]) which contains the same domains (Brouwers et al., 2010), which has been widely adopted (Rosenfeld and Shiffman, 2009) and measures the following domains and dimensions of quality development, as follows:

1. Explicit scope and purpose: The overall objective(s), clinical questions, and target population are explicated.
2. Stakeholder involvement: Patient(s) are involved in guideline development and all audiences are defined clearly and involved in pilot-testing.
3. Rigor of development: Recommendations are linked explicitly to supporting evidence and there is discussion of health benefits or risks; recommendations are reviewed externally before publication and development group provides details of updating.
4. Clarity of presentation: Recommendations are not ambiguous and do consider different possible options; key recommendations are easily identified; and a summary document and patient education materials are provided.
5. Applicability: Organizational changes and cost implications of applying recommendations and review criteria for monitoring guidelines use are explicated.
6. Editorial independence: Views or interests of the funding body have not influenced final recommendations; members of the guideline group have declared possible conflicts of interest. (Increased detail of the AGREE instrument and its relatives is provided within Appendix C). The IOM has asserted that each such attribute "affects the likelihood that guidelines will be perceived as trustworthy and useable

or the probability that they will, if used, help achieve the desired health outcomes" (Graham et al., 2000).

As discussed earlier in this chapter, methodological quality of CPGs has been unreliable and advancing unsatisfactorily for decades, despite the existence of guideline appraisal tools such as AGREE. Specifically, empirical evidence supports that quality of guidelines' development processes suffers from a large number of weaknesses across the variety of aforementioned established quality domains (Grilli et al., 2000; Hasenfeld and Shekelle, 2003; Kryworuchko et al., 2009; Shaneyfelt et al., 1999). Furthermore, existing CPG development appraisal instruments do not capture all relevant quality domains. For example, in Vlayen's systematic review, one quarter of instruments omitted transparency and external review. One quarter excluded certain dimensions of derivation and rating of recommendations, such as patient preferences and patient exclusions. One quarter neglected to address updating, and one quarter failed to include the multidisciplinary composition of a guideline development team. Approximately 85 percent did not capture implementation feasibility and more than 40 percent excluded details of recommendation articulation such as wording clarity. With the exception of the Conference on Guideline Standardization (COGS), none of the tools specifies numeric appraisal of the evidentiary foundations for clinical recommendations (Vlayen et al., 2005). Graham's complementary review of guideline appraisal instruments asserts that overall, there appears to be little evidence underlying inclusion of most theoretical domains reflected in the instruments. Direct empirical underpinnings are omitted from accompanying documentation (Graham et al., 2000).

It is important to underscore that this body of guideline appraisal tools overwhelmingly focuses on process and format. Only a small number attend to particulars of guideline clinical content and clinical value (e.g., quality of evidence and strength of recommendations) (Graham et al., 2000). There is no agreed-on standard put forth for prospective enhancement of high-quality, trustworthy guidelines (Shiffman et al., 2003). Moreover, as appraisal and reporting tools, they are designed for retrospective assessment and documentation of released guidelines rather than prospective application to development of high-quality, trustworthy CPGs (Shiffman et al., 2003). As further elaboration, COGS is limited to reporting of the guideline development process, as its authors attest: "[COGs] is not intended to dictate a particular guideline development methodology . . . we believe that COGS can be used most effectively to identify necessary components that should be documented in guidelines but should not be used (alone) to judge guideline quality or adequacy" (Shiffman et al., 2003, pp. 495–496). The AGREE instrument is the only instrument to have been validated it has wide acceptance; however, it only assesses the quality of reporting and the quality of "some aspects of recommendations" (AGREE, 2001, p. 2) and, like its peers, AGREE fails specifically with regard to evidence quality appraisal (Vlayen et al., 2005). "The AGREE instrument is designed to assess the process of guideline development and how well it is reported. It does not assess the clinical content of the guideline nor the quality of evidence that underpins the recommendations" (AGREE, 2003, p. 18).

Complementing empirical study of the validity of quality appraisal tools and description of their adoption, is literature devoted to the validity of individual quality components within these tools. This work sheds further light on the nuances of deficiencies inherent in the state-of-the-art of development of CPGs, with emphatic attention given to subtle dimensions (e.g., explicit scope and purpose, applicability, editorial independence) and operational details of methodological quality criteria, including conflict of interest, the role of judgment in recommendations derivation, recommendations prioritization, development group composition, patient-centeredness (including patient preferences and comorbidity), and implementation feasibility (Choudhry et al., 2002; Graham et al., 2000; Grol et al., 2003; Guyatt et al., 2010; Shaneyfelt and Centor, 2009; Sniderman and Furberg, 2009).

The standards for development of trustworthy CPGs delineated in the chapters to follow arose from the committee's investigation of the evidence bases synthesized above. Full details of the spectrum of research methods supporting the committee's standards setting are contained in Chapter 1.

REFERENCES

ACCF and AHA (American College of Cardiology Foundation and American Heart Association). 2008. Methodology manual for ACCF/AHA guideline writing committees. In *Methodologies and policies from ACCF/AHA Taskforce on Practice Guidelines*. ACCF and AHA.

AGREE (Appraisal of Guidelines for Research & Evaluation). 2001. *Appraisal of Guidelines for Research & Evaluation (AGREE) Instrument*. The AGREE Collaboration. www.agreecollaboration.org (accessed November 10, 2010).

AGREE. 2003. Development and validation of an international appraisal instrument for assessing the quality of clinical practice guidelines: The AGREE project. *Quality and Safety in Health Care* 12(1):18–23.

AHRQ (Agency for Healthcare Research and Quality). 2008. *U.S. Preventive Services Task Force procedure manual.* AHRQ http://www.healtheducationadvocate.org/Summit/. No. 08-05118-ef. http://www.ahrq.gov/clinic/uspstf08/methods/procmanual.htm (accessed February 12, 2009).

Als-Nielsen, B., W. Chen, C. Gluud, and L. L. Kjaergard. 2003. Association of funding and conclusions in randomized drug trials: A reflection of treatment effect or adverse events? *JAMA* 290(7):921–928.

Antman, E. M., and R. J. Gibbons. 2009. Clinical practice guidelines and scientific evidence. *JAMA* 302(2):143–144; author reply 145–147.

Armstrong, D. 2006. Medical journal spikes article on industry ties. *The Wall Street Journal*, December 26, B1.

Avorn, J. 2005. *Powerful medicines: The benefits, risks, and costs of prescription drugs.* Rev. and updated, 1st Vintage Books ed. New York: Vintage Books.

Baumann, M. H., S. Z. Lewis, and D. Gutterman. 2007. ACCP evidence-based guideline development: A successful and transparent approach addressing conflict of interest, funding, and patient-centered recommendations. *Chest* 132(3):1015–1024.

Beck, C., M. Cody, E. Souder, M. Zhang, and G. W. Small. 2000. Dementia diagnostic guidelines: Methodologies, results, and implementation costs. *Journal of the American Geriatrics Society* 48(10):1195–1203.

Bottles, K. 2010. *Institute for Clinical Systems Improvement (ICSI).* Presented at the IOM Committee on Standards for Developing Trustworthy Clinical Practice Guidelines meeting, January 11, 2010, Washington, DC.

Boyd, C. 2010. *CPGs for people with multimorbidities.* Presented at the IOM Committee on Standards for Developing Trustworthy Clinical Practice Guidelines meeting, January 11, 2010, Washington, DC.

Boyd, C. M., J. Darer, C. Boult, L. P. Fried, L. Boult, and A. W. Wu. 2005. Clinical practice guidelines and quality of care for older patients with multiple comorbid diseases: Implications for pay for performance. *JAMA* 294(6):716–724.

Brouwers, M. C., M. E. Kho, G. P. Browman, J. S. Burgers, F. Cluzeau, G. Feder, B. Fervers, I. D. Graham, J. Grimshaw, S. E. Hanna, P. Littlejohns, J. Makarski, and L. Zitzelsberger. 2010. AGREE II: Advancing guideline development, reporting and evaluation in health care. *Canadian Medical Association Journal* 182(18):E839–842.

Brown, A. 2010. *Clinical practice guidelines: Implications for vulnerable patients: Development of geriatric diabetes guidelines.* Paper presented at the IOM Committee on Standards for Developing Trustworthy Clinical Practice Guidelines meeting, January 11, 2010, Washington, DC.

Burgers, J., R. Grol, N. Klazinga, M. Makela, J. Zaat, and AGREE Collaboration. 2003a. Towards evidence-based clinical practice: An international survey of 18 clinical guideline programs. *International Journal on Quality Health Care* 15(1):31–45.

Burgers, J. S., F. A. Cluzeau, S. E. Hanna, C. Hunt, and R. Grol. 2003b. Characteristics of high-quality guidelines: Evaluation of 86 clinical guidelines developed in ten European countries and Canada. *International Journal of Technology Assessment in Health Care* 19(1):148–157.

Choudhry, N. K., H. T. Stelfox, and A. S. Detsky. 2002. Relationships between authors of clinical practice guidelines and the pharmaceutical industry. *JAMA* 287(5):612–617.

Cluzeau, F. A., and P. Littlejohns. 1999. Appraising clinical practice guidelines in England and Wales: The development of a methodologic framework and its application to policy. *Joint Commission Journal of Quality Improvement* 25(10):514–521.

Cluzeau, F. A., P. Littlejohns, J. M. Grimshaw, G. Feder, and S. E. Moran. 1999. Development and application of a generic methodology to assess the quality of clinical guidelines. *International Journal for Quality in Health Care* 11(1):21–28.

Coates, V. 2010. *National Guidelines Clearinghouse/ECRI Institute*. Paper presented at the IOM Committee on Developing Standards for Trustworthy Clinical Practice Guidelines meeting, January 11, 2010, Washington, DC.

Connecticut Attorney General's Office. 2008. Attorney general's investigation reveals flawed Lyme disease guideline process, IDSA agrees to reassess guidelines, install independent arbiter. Hartford, CT: Connecticut Attorney General's Office.

Coyne, D. W. 2007a. Influence of industry on renal guideline development. *Clinical Journal of the American Society of Nephrology* 2(1):3–7.

Coyne, D. W. 2007b. Practice recommendations based on low, very low, and missing evidence. *Clinical Journal of the American Society of Nephrology* 2(1):11–12.

Drueke, T. B., F. Locatelli, N. Clyne, K. Eckardt, I. C. Macdougall, D. Tsakiris, H. Burger, A. Scherhag, and C. Investigators. 2006. Normalization of hemoglobin level in patients with chronic kidney disease and anemia. *New England Journal of Medicine* 355(20):2071–2084.

Feder, G., M. Eccles, R. Grol, C. Griffiths, and J. Grimshaw. 1999. Clinical guidelines: Using clinical guidelines. *BMJ* 318(7185):728–730.

Ferrette, C. 2008. Lyme disease expert defends research. *The Journal News*, May 6, 1A.

Fervers, B., J. S. Burgers, M. C. Haugh, M. Brouwers, G. Browman, F. Cluzeau, and T. Philip. 2005. Predictors of high quality clinical practice guidelines: Examples in oncology. *International Journal for Quality in Health Care* 17(2):123–132.

Fochtmann, L. 2010. *American Psychiatric Association*. Presented at the IOM Committee on Standards for Developing Trustworthy Clinical Practice Guidelines meeting, January 11, 2010, Washington, DC.

Goldberg, P. 2008. Pragmatists vs. purists: Colon cancer screening guideline triggers debate. *The Cancer Letter* 34(7):1–5.

Graham, I. D., L. A. Calder, P. C. Herbert, A. O. Carter, and J. M. Tetroe. 2000. A comparison of clinical practice guideline appraisal instruments. *International Journal of Technology Assessment in Health Care* 16(4):1024–1038.

Grilli, R., N. Magrini, A. Penna, G. Mura, and A. Liberati. 2000. Practice guidelines developed by specialty societies: The need for a critical appraisal. *The Lancet* 355(9198):103–106.

Grimshaw, J., M. Eccles, and J. Tetroe. 2004. Implementing clinical guidelines: Current evidence and future implications. *The Journal of Continuing Education in the Health Professions* 24(Suppl 1):S31–S37.

Grol, R., F. A. Cluzeau, and J. S. Burgers. 2003. Clinical practice guidelines: Towards better quality guidelines and increased international collaboration. *British Journal of Cancer* 89(Suppl 1): S4–S8.

Grol, R., M. Wensing, and M. Eccles. 2005. *Improving patient care: The implementation of change in clinical practice*.Oxford: Elsevier Butterworth Heinemann.

Guyatt, G., E. A. Akl, J. Hirsh, C. Kearon, M. Crowther, D. Gutterman, S. Z. Lewis, I. Nathanson, R. Jaeschke, and H. Schünemann. 2010. The vexing problem of guidelines and conflict of interest: A potential solution. *Annals of Internal Medicine* 152(11):738–741.

Halperin, J. J., E. D. Shapiro, E. Logigian, A. L. Belman, L. Dotevall, G. P. Wormser, L. Krupp, G. Gronseth, and C. T. Bever, Jr. 2007. Practice parameter: Treatment of nervous system Lyme disease (an evidence-based review): Report of the Quality Standards Subcommittee of the American Academy of Neurology. *Neurology* 69(1):91–102.

Hasenfeld, R., and P. G. Shekelle. 2003. Is the methodological quality of guidelines declining in the U.S.? Comparison of the quality of U.S. Agency for Health Care Policy and Research (AHCPR) guidelines with those published subsequently. *Quality and Safety in Health Care* 12(6):428–434.

Hayward, R. S. A., M. C. Wilson, S. R. Tunis, E. B. Bass, H. R. Rubin, and R. B. Haynes. 1993. More informative abstracts of articles describing clinical practice guidelines. *Annals of Internal Medicine* 118(9):731–737.

The House of Commons Health Committee. 2005. The influence of the pharmaceutical industry. Vol. 1. London, U.K.: The Stationary Office Limited. http://www.parliament.the-stationery-office.co.uk/pa/cm200405/cmselect/cmhealth/42/42.pdf (accessed April 8, 2010).

IDSA (Infectious Diseases Society of America). 2008. *Agreement ends Lyme disease investigation by Connecticut attorney general*. Infectious Diseases Society of America.

IDSA. 2010. *News release: Special review panel unanimously upholds Lyme disease treatment guidelines: April 22, 2010*. http://www.idsociety.org/Content.aspx?id=16556 (accessed November 1, 2010).

Imperiale, T. F., and D. F. Ransohoff. 2010. Understanding differences in the guidelines for colorectal cancer screening. *Gastroenterology* 138(5):1642–1647.

Ingelfinger, J. R. 2007. Through the looking glass: Anemia guidelines, vested interests, and distortions. *Clinical Journal of the American Society of Nephrology* 2(3):415–417.

IOM (Institute of Medicine). 1992. *Guidelines for clinical practice: From development to use*. Edited by M. J. Field and K. N. Lohr. Washington, DC: National Academy Press.

IOM. 2008. *Knowing what works in health care: A roadmap for the nation*. Edited by J. Eden, B. Wheatley, B. McNeil and H. Sox. Washington, DC: The National Academies Press.

IOM. 2009. *Conflict of interest in medical research, education, and practice*. Edited by B. Lo and M. J. Field. Washington, DC: The National Academies Press.

Jacobs, A. 2010. *American College of Cardiology and American Heart Association*. Presented at the IOM Committee on Standards for Developing Trustworthy Clinical Practice Guidelines meeting, January 11, 2010, Washington, DC.

Jacques, L. B. 2010. *Centers for Medicare & Medicaid Services (CMS)*. Presented at the IOM Committee on Standards for Developing Trustworthy Clinical Practice Guidelines meeting, January 11, 2010, Washington, DC.

Johnson, L., and R. B. Stricker. 2009. Attorney general forces Infectious Diseases Society of America to redo Lyme guidelines due to flawed development process. *Journal of Medical Ethics* 35(5):283–288.

Klein, J. O. 2008. Danger ahead: Politics intrude in Infectious Diseases Society of America guideline for Lyme disease. *Clinical Infectious Diseases* 47(9):1197–1199.

Koster, M. A. 2010. *Technology assessment and guidelines unit: Kaiser Permanente Southern California*. Paper presented at the IOM Committee on Standards for Developing Trustworthy Clinical Practice Guidelines meeting, http://www.idsociety.org/Content.aspx?id=16556January 11, 2010, Washington, DC.

Kraemer, J. D., and L. O. Gostin. 2009. Science, politics, and values: The politicization of professional practice guidelines. *JAMA* 301(6):665–667.

Kryworuchko, J., D. Stacey, N. Bai, and I. Graham. 2009. Twelve years of clinical practice guideline development, dissemination and evaluation in Canada (1994 to 2005). *Implementation Science* 4(1):49.

Lederer, E. D. 2007. Development of clinical practice guidelines: Are we defining the issues too narrowly? *Clinical Journal of the American Society of Nephrology* 2(2):207.

Levin, A., and M. Rocco. 2007. KDOQI clinical practice guideline and clinical practice recommendations for anemia in chronic kidney disease: 2007 update of hemoglobin target. *American Journal of Kidney Diseases* 50(3):471–530.

Levin, B., D. A. Lieberman, B. McFarland, R. A. Smith, D. Brooks, K. S. Andrews, C. Dash, F. M. Giardiello, S. Glick, T. R. Levin, P. Pickhardt, D. K. Rex, A. Thorson, S. J. Winawer, A. C. S. C. C. Advis, U. M.-S. T. Force, and A. C. R. C. C. Com. 2008. Screening and surveillance for the early detection of colorectal cancer and adenomatous polyps, 2008: A joint guideline from the American Cancer Society, the US Multi-Society Task Force on Colorectal Cancer, and the American College of Radiology. *CA: A Cancer Journal for Clinicians* 58(3):130–160.

Lewis, S. Z. 2010. *American College of Chest Physicians*. Paper presented at the IOM Committee on Standards for Developing Trustworthy Clinical Practice Guidelines meeting, January 11, 2010, Washington, DC.

McAlister, F., S. van Diepen. R. Padwa, J. Johnson, and S. Majumdar. 2007. How evidence-based are the recommendations in evidence-based guidelines. *PLoS Medicine* 4(8): 1325–1332.

McSweegan, E. 2008. Lyme disease and the politics of public advocacy. *Clinical Infectious Diseases* 47(12):1609–1610.

Milliman Inc. 2009. *Milliman care guidelines*. http://www.milliman.com/expertise/healthcare/products-tools/milliman-care-guidelines/ (accessed June 9, 2009).

New Zealand Guidelines Group. 2001. Handbook for the preparation of explicit evidence-based clinical practice guidelines. http://www.nzgg.org.nz (accessed August 26, 2009).

NICE (National Institute for Health and Clinical Excellence). 2009. *Methods for the development of NICE public health guidance*, 2nd ed. London, UK: NICE.

NKF (National Kidney Foundation). 2001. *Guidelines for anemia of chronic kidney disease*. National Kidney Foundation, Inc. http://www.kidney.org/PROFESSIONALS/kdoqi/guidelines_updates/doqiupan_ii.html (accessed January 21, 2011).

NKF. 2006. KDOQI clinical practice guidelines and clinical practice recommendations for anemia in chronic kidney disease. *American Journal of Kidney Diseases* 47(5, S http://www.idsociety.org/Content.aspx?id=16556uppl 3):S11–S145.

Phrommintikul, A., S. J. Haas, M. Elsik, and H. Krum. 2007. Mortality and target haemoglobin concentrations in anaemic patients with chronic kidney disease treated with erythropoietin: A meta-analysis. *The Lancet* 369(9559):381–388.

Pignone, M., and H. C. Sox. 2008. Screening guidelines for colorectal cancer: A twice-told tale. *Annals of Internal Medicine* 149(9):680–682.

Ray-Coquard, I., T. Philip, M. Lehmann, B. Fervers, F. Farsi, and F. Chauvin. 1997. Impact of a clinical guidelines program for breast and colon cancer in a French cancer center. *JAMA* 278(19):1591–1595.

Remuzzi, G., and J. R. Ingelfinger. 2006. Correction of anemia—payoffs and problems. *New England Journal of Medicine* 355(20):2144–2146.

Rosenfeld, R., and R. N. Shiffman. 2009. Clinical practice guideline development manual: A quality-driven approach for translating evidence into action. *Otolaryngology–Head & Neck Surgery* 140(6, Suppl 1):1–43.

Schünemann, H. J., A. Fretheim, and A. D. Oxman. 2006. Improving the use of research evidence in guideline development: Guidelines for guidelines. *Health Research Policy and Systems* 4:13.

Schünemann, H. J., M. Osborne, J. Moss, C. Manthous, G. Wagner, L. Sicilian, J. Ohar, S. McDermott, L. Lucas, and R. Jaeschke. 2009. An official American Thoracic Society policy statement: Managing conflict of interest in professional societies. *American Journal of Respiratory Critical Care Medicine* 180(6):564–580.

Shaneyfelt, T. M., and R. M. Centor. 2009. Reassessment of clinical practice guidelines: Go gently into that good night. *JAMA* 301(8):868–869.

Shaneyfelt, T., M. Mayo-Smith, and J. Rothwangl. 1999. Are guidelines following guidelines? The methodological quality of clinical practice guidelines in the peer-reviewed medical literature. *JAMA* 281:1900–1905.

Shekelle, P. G., R. L. Kravitz, J. Beart, M. Marger, M. Wang, and M. Lee. 2000. Are nonspecific practice guidelines potentially harmful? A randomized comparison of the effect of nonspecific versus specific guidelines on physician decision making. *Health Services Research* 34(7):1429–1448.

Shiffman, R. N., P. Shekelle, J. M. Overhage, J. Slutsky, J. Grimshaw, and A. M. Deshpande. 2003. Standardized reporting of clinical practice guidelines: A proposal from the conference on guideline standardization. *Annals of Internal Medicine* 139(6):493–498.

SIGN, ed. 2008. *SIGN 50: A guideline developer's handbook.* Edinburgh, Scot.: Scottish Intercollegiate Guidelines Network.

Singh, A. K., L. Szczech, K. L. Tang, H. Barnhart, S. Sapp, M. Wolfson, D. Reddan, and C. Investigators. 2006. Correction of anemia with epoetin alfa in chronic kidney disease. *New England Journal of Medicine* 355(20):2085–2098.

Smith, T. J., and B. E. Hillner. 2001. Ensuring quality cancer care by the use of clinical practice guidelines and critical pathways. *Journal of Clinical Oncology* 19(11):2886–2897.

Sniderman, A. D., and C. D. Furberg. 2009. Why guideline-making requires reform. *JAMA* 301(4):429–431.

Steinbrook, R. 2006. Haemoglobin concentrations in chronic kidney disease. *The Lancet* 368(9554):2191–2193.

Steinbrook, R. 2007. Medicare and erythropoietin. *New England Journal of Medicine* 356(1):4–6.

Strippoli, G. F., S. D. Navaneethan, and J. C. Craig. 2006. Haemoglobin and haematocrit targets for the anaemia of chronic kidney disease. *Cochrane Database of Systematic Reviews* (4):CD003967.

Tregear, M. 2007. Guideline heterogeneity; workshop—part 2. Paper presented at The Fourth Annual Guidelines International Network m Haemoglobin concentrations in chronic kidney disease eeting, August 22–25, 2007, Toronto, Canada.

Turner, T., M. Misso, C. Harris, and S. Green. 2008. Development of evidence-based clinical practice guidelines (CPGs): Comparing approaches. *Implementation Science* 3:45.

USRDS (United States Renal Data System). 2009. *USRDS 2009 annual data report: Atlas of chronic kidney disease and end-stage renal disease in the United States.* Bethesda, MD: National Institute of Diabetes and Digestive and Kidney Diseases.

Van Wyck, D., K. U. Eckardt, K. Uhlig, M. Rocco, and A. Levin. 2007. Appraisal of evidence and control of bias in the Kidney Disease Outcomes Quality Initiative guideline development process. *Clinical Journal of the American Society of Nephrology* 2(1):8–10.

Vlayen, J., B. Aertgeerts, K. Hannes, W. Sermeus, and D. Ramaekers. 2005. A systematic review of appraisal tools for clinical practice guidelines: Multiple similarities and one common deficit. *International Journal of Quality Health Care* 17(3):235–242.

Wormser, G. P., R. J. Dattwyler, E. D. Shapiro, J. J. Halperin, A. C. Steere, M. S. Klempner, P. J. Krause, J. S. Bakken, F. Strle, G. Stanek, L. Bockenstedt, D. Fish, J. S. Dumler, and R. B. Nadelman. 2006. The clinical assessment, treatment, and prevention of lyme disease, human granulocytic anaplasmosis, and babesiosis: clinical practice guidelines by the Infectious Diseases Society of America. *Clinical Infectious Diseases* 43(9):1089–1134.

4

Current Best Practices and Proposed Standards for Development of Trustworthy CPGs: Part 1, Getting Started

Abstract: As stated in Chapter 1, the committee was charged with identifying standards for the production of unbiased, scientifically valid, and trustworthy clinical practice guidelines. The following two chapters describe and present the rationale for the committee's proposed standards, which reflect a review of the literature, public comment, and expert consensus on best practices for developing trustworthy guidelines. The standards and supporting text herein address several aspects of guideline development, including transparency, conflict of interest, guideline development team composition and group process, and finally, the determination of guideline scope and the chain of logic, including interaction with the systematic review team.

INTRODUCTION

Chapters 4 and 5 detail aspects of the clinical practice guideline (CPG) development process, and the committee's related proposed standards, over time, from considerations of transparency and conflict of interest (COI) to updating of guidelines. The proposed standards arose from the committee's compliance with standard-setting methodologies elaborated on in Chapter 1. A standard is defined as a process, action, or procedure that is deemed essential to producing scientifically valid, transparent, and reproducible results. The committee expects its standards to be pilot-tested and evaluated for reliability and validity (including applicability), as described in detail in Chapter 7, and to evolve as the science and experience demand.

This chapter captures aspects of the beginnings of guideline development, including transparency, conflict of interest, guideline development team composition and group process, and determining guideline scope and logic, including interaction with the systematic review (SR) team. The committee hopes its proposed standards serve as an important contribution to advancing the work of numerous researchers, developers, and users of guidelines, and help to clarify where evidence and expert consensus support best practices and where there is still much to learn. An important note is that, although textually discussed, no standards are proposed for certain aspects of the guideline development process, such as determining group processes, guideline scope, chain of logic underlying a guideline, incorporating patients with comorbidities and the impact of cost on rating the strength of recommendations, given that the committee could not conceive any standards applicable to all guideline development groups (GDGs) in these areas at this time.

ESTABLISHING TRANSPARENCY

"Transparency" connotes the provision of information to CPG users that enables them to understand how recommendations were derived and who developed them. Increasing transparency of the guideline development process has long been recommended by authors of CPG development appraisal tools (AGREE, 2001; IOM, 1992; Shaneyfelt et al., 1999) and the following leading guideline development organizations: the U.S. Preventive Services Task Force (USPSTF), National Institute for Health and Clinical Excellence (NICE), American College of Cardiology Foundation/American Heart Association (ACCF/AHA), and American Thoracic Society. However, exactly what needs to be transparent and how transparency should be accomplished has been unclear. The desire to have public access to GDG deliberations and documents must be balanced with resource and time constraints as well as the need for GDG members to engage in frank discussion.

The committee found no comparisons in the literature of GDG approaches to achieving transparency, but did inspect policies of select organizations. The American Academy of Pediatrics transparency policy calls on guideline authors to make an explicit judgment regarding anticipated benefits, harms, risks, and costs (American

Academy of Pediatrics, 2008).[1] According to Schünemann and coauthors (2007, p. 0791) in an article concerning transparent development of World Health Organization (WHO) guidelines, "Guideline developers are increasingly using the GRADE (Grading Recommendations Assessment, Development and Evaluation) approach because it includes transparent judgments about each of the key factors that determine the quality of evidence for each important outcome, and overall across outcomes for each recommendation."

Even clinical decisions informed by high-quality, evidence-based CPG recommendations are subject to uncertainty. An explicit statement of how evidence, expertise, and values were weighed by guideline writers helps users to determine the level of confidence they should have in any individual recommendation. Insufficient or conflicting evidence, inability to achieve consensus among guideline authors, legal and/or economic considerations, and ethical/religious issues are likely reasons that guideline writers leave recommendations vague (American Academy of Pediatrics, 2008). Instead, guideline developers should highlight which of these factors precluded them from being more specific or directive. When a guideline is written with full disclosure, users will be made aware of the potential for change when new evidence becomes available, and will be more likely to understand and accept future alterations to recommendations (American Academy of Pediatrics, 2008). Detailed attention to CPG development methods for appraising, and elucidating the appraisal of, evidentiary foundations of recommendations is provided in Chapter 5.

Transparency also requires statements regarding the development team members' clinical experience, and potential COIs, as well as the guideline's funding source(s) (ACCF and AHA, 2008, AHRQ, 2008; Rosenfeld and Shiffman, 2009). Disclosing potential financial and intellectual conflicts of interest of all members of the development team allows users to interpret recommendations in light of the COIs (American Academy of Pediatrics, 2008). The following section in this chapter discusses in greater detail how to manage COIs among development team members. Ultimately, a transparent guideline should give users confidence that guidelines are based on best available evidence, largely free from bias, clear about the purpose of recommendations to individual patients, and therefore trustworthy.

---

[1]The committee did not inspect whether GDGs followed policies on transparency set in place by their parent organizations (i.e., did AAP guidelines meet their own standard on transparency).

1. **Establishing Transparency**
   1.1 The processes by which a CPG is developed and funded should be detailed explicitly and publicly accessible.

MANAGEMENT OF CONFLICT OF INTEREST

The Institute of Medicine's 2009 report on *Conflict of Interest in Medical Research, Education, and Practice* defined COI as "A set of circumstances that creates a risk that professional judgment or actions regarding a primary interest will be unduly influenced by a secondary interest" (IOM, 2009, p. 46). A recent comprehensive review of COI policies of guideline development organizations yielded the following complementary descriptions of COI: "A divergence between an individual's private interests and his or her professional obligations such that an independent observer might reasonably question whether the individual's professional actions or decisions are motivated by personal gain, such as financial, academic advancement, clinical revenue streams, or community standing" and "A financial or intellectual relationship that may impact an individual's ability to approach a scientific question with an open mind" (Schünemann et al., 2009, p. 565). Finally, intellectual COIs specific to CPGs are defined as "academic activities that create the potential for an attachment to a specific point of view that could unduly affect an individual's judgment about a specific recommendation" (Guyatt et al., 2010, p. 739). Increasingly, CPG developers—including the American Heart Association, American Thoracic Society, American College of Chest Physicians, American College of Physicians, and World Health Organization—all have COI policies encompassing financial and intellectual conflicts (Guyatt et al., 2010; Schünemann et al., 2009).

The concept that COI can influence healthcare decision makers is widely recognized (Als-Nielsen, 2003; Lexchin et al., 2003). Therefore, it is disturbing that an assessment of 431 guidelines authored by specialty societies reported that 67 percent neglected to disclose information on the professionals serving on the guideline development panel, making even rudimentary evaluation of COI infeasible (Grilli et al., 2000). Furthermore, an investigation of more than 200 clinical practice guidelines within the National Guideline Clearinghouse determined that greater than half included no information about financial sponsors of guidelines or financial conflicts of interest of guideline authors (Taylor, 2005). Organizations developing practice guidelines thus need to improve management and reporting of COI (Boyd and Bero, 2000; Campbell, 2007; Jacobs et al., 2004).

Disclosure policies should relate to all potential committee members (including public/patient representatives) and should include all current and planned financial and institutional conflicts of interest. Financial (commercial or noncommercial) COI typically stems from actual or potential direct financial benefit related to topics discussed or products recommended in guidelines. Direct financial commercial activities include clinical services from which a committee member derives a substantial proportion of his or her income; consulting; board membership for which compensation of any type is received; serving as a paid expert witness; industry-sponsored research; awarded or pending patents; royalties; stock ownership or options; and other personal and family member financial interests. Examples of noncommercial financial activities include research grants and other types of support from governments, foundations, or other nonprofit organizations (Schünemann et al., 2009). A person whose work or professional group fundamentally is jeopardized, or enhanced, by a guideline recommendation is said to have intellectual COI. Intellectual COI includes authoring a publication or acting as an investigator on a peer-reviewed grant directly related to recommendations under consideration. Finally, individuals with knowledge of relationships between their institutions and commercial entities with interests in the CPG topic are considered to have institutional COI. These include public/patient representatives from advocacy organizations receiving direct industry funding.

Biases resulting from COI may be conscious or unconscious (Dana, 2003) and may influence choices made throughout the guideline development process, including conceptualization of the question, choice of treatment comparisons, interpretation of the evidence, and, in particular, drafting of recommendations (Guyatt et al., 2010). A recent study of Food and Drug Administration Advisory Committees found that members regularly disclose financial interests of considerable monetary value, yet rarely recuse themselves from decision making. When they did, less favorable voting outcomes regarding the drug in question were observed across the majority of committee meetings (Lurie et al., 2006). A related investigation observed that 7 percent of guideline developers surveyed believed their relationships with industry affected their guideline recommendations; moreover, nearly 20 percent believed that guideline coauthors' recommendations were subject to industry influence (Chaudhry et al., 2002). Regardless of the nature of COI or its effects on guideline development, perception of bias undermines guideline users' confidence in guideline trustworthiness as well as public trust in science (Friedman, 2002).

Direct guideline funding by for-profit organizations also poses COI challenges. The development, maintenance, and revision of CPGs is a costly, labor-intensive endeavor (American Academy of Physicians Assistants, 1997). Many professional societies and other groups developing guidelines rely, at least in part, on commercial sponsors to cover costs. The perception that a for-profit commercial entity, including pharmaceutical and medical device companies in particular, had influenced conclusions and recommendations of a CPG committee could undermine the trustworthiness of the GDG and its CPG (Eichacker et al., 2006; Rothman et al., 2009). Although the 2009 IOM Committee on COI in Medical Research, Education, and Practice found no systematic studies investigating the association between the guideline development process or CPG content and funding source, it did detail cases that raised concern about industry funding influence (IOM, 2009).

The controversy over Eli Lilly's involvement with practice guidelines for treatment of severe sepsis, and the company's marketing campaign for the drug rhAPC, highlight this issue. Although Eli Lilly and the sepsis guideline development group maintain that recommendations were based on high-quality randomized controlled trials (RCTs), many experts contend the group undervalued non-RCT studies of standard therapies and failed to address concerns about rhAPC's adverse side effects. Because Eli Lilly was the predominant funder and many development panel members had relationships with the company, trust in integrity of the guideline recommendations was understandably low (Eichacker et al., 2006).

Some guideline experts have requested that professional medical organizations reject all industry funding for practice guidelines (Rothman et al., 2009) and hold GDG members to the most stringent COI standards (Sniderman and Furberg, 2009). The IOM's 2009 report on conflict of interest suggests that adequate firewalls between funders and those who develop guidelines must exist (IOM, 2009).

However, the most knowledgeable individuals regarding the subject matter addressed by a CPG are frequently conflicted. These "experts" often possess unique insight into guideline-relevant content domains. More specifically, through their research or clinical involvement, they may be aware of relevant information about study design and conduct that is not easily identified. Although expert opinion is not a form of high-quality evidence, the observations of experts may provide valuable insight on a topic; those who have such insight may simply be without substitutes. Optimally GDGs are made up of members who lack COIs. Experts who have unique knowledge about the topic under consideration—but who have COIs—can share their expertise with the GDG as consultants and as reviewers of GDG products, but generally should not serve as members of the GDG.

Strategies for Managing COI

Strategies for managing potential COI range from exclusion of conflicted members from direct panel participation or restriction of roles, to formal or informal consultation, to participation in certain exclusive recommendations, to simple disclosure of COI. Although the 2009 IOM committee on COI found no systematic review of guideline development organizations' conflict-of-interest policies, the committee did identify variations in the COI policies of select organizations. Specifically, COI policies vary with regard to the specific types of information that must be disclosed, who is responsible for managing conflicts and monitoring policy compliance, and whether COI procedures are transparent. Provisions for public disclosure of COI and managing relationships with funders also differ (IOM, 2009).

Although disclosure of guideline development members' financial conflicts has become common practice, many experts are skeptical that disclosure alone minimizes the impact of conflicts (Guyatt et al., 2010). Hence, increasingly rigorous management strategies have been adopted by some organizations (Schünemann et al., 2009). These have included omission of those with COI from guideline development panels (WHO, 2008) and exclusion of conflicted persons from leadership positions (NICE, 2008). The USPSTF currently bars individuals who have earned more than $10,000 per year from medical expert testimony or related endeavors from serving on guideline panels. Lesser financial or intellectual conflicts may require disclosure to other panel members or recusal from specific recommendation deliberations, at the discretion of the USPSTF chair and vice chair and under the aegis of Agency for Healthcare Research and Quality staff (AHRQ, 2008). The ACCF/AHA task force strives to balance conflict of interest, rather than remove it completely, and allows 50 percent of committee members to have industry relationships, but recuses those members from voting on relevant recommendations. The committee chair must also be free of any COI (ACCF and AHA, 2008).

Other COI management approaches—including mandating clearer separation of unconflicted methodologists from the influence of potentially conflicted clinical experts—are reflected in the American College of Chest Physicians Antithrombotic Guidelines

(Guyatt et al., 2010). In this approach, unconflicted methodologists, such as epidemiologists, statisticians, healthcare researchers and/or "guidelineologists" (i.e., those with specific expertise in the guideline development process), lead the formulation of recommendations in collaboration with clinical experts who may be conflicted to a degree that would not preclude them from panel participation. Guyatt and coauthors advocate this strategy, stating that the key to developing unconflicted recommendations is that the responsibility for the final presentation of evidence summaries and rating of quality of evidence rests with unconflicted panel members, and in particular with the methodologist chapter editor (Guyatt et al., 2010). A 2010 examination of state-of-the-art COI management schemata for CPGs, performed by Shekelle et al. (2010), provides detailed insight for developers, as described below.

Preliminary Review and Management of COI

In selecting prospective participants for guideline development, disclosures typically are reviewed prior to the first meeting, and unresolvable conflicts of interest are investigated. The procedures (including step-by-step review and management) are described clearly as part of CPG development policy. Prospective members agree to divest any stocks or stock options whose value could be influenced by the CPG recommendations, and refrain from participating in any marketing activities or advisory boards of commercial entities related to the CPG topic.

Disclosure of COI to Other Panel Members

Once members of a guideline panel have been assembled, any member COI is disclosed and discussed before deliberations begin. Individual participants (including project chairs and panelists) label how COI might affect specific recommendations. Disclosures and conflicts should be reviewed in an ongoing manner by those managing COI.

2. **Management of Conflict of Interest (COI)**
    2.1 Prior to selection of the guideline development group (GDG), individuals being considered for membership should declare all interests and activities potentially resulting in COI with development group activity, by written disclosure to those convening the GDG:
    - **Disclosure should reflect all current and planned com-**

mercial (including services from which a clinician derives a substantial proportion of income), noncommercial, intellectual, institutional, and patient–public activities pertinent to the potential scope of the CPG.

2.2 Disclosure of COIs within GDG:
- All COI of each GDG member should be reported and discussed by the prospective development group prior to the onset of his or her work.
- Each panel member should explain how his or her COI could influence the CPG development process or specific recommendations.

2.3 Divestment
- Members of the GDG should divest themselves of financial investments they or their family members have in, and not participate in marketing activities or advisory boards of, entities whose interests could be affected by CPG recommendations.

2.4 Exclusions
- Whenever possible GDG members should not have COI.
- In some circumstances, a GDG may not be able to perform its work without members who have COIs, such as relevant clinical specialists who receive a substantial portion of their incomes from services pertinent to the CPG.
- Members with COIs should represent not more than a minority of the GDG.
- The chair or cochairs should not be a person(s) with COI.
- Funders should have no role in CPG development.

GUIDELINE DEVELOPMENT GROUP COMPOSITION AND GROUP PROCESS

Guideline development involves technical processes (SRs of relevant evidence), judgmental processes (interpretation of SR and derivation of recommendations), and interpersonal processes (consensus building). The validity of guideline recommendations may be influenced adversely if any one of these processes is biased. There has been much less methodological focus given to studying and optimizing judgmental and interpersonal processes, than on ensuring validity of the technical process. (Gardner et al., 2009; Moreira, 2005; Moreira et al., 2006; Pagliari and Grimshaw, 2002; Pagliari et al., 2001). Fundamentally, the quality of the latter processes depends on composition of the group (whether the right participants have been brought to the table) and group process (whether the process allows all participants to be involved in constructive discourse surrounding implications of the systematic review).

Group Composition

Although the composition across prominent GDGs may vary, most commonly GDGs consist of 10 to 20 members reflecting 3 to 5 relevant disciplines (Burgers et al., 2003b). Clinical disciplines typically represented include both generalists and subspecialists involved in CPG-related care processes. Nonclinical disciplines typically represented include those of methodological orientation, such as epidemiologists, statisticians, "guidelineologists" (i.e., those with specific expertise in the guideline development process), and experts in areas such as decision analysis, informatics, implementation, and clinical or social psychology. It is important that the chair have leadership experience. Public representatives participate in a number of guideline development efforts and may include current and former patients, caregivers not employed as health professionals, advocates from patient/consumer organizations, and consumers without prior direct experience with the topic (Burgers et al., 2003b).

Empirical evidence consistently demonstrates that group composition influences recommendations. In a systematic review of factors affecting judgments achieved by formal consensus development methods, Hutchings and colleague identified 22 studies examining the impact of individual participant specialty or profession. Overall, the authors observed that those who performed a procedure, versus those who did not, were more likely to rate more indications as appropriate for that procedure. In addition, in five individual studies comparing recommendations made by unidisciplinary and multidisciplinary groups, recommendations by multidisciplinary groups generally were more conservative (Hutchings and Raine, 2006). Murphy and colleagues (1998) offer other relevant findings in a systematic review in which they compared guideline recommendations produced by groups of varying composition. The authors concluded that differences in group composition may lead to contrasting recommendations; more specifically, members of a clinical specialty are more likely to promote interventions in which their specialty plays a part. Overall, the authors state: "The weight of the evidence suggests that heterogeneity in a decision-making group can lead to a better performance [e.g., clarity and creativity in strategic decision making due to fewer assumptions about shared values] than homogeneity" (Murphy et al., 1998, p. 33).

Fretheim and colleagues' (2006a) analysis of six studies of CPGs, excluded from Murphy's review, demonstrated that clinical experts have a lower threshold for recommending procedures they perform. Complementary findings provided by Shekelle et al. (1999) discovered that given identical evidence, a single subspecialty group will arrive at contrasting conclusions compared to those of a multidisciplinary group. Finally, an investigation of six surgical procedures by Kahan and colleagues (1996) suggests that 10 to 42 percent of cases considered appropriate for surgery by specialists who performed the procedure were considered inappropriate by primary care providers.

Lomas (1993) explains and offers implications of these findings as follows: first, limited evidentiary foundations for guideline development require supplementation by a variety of stakeholders; second, value conflicts demand resolution; and third, successful introduction of a guideline requires that all key disciplines contribute to development to ensure "ownership" and support. In complementary fashion, the IOM Committee to Advise the Public Health Service on Clinical Practice Guidelines in 1990 offered the following rationale in support of multidisciplinary guideline development groups: (1) they increase the likelihood that all relevant scientific evidence will be identified and critically assessed; (2) they increase the likelihood that practical problems in guideline application will be identified and addressed; and (3) they increase a sense of involvement or "ownership" among audiences of the varying guidelines (IOM, 1990).

Given these empirical and theoretical arguments, there is broad international consensus that GDGs should be multidisciplinary, with representation from all key stakeholders (ACCF and AHA, 2008; AGREE, 2003; NICE, 2009; SIGN, 2008). Rosenfeld and Shiffman (2009, p. S8) capture this sentiment in the following words: "every discipline or organization that would care about implementation [of the guideline] has a voice at the table." This carries practical implications when convening a guideline development panel in terms of panel size, disciplinary balance, and resource support. Small groups may lack a sufficient range of experience. In their 1999 conceptualization of the CPG development process, Shekelle and colleagues (1999) assert that guideline reliability may increase in a multidisciplinary (and hence larger) group due to increased balancing of biases. More than 12 to 15 participants may result in ineffective functioning (Rosenfeld and Shiffman, 2009). Murphy and coauthors' systematic review asserts that "having more group members will increase the reliability of group judgment," but "large groups may cause coordination problems" (Murphy et al., 1998, p. 37). Furthermore, "It is likely that below about 6 participants, reliability (agreement across group members) (Richardson, 1972) will decline quite rapidly, while above about 12, improvements in reliability will be subject to diminishing returns" (Murphy et al., 1998). Of course, the specific number of participants and balance of disciplines should also be influenced by the guideline's focus. Decisions about which categories of participants to involve in the guideline development group are then required. Here, as suggested above, guideline developers often have to weigh desire for wide representation against need for cohesiveness and efficiency.

However, GDG composition typically is either not characterized by a multidisciplinary group or does not even allow for such characterization. Shaneyfelt and colleagues (1999), in their study of 279 guidelines representing a diversity of topics, demonstrated that only 26 percent of guidelines specify development group participants and their areas of expertise. In a complementary investigation of 431 guidelines authored by specialty societies, Grilli and colleagues (2000) discovered that 88 percent of guidelines did not explicitly describe the types of professionals involved in development. Only 28 percent showed evidence of participation of more than one discipline authoring the guideline (Grilli et al., 2000).

Group Processes

A range of professional, cultural, and psychological factors can influence the process and content of guideline development panel meetings (Pagliari et al., 2001). GDGs undergo a socialization process (Tuckman, 1965). For example, during the first few meetings, much attention may be paid to developing interpersonal relations, setting group goals, establishing norms of behavior, and defining explicit and implicit roles. Such group-related issues may need to be addressed before much progress can be made on developing clinical recommendations. Group decision making involves three phases: *orientation* (defining the problem), *evaluation* (discussion of decision alternatives), and *control* (deciding prevailing alternatives) (Bales and Strodtbeck, 1951). Ideal conditions for group decision making are those enabling views of all parties to be expressed and considered before reaching a recommendation acceptable to the majority (Pagliari et al., 2001).

Dysfunctional group processes unduly encourage minority or majority views that may result in invalid or unreliable recommendations. These processes include minority influence (a single member or minority of group members sway the majority, often by capitalizing on small divisions in the group), group polarization (group dynamic leads to more extreme decisions than members would make individually), and "groupthink" (members' desire for unanimity trump objective appraisal of the evidence) (Pagliari et al., 2001). Multidisciplinary groups are particularly at risk here, as members vary in professional status, in the nature or depth of their specialist knowledge, and in their appreciation of roles and modus operandi of professional colleagues (Shekelle et al., 2010).

The risk of these biases can be reduced with careful planning and attention to small-group processes. The aim is to ensure that group processes fundamentally encourage inclusion of all opinions and grant adequate hearing to all arguments (Fretheim et al., 2006b). Although somewhat limited support exists for their effectiveness, informal and formal methods are available to assist in achieving these objectives. Moynihan and Henry surveyed international CPG or health technology assessment organizations and found that 42 percent claimed to apply formal consensus development methods (Moynihan and Henry, 2006). Burgers and coauthors discovered that 38 percent of guideline developers surveyed applied formal rather than informal methods to recommendation formulation (Burgers et al., 2003a).

Among informal approaches, a variety of strategies may be required to encourage positive group processes. Selection of the group leader is critical. Positive group leadership is characterized by an individual who is qualified and experienced in facilitation of optimal group processes (Fretheim et al., 2006b). The United Kingdom's NICE asserts that this individual "needs to allow sufficient time for all members to express their views without feeling intimidated or threatened and should check that all members in the group agree to endorse any recommendations" (NICE, 2009, p. 42). Thus this individual preferably is not an expert or subspecialist in a particular clinical domain (NICE, 2009). Further, the Chair should be selected as someone who is neutral and who has enough expertise in coordinating groups of health professionals and patients/caregivers so that the appointment is acceptable to all (NICE, 2009).

A variant on this leadership form also has received support by guideline development leaders. Although one individual can be responsible for group process and task, if a group is especially large or the task is particularly complex, these support roles may be better divided between two persons, provided both they and the panel are clear about their differing functions (Shekelle et al., 2010). The committee suggests consideration of coleaders, such as a subspecialist and a generalist clinician, or coleaders representing differing clinical disciplines. Another informal approach to improving process centers on the role of technical experts. Technical support, typically found among researchers rather than clinicians, predominantly is required to identify and synthesize evidence, then present it to the GDG in a form allowing for derivation of recommendations. During guideline development, the technical expert should encourage the GDG to scrutinize the guideline repeatedly to guarantee its internal logic and clarity (Shekelle et al., 2010).

Several formal consensus development strategies are available to clinical practice guideline developers. Of these methods, the three most often applied include the Nominal Group Technique (NGT), the Delphi Method, and Consensus Conferences. These approaches reflect a variety of characteristics, including the use of questionnaires to elicit opinion, private elicitation of decisions, and formal feedback on group preferences. The specific character of their application varies in practice (Fretheim et al., 2006b).

As alluded to earlier, there remains a dearth of literature devoted to comparative analysis of the variety of formal and informal group process methods encouraging consensus development for producing guidelines. The comprehensive review by Murphy and coauthors and confirmatory work by Hutchings and Raine (2006) provide some insight into the relative merits of these strategies. In summary, this work suggests that formal methods generally perform as well or better than informal ones. However, the relative effectiveness of one formal method versus another remains an open question (Hutchings and Raine, 2006; Murphy et al., 1998). Finally, Shekelle and Schriger, in comparing formal and informal consensus approaches to development of CPGs to treat low back pain, determined that resultant guidelines were "qualitatively similar," yet certain guideline statements arising from formal methods were relatively "more clinically specific" (Shekelle and Schriger, 1996). Overall, the committee believes that group process is enhanced by inclusion of all opinions relevant to a CPG, and adoption of informal (e.g., group leadership) or formal (e.g., NGT, Delphi Method) methods for ensuring effective group process.

Guideline development leaders argue that it may be appropriate that the cost of guideline development include support for the adoption of methods to increase optimal group functioning (the group process) and achievement of aims (the group task) (Grimshaw et al., 1995).

Patient and Public Involvement

The principals involved in CPG development, typically healthcare professionals and scientific experts, can benefit from the input of patients and the public for several reasons. First, as a matter of transparency, detailed in preceding content, the involvement of one or more consumer representatives provides a window into the process and some assurance that guidelines were not developed "behind closed doors" to suit special interests other than theirs.

Second, patients and laypersons bring perspectives that clinicians and scientists often lack, and require attention to be paid to those individuals most deeply affected by guidelines. This input is important not only in deciding what to recommend, but how to present recommendations in ways that are understandable to patients and respectful of their needs. A study by Devereaux et al. (2001) found that patients and physicians assign different outcome values to stroke versus adverse side effects of treatment. Specifically, "Patients at high risk for atrial fibrillation placed more value on the avoidance of stroke and less value on the avoidance of bleeding than did physicians who treat patients with atrial fibrillation" (Devereaux et al., 2001, p. 1). Sensitivity to what matters most to those living with disease provides important context for decisions about the balance of benefits and harms as well as gaps in scientific evidence.

Third, consumer involvement acts as a safeguard against conflicts of interest that may skew judgment of clinical and scientific experts. The ability of consumers to resist recommendations favoring self-interest of a specialty or research enterprise can be an important countermeasure to imbalance in practice guidelines. Williamson (1998) proposed three types of patient representatives, depending on the contributions and skills each can bring: (1) fellow patients or patient surrogates (e.g., parents, caretakers) who would mainly present their own views; (2) a member of a patient group who presents the organization's position; and (3) patient advocates who present knowledge of patient views. A systematic review found that patients and the public did not differ in their preferences for hypothetical health states (Dolders et al., 2006). This finding suggests that consumer representation in GDGs may serve as a good proxy for patients.

However, involvement of laypersons in practice guideline development may be problematic, particularly if they lack relevant training and scientific literacy. Guideline development panel discussions should rely on clinical, technical, and methodological concepts, and terminology must be understood by consumer representative(s). In some instances explanation is not provided and the consumer representative is unable to follow the discussion. A second challenge occurs when a consumer representative has a personal experience with the disease or an advocacy role interfering with the ability to examine evidence and recommendations dispassionately. Such individuals may have difficulty divorcing their personal narrative or policy agenda from the systematic methods and analytic rules a GDG should follow. A panel's orderly review of evidence and construction of recommendations can be sidelined by consumer representative objections and testimonials. The following findings emerged from observations of varying consumer participation methods in the North of England guideline development program. Individual patients who participated in a GDG contributed infrequently and had problems with the use of technical language. Although they contributed most in discussions of patient education, their contributions were not subsequently put into action. Within a "one off" or one-time meeting, participants again encountered problems with medical terminology and were most interested in sections on patient education and self-management. Their understanding of the use of scientific evidence to derive more cost-effective care practices was unclear (van Wersch and Eccles, 2001). Furthermore, a more recent study suggests that consumers hold many misconceptions about evidence-based health care, and are often skeptical of its value. In fact, one study reported that consumers largely believe that more care—and more expensive care—constitutes better care, and that medical guidelines are inflexible (Carman et al., 2010). These misconceptions may act as barriers to effective shared decision making.

To mitigate these concerns, as with any member of a practice guideline development panel, selection criteria should be applied to choose a consumer representative who can consider the evidence objectively, and make recommendations departing from preconceived views of self or interests. Little is known about how best to select consumers for such tasks, a survey of members of the Guideline International Network Patient and Public Involvement Working Group (G-I-N PUBLIC) concluded that "the paucity of process and impact evaluations limits our current understanding of the conditions under which patient and public involvement is most likely to be effective" (Boivin et al., 2010, p. 1), but several public and private efforts are under way to identify best systematic approaches.[2] Identifying a consumer's interests, experience, and skill subsets in order to match them to the needs of the guideline development group will increase the likelihood of success. Unlike health professionals, most consumers will not have economic incentives or support encouraging their participation. Like health professionals, consumers will respond to efforts that are well organized and led, respect their time and effort, and result in a meaningful outcome. Eventually systematic approaches to consumer involvement will improve the prevailing "opportunistic" approach.

In addition to a patient and consumer advocate on the GDG, some groups elicit patient and public perspectives as part of a larger stakeholder input exercise. For example, a GDG might invite patients or other laypersons to review draft documents or attend a meeting to share perspectives. GDGs can host an open forum in which various stakeholder groups, such as patients, payers, manufacturers, and professional associations, are afforded the opportunity to express their viewpoints, present scientific evidence relevant to the guideline, or raise concerns about the impact or implementation of proposed recommendations. The advantage of this approach is that it exposes the GDG to information it might overlook and provides stakeholders with a sense of "being heard," while allowing the panel to have private deliberations. In the North of England study, the workshop format was relatively resource intensive, but made it possible to explain technical elements of guideline development, enabling patients to engage in the process and make relevant suggestions. A patient advocate serving on a panel felt confident enough to speak and was accustomed to discussions with health professionals and to medical terminology (van Wersch and Eccles, 2001).

NICE has developed comprehensive policies to include consumers in their CPG development process. NICE created a patient involvement unit that emphasizes elicitation of stakeholder orga-

---

[2]AHRQ is currently funding the "Community Forum" effort via a contract with the American Institutes of Research. The Forum provides funding for research on how to organize and deliver diverse stakeholder input into comparative effectiveness research. Several states (Oregon, Washington, Wisconsin, and others) have long involved consumers in activities related to the evaluation of evidence in health decisions. Disease organizations—especially those involving AIDS and Breast Cancer— have demonstrated they can select and train consumers to be effective contributors in guideline processes. Personal communication, J. Santa. 2010. Consumers Union (December 22, 2010).

nization commentary across the development process; patient and caregiver committee representation; patient focus groups, written testimonials, and interviews; dissemination and gathering of feedback regarding NICE guidance to patients by patients and patient organization implementers (Schünemann et al., 2006). Other organizations incorporating consumer and patient perspectives in guideline development processes are the Scottish Intercollegiate Guidelines Network (SIGN), and the UK National Health System Health Technology Assessment Program (Schünemann et al., 2006).

Few empirical accounts show attempts to involve consumers (Carver and Entwistle, 1999). Because frameworks for consumer involvement are based on limited practical experience (Bastian, 1996; Duff et al., 1993), there is little consensus about how and when to involve consumers and what to expect from them during guideline development (van Wersch and Eccles, 1999). In 2006, the WHO Advisory Committee on Health Research conducted a critical review of processes involving consumers in the development of guidelines to derive recommendations for improvement (Schünemann et al., 2007). Although Schünemann and colleagues (2006) identified no evidence for determining how best to involve consumers in CPG development, they did find support for approaches to consumer involvement in the scientific research process. More specifically, a study by Telford and colleagues (2004) identified eight principles for successful consumer involvement in research; specifically, they call for an open and explicit process in which consumers are knowledgeable and/or trained in understanding evidence and are included in all steps of the developmental process. Schünemann and colleagues suggested these findings might be relevant to involving consumers in developing CPGs (Schünemann et al., 2006).

Hazards exist when guidelines are developed without sensitivity to public reactions, especially when a topic may become contentious. Many guidelines with the strongest scientific logic have floundered publicly when recommendations or rationales were misunderstood or ridiculed by patients, the media, or politicians. Therefore, consumers should be involved in all stages of guideline development. Although this is possible, it is not straightforward, and there is a clear need for further work on how this can best be achieved. In whatever form it takes, consumer input is helpful in alerting GDGs to public sentiments, to the need for proper messaging, and to the optics and reception that await recommendations they fashion.

3. **Guideline Development Group Composition**
   3.1 The GDG should be multidisciplinary and balanced, comprising a variety of methodological experts and clinicians, and populations expected to be affected by the CPG.
   3.2 Patient and public involvement should be facilitated by including (at least at the time of clinical question formulation and draft CPG review) a current or former patient, and a patient advocate or patient/consumer organization representative in the GDG.
   3.3 Strategies to increase effective participation of patient and consumer representatives, including training in appraisal of evidence, should be adopted by GDGs.

CLINICAL PRACTICE GUIDELINE—
SYSTEMATIC REVIEW INTERSECTION

The idea that trustworthy clinical practice guidelines should be based on a high-quality SR of the evidence is beyond dispute (ACCF and AHA, 2008; AGREE, 2003; AHRQ, 2008; NICE, 2009; Rosenfeld and Shiffman, 2009; SIGN, 2008). The committee defines a high-quality systematic review as one meeting those standards described by the IOM Committee on Standards for Systematic Reviews of Comparative Effectiveness Research. However, the manner by which GDGs obtain SRs is highly variable, ranging from conducting reviews "in-house," to entering a relationship where the SR is conducted specifically to inform the CPG (with varying levels of interaction between the two groups), to an "asynchronous" arrangement where SR and CPG activities are independent of one another. In this instance, GDGs may use preexisting SRs to inform recommendations (asynchronous isolation model) or, as in the case of the National Institutes of Health Consensus Development Conference, work synchronously with an SR panel, but allow no interaction beyond the original clinical question(s) posed and final product delivered (ACCF and AHA, 2008; AHRQ, 2008; New Zealand Guidelines Group, 2001; NICE, 2009; NIH, 2010; Rosenfeld and Shiffman, 2009). Table 4-1 compares varying modes of interaction between systematic review teams and guideline developers and the membership, benefits, and concerns characteristic of each.

The National Institutes of Health Consensus Development Conference believes interaction between SR and CPG panels mandates complete isolation of experts interpreting and rating the evidence from those formulating guideline recommendations to discourage the clinical experts from biasing the SR results (NIH, 2010).

TABLE 4-1 Models of Interaction Between Clinical Practice Guideline (CPG) Groups and Systematic Review (SR) Teams

Characteristics	Models of Interaction			
	Complete Isolation (synchronous model)	Complete Isolation (asynchronous model)	Limited Interaction	Complete Interaction
Membership	There is no overlap in membership between the CPG team and the SR team	There is generally no overlap in membership, but a member of the SR team may later participate in the CPG	Selected members of the CPG team interact with the SR team to refine the key questions, define review criteria, and interpret evidence; the SR methodologists do not make CPG recommendations	The same individuals conduct the SR, grade the evidence, and generate the guidelines
Theoretical benefits	Prevents biases in one group from influencing the other group	Efficiency of using presynthesized and rated evidence	Ensures that at least the major questions of the CPG team will be addressed by the SR	• Ensures that all issues known between the CPG and SR groups will be addressed in the SR • The CPG team will have a better understanding of the evidence • Efficiency of having the same group review evidence and formulate guidelines

| Concerns | • The CPG team is limited to the questions formulated by the initial question-setting panel; these questions may not be complete or what the CPG team considers important
• The CPG team has no opportunity to interact with SR team to appreciate the nuances of the evidence review
• SR team working without input from CPG team that will use the evidence may not optimally structure the synthesis and reporting of evidence | • SR may not fully address all of the CPG panel's clinical questions.
• SR may not include the latest studies
• SR team working without input from CPG team that will use the evidence may not optimally structure the synthesis and reporting of evidence | • Limited interactions may result in some areas being inadequately addressed in the SR
• The subgroup of the CPG team that interacts with the SR team may be biased or lack expertise in specific topics, or it may not cover all the questions and concerns of the entire CPG subgroup | • May introduce bias into the evidence review
• Unlikely that the same individuals have the time or skills to conduct both SRs and CPG |

SOURCE: Lau (2010).

The committee is critical of the isolationist approach because it inhibits knowledge exchange between clinical content experts and methodologists, potentially degrading their abilities to appreciate the nuances of evidence and clinical questions pertinent to the formulation of recommendations.

The committee understands many GDGs of small professional societies review and rate evidence internally, as the interactive approach is infeasible for those with limited resources. However, these developers may not include methodological experts, and may lack training and skills in high-quality SR conduct. The committee believes that if required to maintain standards set by the IOM's Committee on Standards for Systematic Reviews of Comparative Effectiveness Research, many such organizations would require alternate means to secure evidence in support of recommendations. The committee encourages small professional societies to partner with other guideline development organizations or use publicly funded SRs developed by the new federally funded private agency, the Patient-Centered Outcomes Research Institute (PCORI); PCORI is mentioned again in Chapter 7.

Organizations such as the USPSTF and Kidney Disease: Improving Global Outcomes contract with an outside systematic review team to support their CPG development, but work closely with SR methodologists throughout the SR. The emphasis here is on increased intersection at multiple critical points across the SR process. Hence, the model allows for interaction between systematic review teams and guideline developers in response to developers' concerns during literature review related to clinical questions or study parameters. In addition, interpretation and rating of the evidence requires particularly close interaction between systematic review teams and GDGs, as does derivation of clinical recommendations.

The following elaborates the "complete interaction" model of guideline developers and SR methodologists and further specifies the nature of intersection. The committee believes that an ongoing, interactive relationship between systematic review teams and guideline developers will increase validity and trustworthiness of the guideline development process. At the same time, the committee is aware that many variants of this model may be suitable across differing CPG development contexts. Prior to the first meeting, and as needed throughout the process, methodologists from the SR team may provide training to guideline development members on topics such as literature selection and the rating of evidence and recommendations. Reciprocally, clinical experts from the guideline group assist SR methodologists on the nuances of clinical questions, selection criteria (e.g., varying biases across United States and European Union investigations), and interpretation of study design and results. By the first meeting of the GDG and SR methodologists, understanding and agreement on the above topics as well as scope (breadth and depth) of the SR and supportive resources should be reached. At the second meeting, SR team members should present their findings to the GDG and the teams should jointly interpret evidence and discuss rating its quality. At this point, guideline developers may request more information (e.g., observational data for subpopulations or for harms), and highlight subtleties in research findings overlooked by SR methodologists (e.g., need to assign greater weight to quality of provider, drug dose, or adherence issues than to allocation blinding), which may alter evidence interpretations. In the interim, SR members may refine evidence tables, perform additional analyses requested by guideline developers, and provide feedback on developers' evidence interpretations. When incorporating any new findings and interpretations, guideline development and SR group members may discuss draft guidelines and clinical recommendations' ratings at the final meeting. Overall, across this entire process, requests for data or discussion are bidirectional.

The committee thoughtfully deliberated the extent to which it felt justified prescribing a detailed CPG development methodology across all aspects of the development process, including the intersection of SR and CPG activities. As with any collaborative research enterprise there often is very subtle negotiation, among varying persuasions, regarding what shall be investigated and how. The committee decided a highly specified prescription was inappropriate given the emergent state-of-the-art of CPG development and a commitment to standards' generalizablity.

4. **Clinical Practice Guideline–Systematic Review Intersection**
   4.1 Clinical practice guideline developers should use systematic reviews that meet standards set by the Institute of Medicine's Committee on Standards for Systematic Reviews of Comparative Effectiveness Research.
   4.2 When systematic reviews are conducted specifically to inform particular guidelines, the GDG and systematic review team should interact regarding the scope, approach, and output of both processes.

DETERMINING GUIDELINE SCOPE AND
REQUISITE CHAIN OF LOGIC

Guideline development groups determine scope and logic (formulation of key clinical questions and outcomes) of CPGs in a variety of ways. Though the committee found no one approach rose to the level of a standard, it recognizes the importance of various associated components to the guideline development process. The committee therefore considered factors important in determining guideline scope, as well as the development of an analytical model to assist in identification of critical clinical questions and key outcomes, and exploration of the quality of varying evidence in a chain of reasoning.

Elaborating Scope

When elaborating guideline scope, GDG members need to consider a variety of clinical issues, including benefits and harms of different treatment options; identification of risk factors for conditions; diagnostic criteria for conditions; prognostic factors with and without treatment; resources associated with different diagnostic or treatment options; the potential presence of comorbid conditions; and patient experiences with healthcare interventions. These issues must be addressed in the context of a number of factors, including target conditions, target populations, practice settings, and audience (Shekelle et al., 2010).

Analytic Framework

To define which clinical questions must be answered to arrive at a recommendation, which types of evidence are relevant to the clinical questions, and by what criteria that evidence will be evaluated and lead to clinical recommendations, GDGs optimally specify a chain of reasoning or logic related to key clinical questions that need to be answered to produce a recommendation on a particular issue. Failure to do so may undermine the trustworthiness of guidelines by neglecting to define at the outset the outcomes of interest, specific clinical questions to be answered, and available evidence. The absence of these guideposts can become apparent as guideline development work unfolds. Failure to define key questions and failure to specify outcomes of interest and admissible evidence can result in wasted time, money, and staff resources to gather and analyze evidence irrelevant to recommendations. Poorly defined outcomes can obscure important insights in the evidence review process, resulting in incomplete or delayed examination of relevant evidence. Disorganized analytic approaches may result in the lack of a crisp, well-articulated explanation of the recommendations' rationale. Poorly articulated or indirect evidence chains can make it difficult to discern which parts of the analytic logic are based on science or opinion, the quality of that evidence, and how it was interpreted. Readers can be misled into thinking that there is more (or less) scientific support for recommendations than actually exists. The ambiguity can also cause difficulty in establishing research priorities (Shekelle et al., 2010; Weinstein and Fineberg, 1980).

The visual analytic framework described here is one of a variety of potential approaches; the particular model is less important than the principles on which it is based. These principles include the need for guideline developers to take the following actions: (1) make explicit decisions at the outset of the analytic process regarding the clinical questions that need to be answered and the patient outcomes that need to be assessed in order to formulate a recommendation on a particular issue; (2) have a clear understanding of the logic underlying each recommendation; (3) use the analytic model for keeping the GDG "on track"; (4) be explicit about types of evidence or opinion, as well as the value judgments supporting each component of the analytic logic; and (5) transmit this information with clarity in the guideline's rationale statement (discussed hereafter).

Explication of Outcomes

Guideline developers must unambiguously define outcomes of interest and the anticipated timing of their occurrence. Stating that a practice is "clinically effective" is insufficient. Specification of the outcomes (including magnitude of intervention benefits and harms) and time frames in which they are expected to occur, as reflected in a clinical recommendation, is required. The GDG must decide which health outcomes or surrogate outcomes will be considered. A health outcome, which can be acute, intermediate, or long term, refers to direct measures of health status, including indicators of physical morbidity (e.g., dyspnea, blindness, functional status, hospitalization), emotional well-being (e.g., depression, anxiety), and mortality (e.g., survival, life expectancy). Eddy defines these as "outcomes that people experience (feel physically or mentally) and care about" (Eddy, 1998, p. 10). This is a critical area for serious consideration of consumer input. Health outcomes are the preferred metric, but surrogate outcomes are sometimes used as proxies for health outcomes. Surrogate outcomes are often physiologic variables, test results, or other measures that are not themselves health outcomes, but that have established pathophysiologic relationships with those outcomes. The validity of a surrogate endpoint must be well established in order to accept it as a proxy for a health outcome endpoint. For example, for AIDS, the need for ventilator support, loss of vision, and death would be acute, intermediate, and long-term outcomes respectively, while increased CD4 cell counts or decreased viral-load measures represent surrogate outcomes (Fleming and DeMets, 1996). Guideline developers must determine which of these outcome classes must be affected to support a recommendation.

One Example of Guideline Logic:
The Analytic Graphical Model

These potentially complex interrelationships can be visualized in a graphic format. A recent example of an analytic framework (Figure 4-1) was developed by the USPSTF in consideration of its guideline for osteoporosis screening (Nelson et al., 2010).

This diagrammatic approach, first described in the late 1980s, emerged from earlier advances in causal pathways (Battista and Fletcher, 1988), causal models (Blalock, 1985), influence diagrams (Howard and Matheson, 1981), and evidence models (Woolf, 1991).

Construction of the diagram begins with listing the outcomes the GDG has identified as important. This list of benefits and harms reflects key criteria the development group must address in arriving at a recommendation. Surrogate outcomes considered reliable and valid outcome indicators may then be added to the diagram. The interconnecting lines, or linkages, appearing in Figure 4-1 represent critical premises in logic or reasoning that require confirmation by

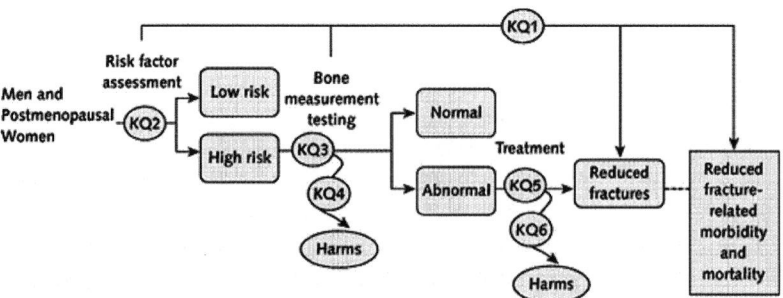

FIGURE 4-1 Analytic framework and KQs.
NOTE: KQ = key question.
SOURCE: Nelson et al. (2010).

evidence review to support related recommendations. KQ1 is the overarching question—does risk factor assessment or bone measurement testing lead to reduced fracture-related morbidity and mortality? KQ2 (Is the patient "low risk" or "high risk" for fracture-related morbidity and mortality?), KQ3 (If a patient is "high risk" for fracture-related morbidity and mortality are bone measurement test results normal or abnormal?), KQ4 (If a patient is "high risk" for fracture-related morbidity and mortality, do harms associated with bone measurement testing outweigh benefits?), KQ5 (If patient bone measurement testing is abnormal, will treatment result in reduced fractures?), and KQ6 (If patient bone measurement is abnormal, do treatment harms outweigh benefits?) are questions about intermediate steps along the guideline logic or reasoning path concerning the accuracy of risk factor assessment and bone measurement testing, and potential benefits and harms of testing and treatment of persons identified as abnormal (Shekelle et al., 2010).

Specification of the presumed relationships among acute, intermediate, long-term, and surrogate outcomes in a visual analytic model serves a number of useful purposes. It forces guideline developers to make explicit, a priori decisions about outcomes of interest in the derivation of a recommendation. It allows others to judge whether important outcomes are overlooked (Harris et al., 2001). It makes explicit a development group's judgments regarding the validity of various indicators of outcome. The proposed interrelationships depicted in the diagram reveal group members' assumptions pertinent to pathophysiologic relationships. They also allow others to make a general determination of whether the correct questions were asked at the outset (IOM, 2008).

Filling in the Evidence

Linkages in the visual reasoning model provide a "road map" to guide the evidence review. They specify a list of questions that must be answered to derive recommendations. This focused approach, in which evidence review is driven by key questions, is more efficient than broad reviews of a guideline topic. A common error among guideline developers is to conduct an amorphous literature search with broad inclusion criteria. Because hundreds to thousands of data sources usually are available on any guideline topic, such an approach often retrieves many irrelevant citations. A targeted approach is more expeditious, less costly, and directed only to the specific issues that are priorities to be addressed in confirming the rationale for recommendations (AHRQ, 2009; Slavin, 1995).

In addition to defining questions to be answered in the literature review, linkages in the analytic framework keep the review process on track. Linkages serve as placeholders for documenting whether supporting evidence has been uncovered for a particular linkage and the nature of that evidence. By identifying which linkages have been "filled in" with evidence, the analytic framework provides a flow-chart for tracking progress in evidence identification. It also serves as a checklist to ensure that important outcomes of interest are not neglected in the evidence review process (Harris et al., 2001).

Although the linkages define questions to be answered and provide placeholders for documenting results, they do not define the quality of evidence or its implications for recommendations. However, this graphical exercise may serve as a preliminary founda-tion for deriving clinical recommendations. Scanning linkages in the model directs CPG developers to each of the specific components of their reasoning that require evidence in support of recommenda-tions, an assessment of the quality of that evidence, and an appraisal of the strength of a recommendation that can be made. The com-plexity of the quality of evidence and strength of recommendation appraisal activities is discussed fully in Chapter 5.

With regard to the greater state of the art of CPGs, the analytic model highlights most important outcomes that, depending on the quality of available evidence, require consideration by future inves-tigators in establishing effectiveness of a clinical practice and the demand for guidelines. This information is essential, in an era of limited research resources, to establish priorities and direct out-comes research to fundamental questions. Finally, outcomes identi-fied in the analytic model also provide a template for evaluating effects of guidelines on quality of care (Shekelle et al., 2010).

The Rationale Statement

The composition of a clear rationale statement is facilitated by the analytic framework. The rationale statement summarizes the benefits and harms considered in deriving the recommendation, and why the outcomes were deemed important (including consideration of patient preferences); the GDG's assumptions about relationships among all health and surrogate outcomes; and the nature of evi-dence upholding linkages. If the review uncovered linkages lacking supportive evidence, the rationale statement can speak to the role that opinion, theory, or clinical experience may play in arriving at a recommendation. The rationale statement may thereby provide clinicians, policy makers, and other guideline users with credible insight into underlying model assumptions. It also avoids misleading generalizations about the evidence, such as claiming a clinical practice is supported by "randomized controlled trials" when such evidence supports only one linkage in the analytic model. By sharing the blueprint for recommendations, the linkages in the analytic logic allow various developers to identify pivotal assumptions about which they disagree (Shekelle et al., 2010).

REFERENCES

ACCF and AHA (American College of Cardiology Foundation and American Heart Association). 2008. Methodology manual for ACCF/AHA guideline writing committees. In *Methodologies and policies from ACCF/AHA Taskforce on Practice Guidelines*. ACCF and AHA.

AGREE (Appraisal of Guidelines for Research & Evaluation). 2001. Appraisal of Guidelines for Research & Evaluation (AGREE) instrument.

AGREE. 2003. Development and validation of an international appraisal instrument for assessing the quality of clinical practice guidelines: The AGREE project. *Quality and Safety in Health Care* 12(1):18–23.

AHRQ (Agency for Healthcare Research and Quality). 2008. *U.S. Preventive Services Task Force procedure manual*. AHRQ Pub. No. 08-05118-ef. http://www.ahrq.gov/clinic/uspstf08/methods/procmanual.htm (accessed February 12, 2009).

AHRQ. 2009. *Methods guide for comparative effectiveness reviews* (accessed January 23, 2009).

Als-Nielsen, B., W. Chen, C. Gluud, and L. L. Kjaergard. 2003. Association of funding and conclusions in randomized drug trials: A reflection of treatment effect or adverse events? *JAMA* 290:921–928.

American Academy of Pediatrics. 2008. Toward transparent clinical policies. *Pediatrics* 121(3):643–646.

American Academy of Physicians Assistants. 1997. *Policy brief: Clinical practice guidelines*. http://www.aapa.org/gandp/cpg.html (accessed May 21, 2007).

Bales, R. F., and F. L. Strodtbeck. 1951. Phases in group problem-solving. *Journal of Abnormal Social Psychology* 46(4):485–495.

Bastian, H. 1996. Raising the standard: Practice guidelines and consumer participation. *International Journal of Quality Health Care* 8(5):485–490.

Battista, R. N., and S. W. Fletcher. 1988. Making recommendations on preventive practices: Methodological issues. *American Journal of Preventive Medicine* 4(4 Suppl):53–67; discussion 68–76.

Blalock, H. J., ed. 1985. *Causal models in the social sciences*, 2nd ed. Chicago. IL: Aldine.

Boivin, A., K. Currie, B. Fervers, J. Gracia, M. James, C. Marshall, C. Sakala, S. Sanger, J. Strid, V. Thomas, T. van der Weijden, R. Grol, and J. Burgers. 2010. Patient and public involvement in clinical guidelines: International experiences and future perspectives. *Quality and Safety in Health Care* 19(5):e22.

Boyd, E. A., and L. A. Bero. 2000. Assessing faculty financial relationships with industry: A case study. *JAMA* 284(17):2209–2214.

Burgers, J., R. Grol, N. Klazinga, M. Makela, J. Zaat, and AGREE Collaboration. 2003a. Towards evidence-based clinical practice: An international survey of 18 clinical guideline programs. *International Journal on Quality Health Care* 15(1):31–45.

Burgers, J. S., R. P. Grol, J. O. Zaat, T. H. Spies, A. K. van der Bij, and H. G. Mokkink. 2003b. Characteristics of effective clinical guidelines for general practice. *British Journal of General Practice* 53(486):15–19.

Campbell, E. G. 2007. Doctors and drug companies—scrutinizing influential relationships. *New England Journal of Medicine* 357(18):1796–1797.

Carman, K. L., M. Maurer, J. M. Yegian, P. Dardess, J. McGee, M. Evers, and K. O. Marlo. 2010. Evidence that consumers are skeptical about evidence-based health care. *Health Affairs* 29(7):1400–1406.

Carver, A., and V. Entwistle. 1999. Patient involvement in sign guideline development groups. Edinburgh, Scot.: Scottish Association of Health Councils.

Chaudhry, S., S. Schroter, R. Smith, and J. Morris. 2002. Does declaration of competing interests affect readers' perceptions? A randomised trial. *BMJ* 325(7377):1391–1392.

Dana, J. 2003. Harm avoidance and financial conflict of interest. *Journal of Medical Ethics* Online Electronic Version:1–18.

Devereaux, P. J., D. R. Anderson, M. J. Gardner, W. Putnam, G. J. Flowerdew, B. F. Brownell, S. Nagpal, and J. L. Cox. 2001. Differences between perspectives of physicians and patients on anticoagulation in patients with atrial fibrillation: Observational study. *BMJ* 323(7323):1218–1221.

Dolders, M. G. T., M. P. A. Zeegers, W. Groot, and A. Ament. 2006. A meta-analysis demonstrates no significant differences between patient and population preferences. *Journal of Clinical Epidemiology* 59(7):653–664.

Duff, L. A., M. Kelson, S. Marriott, A. Mcintosh, S. Brown, J. Cape, N. Marcus, and M. Traynor. 1993. Clinical guidelines: Involving patients and users of services. *British Journal of Clinical Governance* 1(3):104–112.

Eddy, D. 1998. Performance measurement: Problems and solutions. *Health Affairs* 17(4):7–25.

Eichacker, P. Q., C. Natanson, and R. L. Danner. 2006. Surviving sepsis—practice guidelines, marketing campaigns, and Eli Lilly. *New England Journal of Medicine* 355(16):1640–1642.

Fleming, T. R., and D. L. DeMets. 1996. Surrogate end points in clinical trials: Are we being misled? *Annals of Internal Medicine* 125(7):605–613.

Fretheim, A., H. J. Schünemann, and A. D. Oxman. 2006a. Improving the use of research evidence in guideline development: Group composition and consultation process. *Health Research Policy and Systems* 4:15.

Fretheim, A., H. J. Schünemann, and A. D. Oxman. 2006b. Improving the use of research evidence in guideline development: Group processes. *Health Research Policy and Systems* 4:17.

Friedman, P. J. 2002. The impact of conflict of interest on trust in science. *Science and Engineering Ethics* 8(3):413–420.

Gardner, B., R. Davidson, J. McAteer, and S. Michie. 2009. A method for studying decision-making by guideline development groups. *Implementation Science* 4(1):48.

Grilli, R., N. Magrini, A. Penna, G. Mura, and A. Liberati. 2000. Practice guidelines developed by specialty societies: The need for a critical appraisal. *The Lancet* 355(9198):103–106.

Grimshaw, J., M. Eccles, and I. Russell. 1995. Developing clinically valid practice guidelines. *Journal of Evaluation in Clinical Practice* 1(1):37–48.

Guyatt, G., E. A. Akl, J. Hirsh, C. Kearon, M. Crowther, D. Gutterman, S. Z. Lewis, I. Nathanson, R. Jaeschke, and H. Schünemann. 2010. The vexing problem of guidelines and conflict of interest: A potential solution. *Annals of Internal Medicine* 152(11):738–741.

Harris, R. P., M. Helfand, S. H. Woolf, K. N. Lohr, C. D. Mulrow, S. M. Teutsch, and D. Atkins. 2001. Current methods of the U.S. Preventive Services Task Force: A review of the process. *American Journal of Preventive Medicine* 20(3 Suppl):21–35.

Howard, R., and J. Matheson, eds. 1981. *Readings on the principles and applications of decision analysis.* Menlo Park, CA: Strategic Decisions Group.

Hutchings, A., and R. Raine. 2006. A systematic review of factors affecting the judgments produced by formal consensus development methods in health care. *Journal of Health Services Research and Policy* 11(3):172–179.

IOM (Institute of Medicine). 1990. *Clinical practice guidelines: Directions for a new program.* Edited by M. J. Field and K. N. Lohr. Washington, DC: National Academy Press.

IOM. 1992. *Guidelines for clinical practice: From development to use.* Edited by M. J. Field and K. N. Lohr. Washington, DC: National Academy Press.

IOM. 2008. *Knowing what works in health care: A roadmap for the nation.* Edited by J. Eden, B. Wheatley, B. McNeil, and H. Sox. Washington, DC: The National Academies Press.

IOM. 2009. *Conflict of interest in medical research, education, and practice.* Edited by B. Lo and M. J. Field. Washington, DC: The National Academies Press.

Jacobs, A. K., B. D. Lindsay, B. J. Bellande, G. C. Fonarow, R. A. Nishimura, P. M. Shah, B. H. Annex, V. Fuster, R. J. Gibbons, M. J. Jackson, and S. H. Rahimtoola. 2004. Task force 3: Disclosure of relationships with commercial interests: Policy for educational activities and publications. *Journal of American College of Cardiology* 44(8):1736–1740.

Kahan, J. P., R. E. Park, L. L. Leape, S. J. Bernstein, L. H., Hilborne, L. Parker, C. J. Kamberg, D. J. Ballard, and R. H. Brook. 1996. Variations by specialty in physician ratings of the appropriateness and necessity of indications for procedures. *Medical Care* 34(6):512–523.

Lau, J. 2010. Models of interaction between clinical practice guidelines (CPG) groups and systematic review (SR) teams. Presented at IOM Committee on Standards for Developing Trustworthy Clinical Practice Guidelines meeting, January 12, Washington, DC.

Lexchin, J., L. A. Bero, B. Djulbegovic, and O. Clark. 2003. Pharmaceutical industry sponsorship and research outcome and quality: Systematic review. *BMJ* 326(7400):1167–1170.

Lomas, J. 1993. Making clinical policy explicit. Legislative policy making and lessons for developing practice guidelines. *International Journal of Technology Assessment in Health Care* 9(1):11–25.

Lurie, P., C. M. Almeida, N. Stine, A. R. Stine, and S. M. Wolfe. 2006. Financial conflict of interest disclosure and voting patterns at Food and Drug Administration drug advisory committee meetings. *JAMA* 295(16):1921–1928.

Moreira, T. 2005. Diversity in clinical guidelines: The role of repertoires of evaluation. *Social Science and Medicine* 60(9):1975–1985.

Moreira, T., C. May, J. Mason, and M. Eccles. 2006. A new method of analysis enabled a better understanding of clinical practice guideline development processes. *Journal of Clinical Epidemiology* 59(11):1199–1206.

Moynihan, R., and D. Henry. 2006. The fight against disease mongering: Generating knowledge for action. *PLoS Medicine* 3(4):e191.

Murphy, E., R. Dingwall, D. Greatbatch, S. Parker, and P. Watson. 1998. Qualitative research methods in health technology assessment: A review of the literature. *Health Technology Assessment* 2(16):vii–260.

Nelson, H. D., E. M. Haney, T. Dana, C. Bougatsos, and R. Chou. 2010. Screening for osteoporosis: An update for the U.S. Preventive Services Task Force. *Annals of Internal Medicine* 153(2):99–111.

New Zealand Guidelines Group. 2001. Handbook for the preparation of explicit evidence-based clincal practice guidelines. http://www.nzgg.org.nz (accessed August 26, 2009).

NICE (National Institute for Health and Clinical Excellence). 2008. *A code of practice for declaring and dealing with conflicts of interest.* London, UK: NICE.

NICE. 2009. *Methods for the development of NICE public health guidance,* 2nd ed. London, UK: NICE.

NIH (National Institutes of Health). 2010. *About the consensus development program.* http://consensus.nih.gov/aboutcdp.htm (accessed July 20, 2010).

Pagliari, C., and J. Grimshaw. 2002. Impact of group structure and process on multidisciplinary evidence-based guideline development: An observational study. *Journal of Evaluation in Clinical Practice* 8(2):145–153.

Pagliari, C., J. Grimshaw, and M. Eccles. 2001. The potential influence of small group processes on guideline development. *Journal of Evaluation in Clinical Practice* 7(2):165–173.

Richardson, F. M. 1972. Peer review of medical care. *Medical Care* 10(1):29–39.

Rosenfeld, R., and R. N. Shiffman. 2009. Clinical practice guideline development manual: A quality-driven approach for translating evidence into action. *Otolaryngology–Head & Neck Surgery* 140(6 Suppl 1):1–43.

Rothman, D. J., W. J. McDonald, C. D. Berkowitz, S. C. Chimonas, C. D. DeAngelis, R. W. Hale, S. E. Nissen, J. E. Osborn, J. H. Scully, Jr., G. E. Thomson, and D. Wofsy. 2009. Professional medical associations and their relationships with industry: A proposal for controlling conflict of interest. *JAMA* 301(13):1367–1372.

Schünemann, H. J., A. Fretheim, and A. D. Oxman. 2006. Improving the use of research evidence in guideline development: Integrating values and consumer involvement. *Health Research Policy and Systems* 4:22.

Schünemann, H. J., S. R. Hill, M. Kakad, G. E. Vist, R. Bellamy, L. Stockman, T. F. Wisloff, C. Del Mar, F. Hayden, T. M. Uyeki, J. Farrar, Y. Yazdanpanah, H. Zucker, J. Beigel, T. Chotpitayasunondh, T. H. Tran, B. Ozbay, N. Sugaya, and A. D. Oxman. 2007. Transparent development of the WHO rapid advice guidelines. *PLoS Medicine* 4(5):0786–0793.

Schünemann, H. J., M. Osborne, J. Moss, C. Manthous, G. Wagner, L. Sicilian, J. Ohar, S. McDermott, L. Lucas, and R. Jaeschke. 2009. An official American Thoracic Society policy statement: Managing conflict of interest in professional societies. *American Journal of Respiratory Critical Care Medicine* 180(6):564–580.

Shaneyfelt, T., M. Mayo-Smith, and J. Rothwangl. 1999. Are guidelines following guidelines? The methodological quality of clinical practice guidelines in the peer-reviewed medical literature. *JAMA* 281:1900–1905.

Shekelle, P. G., and D. L. Schriger. 1996. Evaluating the use of the appropriateness method in the Agency for Health Care Policy and Research clinical practice guideline development process. *Health Services Research* 31(4):453–468.

Shekelle, P. G., S. H. Woolf, M. Eccles, and J. Grimshaw. 1999. Clinical guidelines. Developing guidelines. *BMJ* 318(7183):593–596.

Shekelle, P. G., H. Schünemann, S. H. Woolf, M. Eccles, and J. Grimshaw. 2010. State of the art of CPG development and best practice standards. In *Committee on Standards for Developing Trustworthy Clinical Practice Guidelines comissioned paper.*

SIGN (Scottish Intercollegiate Guidelines Network), ed. 2008. *SIGN 50: A guideline developer's handbook.* Edinburgh, Scot.: SIGN.

Slavin, R. E. 1995. Best evidence synthesis: An intelligent alternative to meta-analysis. *Journal of Clinical Epidemiology* 48(1):9–18.

Sniderman, A. D., and C. D. Furberg. 2009. Why guideline-making requires reform. *JAMA* 301(4):429–431.

Taylor, I. 2005. Academia's "misconduct" is acceptable to industry. *Nature* 436(7051): 626.

Telford, R., J. D. Boote, and C. L. Cooper. 2004. What does it mean to involve consumers successfully in NHS research? A consensus study. *Health Expectations* 7(3):209–220.

Tuckman, B. W. 1965. Developmental sequence in small groups. *Psychology Bulletin* 63:384–399.

van Wersch, A., and M. Eccles. 1999. Patient involvement in evidence-based health in relation to clinical guidelines. In *The evidence-based primary care handbook*. Edited by M. Gabbay. London, UK: Royal Society of Medicine Press Ltd. Pp. 91–103.

van Wersch, A., and M. Eccles. 2001. Involvement of consumers in the development of evidence based clinical guidelines: Practical experiences from the north of England evidence based guideline development programme. *Quality in Health Care* 10(1):10–16.

Weinstein, M. C., and H. V. Fineberg. 1980. *Clinical decision analysis*. Philadelphia, PA: W. B. Saunders.

WHO (World Health Organization). 2008. *WHO handbook for guideline development*. Geneva, Switz.: WHO.

Williamson, C. 1998. The rise of doctor–patient working groups. *BMJ* 317(7169):1374–1377.

Woolf, S. 1991. *AHCPR interim manual for clinical practice guideline development*. AHCPR Pub. No. 91-0018. Rockville, MD: U.S. Department of Health and Human Services.

5

Current Best Practices and Standards for Development of Trustworthy CPGs: Part II, Traversing the Process

Abstract: This chapter is devoted to the remaining steps in the guideline development process, including standards for establishing evidence foundations for and rating of strength of recommendations, articulation of recommendations, external review, and updating. **The committee believes clinical practice guidelines (CPGs) should comply with all eight proposed standards contained within Chapters 4 and 5 to be considered trustworthy. The committee recommends that CPG developers adhere to these standards, and that CPG users adopt CPGs compliant with these standards.** However, the committee is sympathetic to the time and other resource requirements the standards require. Complying with the full body of standards may not be feasible immediately for guideline developers, and a process of evolutionary adoption over time may be more practicable. Importantly, whether evidence is lacking or abundant in a particular clinical domain, the committee expects guideline development groups to aspire to meet all standards.

INTRODUCTION

Like Chapter 4, Chapter 5 arose from the committee's adoption of standards-setting methodologies elaborated in Chapter 1. This chapter is devoted to the remaining domains of the guideline

109

development process: establishing evidence foundations for and rating strength of recommendations, articulation of recommendations, external review, and updating.

ESTABLISHING EVIDENCE FOUNDATIONS FOR AND RATING STRENGTH OF RECOMMENDATIONS

Appraising Evidence Quality and Recommendation Strength: Fundamentals

Clinical practice guidelines (CPGs) fundamentally rest on appraisal of the quality of relevant evidence, comparison of the benefits and harms of particular clinical recommendations, and value judgments regarding the importance of specific benefits and harms. Historically, value judgments regarding potential outcomes have been made implicitly rather than explicitly, and the basis for judgments regarding the quality of evidence and strength of a recommendation has often been unclear. As a result, many CPG developers now apply formal approaches to appraising both the evidence quality and the strength of recommendations (Ansari et al., 2009; Schünemann et al., 2006a; Shekelle et al., 2010).

Although much has been written about the concept of "quality of evidence," there continues to be considerable variability in what the term is used to describe. Ultimately the term "quality of evidence" is used to describe the level of confidence or certainty in a conclusion regarding the issue to which the evidence relates. And, historically, as detailed hereafter, the notion of quality has emphasized research design, so that evidence quality evaluations arose from the inherent rigor (e.g., RCT vs. uncontrolled case series) of study designs. This certainty or confidence is frequently expressed by assigning a score, rating, or grade (typically in the form of numerals, letters, symbols, or words) to the quality of evidence. Although critically important, it must be underscored that evidence quality as it often has been construed, is not the only factor that needs to be considered when drawing a conclusion regarding optimal clinical practice. Other considerations include the relevance of available evidence to a patient with particular characteristics; the quantity (i.e., volume and completeness) and consistency (i.e. conformity of findings across investigations) of available evidence; and the nature and estimated magnitude of particular impacts of an individual clinical practice and value judgments regarding the relative importance of those different impacts (Verkerk et al., 2006).

　　　Clinical practice recommendations typically are based on consideration of a body of evidence, as well as clinical judgments extending from experience and potential variation in patient preferences. For example, high-quality evidence from well-designed and -conducted clinical trials demonstrates that administration of oral anticoagulants to patients with a first spontaneous deep vein thrombosis reduces risk of recurrent thromboembolic events. Yet, differences in patient risk of bleeding complications and in patient value judgments regarding harms associated with oral anticoagulation therapy, including bleeding risk and the inconvenience related to taking medication and monitoring anticoagulation levels, permit only a weak recommendation regarding whether all patients with a first spontaneous deep vein thrombosis should be treated with oral anticoagulants (Buller et al., 2004).

　　　Economic value also can be included in the strength of recommendation decision process, as it relates to patients' out-of-pocket costs or overall healthcare spending. For a health care intervention to have value, clinical and economic benefits need to be greater than clinical harms and economic costs. Although value is a common term in health care, it has not been defined or studied in a way that is accepted well by the majority of members of the health care evidence community. Value rarely is considered in CPGs, yet the committee acknowledges that patient preferences are often based in part on out-of-pocket costs that may affect their personal decisions about alternative care options (Luce et al., 2010).

　　　Consideration of these latter factors, as well as the fact that evidence regarding several different issues needs to be considered by CPG developers, has given rise to the concept of strength of a recommendation regarding a particular patient management issue. Strength of a recommendation needs to reflect the degree of confidence that all patients would have so they would conclude that desirable outcomes of a recommendation outweigh the undesirable. Like evidence quality, this certainty or confidence is captured by a score, rating, or grading (commonly taking the form of numerals, letters, symbols, or words) assigned to the clinical recommendation (Swiglo et al., 2008).

　　　The appraisal of CPG evidence and recommendations presents considerable complexity, and a number of alternative strategies have been developed for these purposes. The literature demonstrates variability in rating the same evidence when employing varying appraisal systems, and variability in rating when identical systems are applied to identical evidence by different individuals (Ferreira et al., 2002). Judgments employed in translating evidence into a clinical recommendation are even more variable than those applied to evidence quality because their subjectivity (e.g., comparing disparate benefits and harms) is even greater (Calonge and Harris, 2010). Yet, the literature also suggests that a reduction in variability may be achieved by employment of structured, explicit approaches (Uhlig et al., 2006).

Additionally, there is a consensus among most guideline developers that standardized rating of evidence quality facilitates the balancing of benefits and harms requisite to healthcare decision making and guideline recommendation formulation. Furthermore, some have argued that an explicit, systematic scheme for assessing evidence quality and strength of recommendations likely results in reduced errors in judgment, increased facility in evaluating such judgments, and improved communication of related content by guideline developers (Atkins et al., 2004). CPG users need to understand the evidentiary basis of and value judgments associated with particular recommendations (Schünemann et al., 2006a). Over the past decade, guideline developers have recognized the value of providing an efficient summary of the strength of recommendations, and quality of evidence buttressing them, in enhancing clinicians' comprehension of a CPG's basic clinical message (Swiglo et al., 2008). Moreover, a small empirical literature suggests that adopters of clinical guidelines' healthcare recommendations prefer detailed, explicit knowledge about the underlying quality of evidence and strength of recommendations (Akl et al., 2007; Shekelle et al., 2010).

Rating Quality of Evidence and Strength of Recommendation: State of the Art

Rating of healthcare recommendations, specifically, began with the Canadian Task Force on the Periodic Health Examination more than three decades ago (Anonymous, 1979). The scheme was founded on study design exclusively, with randomized controlled trials (RCTs) classified as good (Level 1) evidence; cohort and case control studies as fair (Level II); and expert opinion classified as poor (Level III) evidence. Recommendation strength was derived from the quality of evidence so that a strong recommendation (i.e., A) was based on good (i.e., Level I) evidence. The attractiveness of the Canadian Task Force approach was its simplicity and attendant ease of comprehension, application, and presentation. However, this approach did not consider how well a particular type of study (e.g., RCT) was designed or executed or the number of patients included in particular studies. Furthermore, the rating applied only to the quality of evidence. The Canadian Task Force made no effort to rate the strength of their recommendations (e.g., balance of benefits and harms) (Atkins et al., 2004).

Numerous systems for appraising quality of evidence and strength of recommendations have evolved since, representing efforts of multiple, varied entities involved in guideline development. These systems range from the simple, founded exclusively on research design, and ignoring methodological details of studies, consistency of effects, and clinical relevance and generalizability of the patient population that was studied, to the more structured, which move beyond research design to the complexity of methods and the subjectivity of their appraisal. These schemes also vary with respect to the audiences and clinical foci they address. However, overall, the approaches include a strategy for rating the evidence, resulting in the assignment of an ordinal score (e.g., good, fair, poor; A, B, C; 1++, 1+, 1–, 2++, 2+, 2–, 3, 4) driven by methodological quality (e.g., RCTs without important limitations, RCTs with important limitations, observational studies, case series) of the available evidence. The second component they share is a strategy for rating recommendation strength resulting in assignment of a dichotomous or ordinal score (e.g., strong recommendation, weak recommendation; A, B, C, D; GRADE I, GRADE II, GRADE III) derived from consideration of evidence quality and the trade-offs between recommendation benefits and harms.

In general, when CPG developers are confident that the beneficial effects of a recommendation adherence outweigh the harms, a strong recommendation can be made. A strong recommendation commonly depends on high- or moderate-quality evidence regarding important patient outcomes. Much less often, CPG developers may offer strong recommendations on the basis of low- to very low-quality evidence. This occurrence is the result of guideline development group (GDG) confidence that benefits of a recommendation outweigh harms or vice versa. On the other hand, a weak recommendation commonly arises from development group judgment that the benefits of a recommendation outweigh harms; however, their confidence in this balance is not high (e.g., benefits and harms closely balanced, uncertain balance of benefits and harms). Hence, low or very low, or even very high evidence quality may result in weak recommendations due to a complex or uncertain benefits/harms trade-off (Swiglo et al., 2008). Further specifications of rating schemes are captured within a selection of prominent approaches provided in Appendix D.

Although the literature argues in support of a mechanism for scoring quality of evidence and strength of recommendations, and a vast majority of GDGs apply one, we noted earlier the specific challenges in their application (Schünemann et al., 2006a). In addition, there is widespread agreement that the area of appraisal overall is "besieged with problems" (Kavanagh, 2009). In 2004, Atkins and colleagues conducted a comparison of six well-respected systems, those of the American College of Chest Physicians, Australian National Health and Medical Research Council, Oxford Center for Evidence-Based Medicine, Scottish Intercollegiate Guidelines Network, U.S. Preventive Services Task Force, and U.S. Task Force on Community Preventive Services (Atkins et al., 2004). Atkins and colleagues (2004) identified a number of additional systems in use by 51 organizations, which have developed from 2 to greater than 10 CPGs and applied an explicit scheme to assess the quality of evidence or strength of recommendations. These additional systems reflect those six approaches fully investigated by the authors, with slight variations. The authors' findings are based on assessments of all 6 systems by 12 independent evaluators applying 12 indicators of system "sensibility" or overall utility. These authors' analyses uncovered poor agreement among assessors (Atkins et al., 2004), and still others claim the discord is indicative of the questionable validity of any unique scheme (Kavanagh, 2009).

Atkins and coauthors (2004) offer detailed qualitative insight into the state of the art of evidence quality and recommendation strength assessment. Their evaluation indicates the following:

1. No one system was uniformly endorsed as clear and simple, and the clearer a system, the less likely it was simple to apply.
2. For most approaches data necessary to employ them would at least sometimes be unavailable.
3. All systems were missing at least one critical dimension.
4. Although certain systems were considered to have some ability to discriminate, none of the systems was regarded as likely to clearly articulate the difference between quality of evidence and strength of recommendations.
5. There was uncertainty regarding the reproducibility of the assessment using any of the tools (Atkins et al., 2004).

Based on these findings and in pursuit of an improved strategy for evidence quality and strength of recommendations appraisal, the Grades of Recommendation Assessment, Development and Evaluation (GRADE) was published in 2004 (Atkins, 2004). GRADE has been adopted "unchanged or with only minor modifications" by a large number and variety of organizations, including governments, professional medical societies, and UpToDate, a medical resource accessed online that is used by a majority of U.S. academic medical centers (Schünemann et al., 2006b). GRADE's advantages include its (1) applicability across a great variety of clinical areas (e.g., prevention and therapy); (2) accounting for individual preferences and values; and (3) treatment of the quality of evidence and the strength of recommendation in a transparent, explicit manner. CPGs and recommendations applying the approach typically increase users' understanding of the rationale for CPG recommendations' derivation (Calonge and Harris, 2010).

However, as in the case of the larger body of appraisal tools, criticism has been directed at GRADE, much of it reflecting the issues raised herein. As indicated above, a feature common to all rating systems is the part played by individual judgment, and although judgment criteria are well specified in GRADE, the identical body of evidence can be appraised differently by judges with different individual biases or values. Furthermore, although GRADE explicitly describes the means by which a recommendation is achieved, the system may result in discordance in translating evidence into recommendations among GDGs and potentially within a single group across varying clinical actions (Calonge and Harris, 2010). In fact, empirical assessment of the reliability of GRADE, conducted by the authors of the system, has resulted in findings of very low interrater agreement for quality of evidence judgments. Furthermore, although theoretical underpinnings of GRADE are provided in multiple publications (Atkins, 2004; Atkins et al., 2004, 2005; Guyatt et al., 2006a,b, 2008b; Schünemann et al., 2006b), empirical assessment of the validity of GRADE is absent from the literature.

Derived from GRADE is the American College of Physicians (ACP) system for appraising evidence quality and strength of recommendations. The ACP judges evidence to be of high quality when it is based on one or more well-designed and well-conducted RCTs, giving rise to consistent findings directly applicable to the target population (Qaseem et al., 2010). Moderate-quality evidence is that derived from RCTs characterized by significant deficiencies (e.g., large losses to follow-up, lack of blinding); indirect evidence arising from similar populations; and RCTs that include a small number of subjects or observed events. Additionally, well-designed and non-randomized controlled trials, well-designed cohort or case control analytic studies, and multiple time-series designs comprise moderate-quality evidence. Low-quality evidence commonly derives from observational investigations; yet such evidence may be regarded as moderate or perhaps high, as determined by specifics of research methods (e.g., dose–response relationship, large observed effect). ACP guideline recommendations are graded as strong or weak. A strong recommendation indicates that benefits clearly outweigh harms, or harms clearly outweigh benefits. Weak recommendations result from precariously balanced benefits and harms or a high level of uncertainty regarding magnitude of benefits and harms. Lastly, in the case of a dearth of, conflicting, or poor quality of evidence driving support of or opposition to clinical action, the ACP rates the recommendation as "insufficient evidence to determine net benefits or risks" because the balance of benefits and harms cannot be achieved (Qaseem et al., 2010, p. 196).

The ACP's detailed interpretation of its system for grading the quality of evidence and strength of recommendations, provided in Table 5-1 below, depicts and defines elements basic to appraisal and understanding relationships between evidence quality and recommendation strength. It also highlights the implications of those relationships for clinical practice.

Currently available approaches to rating evidence quality and strength of recommendation are of utility, but not adequate. They provide transparent, systematic frameworks for clinical recommendations' derivation extending from consideration of evidence quality, in contrast to an unsystematic, implicit, non-transparent, intuitive approach. With this, these strategies allow for inspection of the methods and judgments involved in translating evidence into clinical recommendations, thereby increasing trustworthiness of CPGs (Ansari et al., 2009; Calonge and Harris, 2010; Kavanagh, 2009).

As one aspect of establishing evidence foundations for, and ultimately deriving, evidence-based, clinically valid recommendations, the committee supports adoption of systematic methods for rating quality of evidence and strength of recommendations, which include the elements discussed above.

Integrating Guideline Development Group Values

Explaining Variation in Evidence Interpretation

CPG development usually requires interpretation of evidence regarding many different issues. Therefore, recommendations addressing the same topic may vary among guidelines. This is especially the case in the setting of low-quality evidence because judgment is more likely to come into play when evidence is limited or of low quality (Burgers et al., 2002).

TABLE 5-1 Interpretation of the American College of Physicians' Guideline Grading System

Grade of Recommendation	Benefit Versus Risks and Burdens	Methodological Quality of Supporting Evidence	Interpretation	Implications
Strong recommendation; high-quality evidence	Benefits clearly outweigh risks and burden or vice versa	Randomized Clinical Trials (RCTs) without important limitations or overwhelming evidence from observational studies	Strong recommendation; can apply to most patients in most circumstances without reservation	For patients, would want the recommended course of action and only a small proportion would not; a person should request discussion if the intervention was not offered
Strong recommendation; moderate-quality evidence	Benefits clearly outweigh risks and burden or vice versa	RCTs with important limitations (inconsistent results; methodological flaws; indirect, imprecise, or exceptionally strong evidence from observational studies)		For clinicians, most patients should receive the recommended course of action For policy makers, the recommendation can be adopted as a policy in most situations
Strong recommendation; low-quality evidence	Benefits clearly outweigh risks and burden or vice versa	Observational studies or case series	Strong recommendation, but may change when higher quality evidence becomes available	
Weak recommendation; high-quality evidence	Benefits closely balanced with risks and burden	RCTs without important limitations or overwhelming evidence from observational studies	Weak recommendation; best action may differ depending on circumstances or patients' or societal values	For patients, most would want the recommended course of action, but some would not—a decision may depend on an individual's circumstances

continued

TABLE 5-1 Continued

Grade of Recommendation	Benefit Versus Risks and Burdens	Methodological Quality of Supporting Evidence	Interpretation	Implications
Weak recommendation; moderate-quality evidence	Benefits closely balanced with risks and burden	RCTs with important limitations (inconsistent results, methodological flaws, indirect, or imprecise) or exceptionally strong evidence from observational studies		For clinicians, different choices will be appropriate for different patients, and a management decision consistent with a patient's values, preferences, and circumstances should be reached For policy makers, policy making will require substantial debate and involvement of many stakeholders
Weak recommendation; low-quality evidence	Uncertainty in the estimates of benefits, risks, and burden; benefits, risks, and burden may be closely balanced	Observational studies or case Series	Very weak recommendations; other alternatives may be equally reasonable	
Insufficient	Balance of benefits and risks cannot be determined	Evidence is conflicting, poor quality, or lacking	Insufficient evidence to recommend for or against routinely providing the service	For patients, decisions based on evidence from scientific studies cannot be made; for clinicians, decisions based on evidence from scientific studies cannot be made; for policy makers, decisions based on evidence from scientific studies cannot be made

SOURCE: Qaseem et al. (2010).

Eisinger and coauthors (1999) investigated U.S. and French consensus statements regarding breast and ovarian cancer that identified important distinctions in clinical recommendations, particularly given clinical uncertainty. Both consensus statements indicated that mastectomy and oophorectomy are reasonable options for women at high cancer risk, even given inadequate evidence and demonstrations of later breast or ovarian cancer development in women undergoing the procedures. However, the recommendations are vastly different. The French guidelines assert that physicians should "oppose" prophylactic mastectomy in women under age 30 and prophylactic oophorectomy under age 35, and these treatment options should be considered only when a breast cancer risk is greater than 60 percent and an ovarian cancer risk is greater than 20 percent. In the United States, informed choice is adequate justification to perform both surgeries. Eisinger and coauthors (1999) suggested that clinician opposition to delegating decision making to patients is less palatable to the French medical community. Simultaneously, this viewpoint would be perceived as paternalistic to American patients and providers who are embedded in a context where patient preferences and participatory decision making are highly valued. However, even within national borders, credible guideline development groups reach contrasting conclusions despite a common evidence base, as Box 5-1 illustrates.

Burgers and colleagues investigated 15 Type 2 diabetes CPGs from 13 countries in an attempt to identify variables influential to clinical recommendations (Burgers et al., 2002). In essence, the authors corroborated prior findings in determining that research evidence is not always the most important contributor to practice guideline recommendation content. Instead their results demonstrate there is little consistency in studies selected for review. References serving as evidentiary foundations for recommendations were highly variable across 15 guidelines investigated. Specifically, when considering a single CPG, only 18 percent of citations were consistent with those of any other guideline. Only 1 percent of citations were overlapping across six or more guidelines. In spite of this, the level of guideline recommendation concordance was strong, with a high degree of international consensus on the clinical care of Type 2 diabetes. Burgers and coauthors assert that "Guideline development is a social as well as technical process that is affected by access to and choice of research evidence and decisions about the interpretation of evidence and formulation of recommendations . . . guidelines go beyond simple reviews of available evidence and necessarily reflect value judgments in considering all the issues

---

BOX 5-1
Guidelines with Conflicting Recommendations

The North American Society for Pediatric Gastroenterology, Hepatology and Nutrition (NASPHGAN), the National Institutes of Health (NIH) Consensus Development Conference on Celiac Disease, and the American Gastroenterological Association's recommendations conflict on the common scenario of whether to screen an asymptomatic sibling of a patient recently diagnosed with celiac disease. The likely cause of discrepancy is differing positions on how to value benefits of screening (reduced risk of lymphoma, reversal of undetected nutritional deficiency, and improvement in general well-being) against potential harms (inconvenience of maintaining a gluten-free diet and adverse psychological effects of chronic disease diagnosis) to an asymptomatic individual. NASPHGAN concludes that benefits outweigh potential harms and thus recommends screening, while the NIH concludes the opposite, and the American Gastroenterological Association resides between the two, advocating shared decision making between provider and patient.

SOURCES: Elson et al. (2004); Hill et al. (2005); Rostom et al. (2006).

---

relevant to clinical decision making" (Burgers et al., 2002, p. 1937). Michie et al. (2007) also discussed an investigation conducted by Hemingway and colleagues that led to the discovery that two independent expert panels provided with identical research evidence on angina derived contrasting therapeutic recommendations. Of note, the authors identified a twofold difference between panels in their estimates of therapeutic underuse for some patient subgroups (Michie et al., 2007).

Hence, the literature asserts that guideline recommendations do not always emerge directly from empirical evidence reviewed by a GDG. Bodies of complementary work offer some explanatory insight regarding this phenomenon, as well as the variety of strategies that GDGs might employ to address it. In an exploration of the relationship between research evidence and GDG clinical judgment, Raine and coauthors (2004) found agreement between the evidence and clinical judgments 51 percent of the time. Factors identified as influential in the divergence of evidence and recommendations included: weak or non-applicable evidence; clinical experience; patient preferences; treatment availability; and clinician values. Overall, in examining explanations for the disagreement, the authors found greater concordance if evidence upheld clinical experience and beliefs. Acceptance of evidence was more likely if it agreed with current clinical practice. With inconsistency between clinical experience and beliefs, and the scientific evidence, the former appeared to prevail. These authors concluded, "Our findings support the idea that evidence is used to confirm preexisting opinions rather than change them. Guidelines cannot be deduced from research evidence alone. Statements about what should be done in particular circumstances necessarily depend on interpretation of the evidence and on clinicians' experience, beliefs, and values" (Raine et al., 2004, p. 436).

More specifically, the literature addresses the influence of particular scientific evidentiary contexts on recommendation-related decision making. Typically, when the science clearly demonstrates that there is a substantial net benefit (benefit minus harms) of an intervention (e.g., coronary artery bypass graft for left main coronary artery disease), or that an intervention is ineffective or harmful (e.g., bone marrow transplant for breast cancer), the need to consider values and preferences may be less important. However, two circumstances commonly occur in guideline development that require sensitivity to personal preferences and subjective judgments.

First, when evidence is unclear, judgments about magnitude of intervention effects are often swayed by subjective impressions regarding study quality or alternative weights applied to benefits and harms. For example, a number of randomized controlled trials have evaluated the effectiveness of screening mammography in detection of breast cancer, with widely varying effect sizes (Nelson et al., 2009). This variation may explain why, for two decades, experts with differing opinions about randomized clinical trial methodology have reached discordant conclusions regarding quality of evidence and mammography-related, age-specific mortality reduction (Woolf, 2010).

In the presence of scientific uncertainty, judgments based on other considerations often, and sometimes legitimately, assume greater importance. So, guideline developers commonly consider clinical experience, expert opinion, and personal judgments regarding potential harms of the intervention versus potential harms of inaction. These judgments inevitably color their characterization of the evidence and derivation of recommendations (Woolf and George, 2000). In some instances, groups opt for neutrality, stating that evidence is insufficient to make a recommendation (Calonge and Randhawa, 2004). In other circumstances, such as when the condition poses great risk or there is little potential intervention harm, the GDG may recommend the intervention despite inadequate evidence. Given the opposite situation, when concerns about potential harms are heightened, a GDG may recommend against an intervention pending more convincing evidence (Cuervo and Clarke, 2003).

Second, even when effect size is large and clear, the judgment of whether benefits outweigh harms can be subjective (Kassirer and Pauker, 1981). Individuals given identical data regarding probabilities of benefits and harms can reach contrasting conclusions about net benefit due to different values, or utilities, assigned to outcomes (Kassirer, 1994; Pauker and Kassirer, 1997; Shrier et al., 2008). For example, the risk of developing urinary incontinence from surgery for prostate cancer may be less disconcerting to an oncologist or patient focused on the hazard of cancer than to a clinician or patient more concerned about quality of life than life expectancy. These subjective judgments are neither right nor wrong, but they importantly influence conclusions about net benefit and hence a panel's recommendations.

Whatever choices are made, it is best for developers to be transparent and explicit about value judgments (Carlsen and Norheim, 2008). The rationale for concluding that evidence is strong, weak, or equivocal should be detailed. Additionally, concerns about study methodology, including outcomes assessment, should be outlined to explain the GDG's rationale and direct future research in addressing evidentiary limitations. For example, guideline developers' recent citing of contamination of control groups as weaknesses in intervention studies should encourage future investigators to devise methodological innovations to overcome this problem (Shekelle et al., 2010).

Dealing with Close Calls

Panels have two options for dealing with close calls and recommendations involving difficult benefits/harms trade-offs. First, the GDG, with deep knowledge of the clinical topic and underlying science, can attempt to infer how most patients, faced with the same information, would react. Here guideline developers act as proxies for patients; the advantage of this approach is that the GDG has mastery of relevant details often beyond most patients' ability to digest or most busy clinicians' ability to explain. The disadvantages are its inherent paternalism and the risk of GDG misjudgments (Laine and Davidoff, 1996). Guideline developers may not be representative of ordinary clinicians or patients, may have backgrounds and biases skewing perspectives about intervention safety or benefits, and may do a poor job of inferring patient reaction (Bruera et al., 2002; Holmes et al., 1987; Teno et al., 1995). Studies have documented considerable heterogeneity in patient preferences (Ogan et al., 2001; Pignone et al., 1999). Across a sample of patients faced with identical information, individuals will make different choices about the relative importance of pros and cons and clinical options preferred. Hence, a panel deciding on behalf of patients will inevitably advocate an option that a subset or subsets of patients would not prefer (Woolf, 1997).

The second option for addressing close calls is to eschew a blanket recommendation and instead encourage shared or informed decision-making, in which patients discuss trade-offs with their clinicians and make individual decisions based on personal preferences (Braddock et al., 1999; Frosch and Kaplan, 1999; Kassirer, 1994). The advantage of this approach is its respect for individual choice; here, guidelines become tools for patient empowerment, engagement, and activation (Coulter, 2002; Hibbard, 2003; Sox and Greenfield, 2010). Moreover, a large body of literature devoted to determinants of individual health behavior demonstrates that, relative to the uninformed, well-informed patients who actively participate in their care make improved decisions and engage in other positive health-related behaviors (Gochman, 1988). Additionally, in their 2010 commentary in *JAMA* on quality of care, Sox and Greenfield further note that "Informed choice under uncertainty is an ideal to strive for, especially because it enhances the exercise of the patient's right of self-determination, which is a cornerstone of medical ethics. A well informed decision also incorporates the difficult to measure variables—an individual's probabilities and preferences" (p. 2403).

The disadvantage of shared decision making is that patients and clinicians may not embrace these roles or may be incapable of fulfilling them (Deber et al., 1996; Strull et al., 1984). Some patients appreciate making their own decisions; others find it overwhelming, preferring clinicians or "experts" to guide them. Absorbing necessary information—understanding the health condition, available options, scientific evidence, and the probability and magnitude of benefits and harms—is challenging (Wills and Holmes-Rovner, 2003; Woloshin et al., 2001). Decision aids have been developed—in written, video, electronic, and online forms—to present such information in a scientifically accurate, understandable, and balanced way (O'Connor et al., 2005). Accessibility and usefulness of decision aids is an active area of research (Kaplan and Ware, 1995; O'Connor et al., 2009).

Clinicians' barriers to use of shared decision making begin with skepticism about its utility (McNutt, 2004). Clinicians, easily influenced by their own subjective value judgments and memorable experiences with patients who suffered or benefitted from an intervention or its omission, may resist a guideline that gives patients options to make choices (Shekelle et al., 2010). They may also lack time and knowledge to explain evidence bases for available options, as well as decision aids or counseling staff to provide further details, and they are not compensated for extended patient discussions required by informed decision making (Bogardus et al., 1999). Many clinicians fear medicolegal liability and allegations of negligence if they accommodate patient choice that goes awry (Merenstein, 2004).

Both options for addressing close calls are applied to CPGs and both have limitations. Whichever approach a GDG adopts, transparency and clarity are crucial. If a panel acts as patient proxy, value judgments in assessing net benefit should be explained so that others can judge their merit. Furthermore, an acknowledgment of the heterogeneity of patient preferences should be explicated. Typically, the latter is achieved by pairing recommendations with "disclaimer" language for patients or clinical circumstances where recommendations might not apply. For example, a guideline might recommend a treatment with complex trade-offs but add, "the treatment may be inappropriate in certain individual circumstances" or "patients should be informed about the risks before treatment is considered" (Shekelle et al., 2010). Of course, these recommendation expressions are not only applicable to "close calls." If the panel eschews a specific recommendation and advocates shared decision making, it is useful to have the guideline include details regarding content of the relevant patient–clinician conversation. The guideline panel is likely to have clarity respecting preference-sensitive issues influencing the benefit/harm trade-off. Hence, content relevant to shared decision making, the underlying evidence, the role of decision aids, and other suggestions for incorporating personal preferences into the decision-making process optimally are included in guideline textual discussion (Shekelle et al., 2010).

5. **Establishing Evidence Foundations for and Rating Strength of Recommendations**
    5.1 **For <u>each</u> recommendation, the following should be provided:**
        • **An explanation of the reasoning underlying the recommendation, including**
            o **A clear description of potential benefits and harms**
            o **A summary of relevant available evidence (and evidentiary gaps), description of the quality (in-**

cluding applicability), quantity (including completeness), and consistency of the aggregate available evidence
   o   An explanation of the part played by values, opin-
       ion, theory, and clinical experience in deriving the
       recommendation
   •   A rating of the level of confidence in (certainty regard-
       ing) the evidence underpinning the recommendation
   •   A rating of the strength of the recommendation in
       light of the preceding bullets
   •   A description and explanation of any differences of
       opinion regarding the recommendation

Incorporating Patients with Comorbidity

A recent topic of interest in developing practice guidelines
is consideration of patients with multiple medical conditions, an
increasingly important issue as the population ages. This has given
rise to a small emergent literature (Shekelle et al., 2010). Most guidelines are developed for the management of a single disease, rather
than for people with several disease(s), stated Boyd and colleagues
(2005) in their assessment of the applicability of clinical practice
guidelines for a hypothetical 79-year-old woman with five chronic
conditions: osteoporosis, osteoarthritis, diabetes, hypertension, and
chronic obstructive pulmonary disease. Boyd and coauthors noted
that CPGs for these conditions, with the exception of diabetes, did
not discuss recommendations for management of patients with
other chronic conditions. When Boyd and colleagues applied the
relevant guidelines to their hypothetical patient, they found the
patient would need to be advised of 7 self-management tasks, a
clinician would be responsible for performing 18 tasks, the patient
would be advised to take 12 separate medications in 19 doses per
day, and certain medications recommended for one condition could
interact with or exacerbate symptoms or medication side effects
for other conditions (e.g., non-steroidal anti-inflammatory drugs
[NSAIDs] for osteoarthritis potentially raising the blood pressure
in hypertension; hydrochlorothiazide for hypertension potentially
raising glucose levels in diabetes). Boyd and colleagues (2005) concluded that applying current clinical practice guidelines to patients
with multiple health conditions may have undesirable effects.

Since then, the challenges of developing practice guidelines for
patients with multiple chronic conditions has received a great deal
of discussion (the Boyd article had been cited 431 times by early
2010) and, as indicated above, a related literature is amassing. Signif-

icant strides have been made in tailoring clinical recommendations to comorbid conditions, particularly in certain clinical areas, such as diabetes and prostate cancer. Yet, Boyd (2010) noted as recently as 2009 that the current standards of guideline development do not induce CPG developers to provide tools for adapting their recommendations to the patient with many comorbidities or prioritize the most important recommendations within a single disease or between diseases (Boyd, 2010).

One justification for omission of patients with comorbidity from CPGs is that clinical trials commonly used as evidence bases often exclude patients with multiple chronic conditions (Tinetti et al., 2004). At the same time, determining whether the result of a trial applies to an individual with comorbidity can be difficult, even when these patients are not explicitly excluded. A trial's summary results may not apply to all patients in the trial, and how to make average trial results applicable to complex patients has not yet been sufficiently resolved, particularly in those with comorbidity (Boyd, 2010).

Consequently, little literature addresses the effect(s) that other health conditions may have on treatments and outcomes of care for a particular condition—knowledge that likely would translate into differences in guideline treatment recommendations. The exception to this rule is diabetes, where data are available regarding outcome differences for patients with hypertension and cardiovascular disease, for optimal blood pressure control and LDL levels. For example, a 2009 study of patients with Type 2 diabetes found that those with high levels of comorbidity are likely to receive diminished cardiovascular benefit from intensive blood glucose control (Greenfield et al., 2009). These data have been translated into differential treatment recommendations in clinical practice guidelines.

Likewise, Boyd and colleagues have developed a framework for conceptualizing disease severity in older adults, which includes the effect of disease severity on other diseases (Boyd et al., 2007). Because treating one condition optimally (e.g., using increased doses of NSAIDs for osteoarthritis) may cause an increased risk of side effects (gastrointestinal bleeding) that can be mitigated by adding another medication (proton pump inhibitors) that has a possible deleterious impact on outcomes of another health condition (use of clopidogrel in patients who have had coronary artery revascularization interventions), weighing the risks and benefits of treatments across a patient's health conditions is necessary, and likely will involve discussion with the patient about the relative importance of different potential outcomes. Guideline development incorporating patient viewpoints has been advocated (Krahn and Naglie, 2008). Tinetti et al. discuss the tension between one major goal of guidelines, to reduce practice variation among providers, and the necessity of appropriate variation in care due to differing disease burden and preferences of patients. Emerging evidence suggests that older patients and those with multiple morbidities value health outcomes such as long-term survival, risk of physical and cognitive morbidity, and risk of adverse effects differently from other populations (Tinetti et al., 2004).

Boyd (2010) further advises that when guideline developers are in the process of developing guidelines, they should explicitly discuss patients with multiple morbidities by considering the following questions (Boyd, 2010):

- Were individuals with multiple morbidities in the studies considered?
- What is the quality of evidence for those with comorbidities?
- Is there within-trial heterogeneity of treatment effect?
- What are goals of therapy?
- What are highest priorities if recommendations cannot all be done in a person with comorbidities?
- How should patient preferences be discussed and incorporated?
- What interactions are common or important given highly prevalent comorbid conditions?
- What is the complexity of the recommended medication regimen?
- What is the burden of therapy?

The literature suggests that developers with sufficient resources may wish to go further:

- Determine the most relevant chronic conditions coexisting with the condition of guideline topic (these data normally come from descriptive studies of frequencies of health conditions). Attempt to assess the importance of a coexisting condition by capturing how commonly it exists and how severely it may interfere with the management of the CPG related disease.
- Search for evidence about the effect(s) that presence of one of these common comorbidities or their management has on management of the topic condition.
- Report on the presence or absence of such evidence.

- Specifically search for and report on evidence about patient values.
- Explicitly consider the available evidence exploring comorbidities management options and patient values (Shekelle et al., 2010).

ARTICULATION OF RECOMMENDATIONS

An important aspect of developing recommendations favorably influencing care is the wording used for them. Guideline users have lamented recommendations that are vague or nonspecific, using what they refer to as "weasel words," as in "Patients with such and such should be offered the intervention *if clinically appropriate*" or "Clinicians should follow up with patients given the intervention every 4 weeks, or sooner *if necessary*." In such instances clinicians attempting to use the guideline may have difficulty applying it, or be uncertain about what constitutes "clinically appropriate" or "if necessary." Grol and colleagues found that among Dutch general practitioners, vague or nonspecific guideline recommendations were followed 35 percent of the time, while "clear" recommendations were followed 67 percent of the time (Grol et al., 1998). An experimental study using vignettes of patients with back pain found that specific guidelines produced more appropriate and fewer inappropriate orders for electrodiagnostic tests (tests that measure the speed and degree of electrical activity in muscles and nerves to diagnose damage) than did vague guidelines (Shekelle et al., 2000). Michie and Johnston, using evidence from psychological research, went so far as to conclude that the "most cost-effective intervention to increase guideline implementation is rewriting guidelines in behaviorally specific terms" (Michie and Johnston, 2004, p. 328).

However, standardized recommendation wording does not exist (Oxman et al., 2006). This deficit is reflected in results of an evaluation by Hussain and colleagues (2009) of more than nearly 1,300 randomly selected recommendations (out of over 7,500) from the National Guideline Clearinghouse. Recommendations were presented with great inconsistency within and across guidelines, and 31.6 percent did not present actions that could be executed. More than half (52.6 percent) did not indicate strength of recommendation (Hussain et al., 2009).

The editorial board of the National Guideline Clearinghouse "encourages [guideline] developers to formulate recommendation statements that are 'actionable'and that employ active voice, rather than passive voice" (NGC, 2010b). The UK National Institute for

Health and Clinical Excellence (NICE) believes recommendations should be clear and concise, but include sufficient information so they may be understood without reference to other supporting material (NICE, 2009).

Rosenfeld and Shiffman's guideline development manual asserts that the goal of clear and identifiable recommendations is achieved by designing a guideline around *key action statements* and elaborated by text, evidence profiles, and strength of recommendation ratings. The authors assert that recommendation statements commonly are vague, unspecified, and not ready for execution. Key action statements are defined as activity-based prescriptions for specific clinician behavior. Hence, they should imply action operations that can support performance or other quality measures. These statements should be brief and precise. Finally, Rosenfeld and Shiffman submit that recommendations should have clarity respecting under what circumstances who should do what to whom, with what level of obligation. Associated text underscores *why* the recommendation is important and *how* it should be enacted (Rosenfeld and Shiffman, 2009).

Clarity and precision in guidelines are desirable not only to facilitate implementation by clinicians and patients, but also for incorporation into decision support tools (e.g., prompts used by electronic medical records, standing orders, checklists) to facilitate guideline implementation. Programmers writing code to transform guideline knowledge often are frustrated by lack of clarity regarding whether a service is or is not recommended, the precise type of patient for whom it is recommended, and other details necessary for programming rules. The former and related notions are discussed at length in Chapter 6. Similarly, quality review organizations or payers who seek to reward guideline-consistent care find underspecified guidelines unhelpful in developing performance indicators.

However, guideline developers adhering to evidence-based methods for formulating guideline recommendations may find evidence foundations inadequate to justify recommendation precision. Vagueness or underspecification sometimes reflects limited available evidence. For example, evidence indicates that Pap smears of the cervix are effective when done every 1 to 3 years and that mammographic screening in women ages 50 and older can reduce mortality whether it is performed annually or every other year. For certain screening tests there simply is inadequate evidence to specify any interval or define risk groups for whom screening is appropriate. When research has not determined one interval is more effective than another, developing a precise recommendation may satisfy demands for "clear" guidelines, assist computer programmers, and give review organizations and malpractice attorneys a clear benchmark for classifying care as inappropriate or negligent, but it departs from evidence. In articulating recommendations, the guideline developer keenly feels the constant tension between providing guidance that is as unambiguous as possible and the need to not reach beyond the science (Hussain et al., 2009).

In line with other efforts to address this struggle, the GRADE Working Group recommends semantic separation of strong and conditional ("weak") recommendations. Hence, following the GRADE Working Group and other authors, a strong recommendation would be introduced by the terms "We recommend . . . " or "Clinicians should . . . " and a conditional recommendation would begin with the terms "We suggest . . . ", "We conditionally recommend . . . ", or "Clinicians might . . . " (Guyatt et al., 2008a). The population, intervention, and comparator should be included in the recommendation or be easily deduced from surrounding text. A 2010 study by Lomotan and coauthors investigated the level of obligation conveyed to clinicians by deontic terms ("should," "may," "must," and "is indicated"). The authors concluded that while "must" conveyed the strongest level of obligation, guideline developers rarely use the term, except in cases of a clear legal standard or potential for imminent patient harm. "Should," by contrast, was the most common deontic verb found in the authors' sample, and they believe it appropriately conveys an intermediate level of obligation between "must" and "may" (Lomotan et al., 2010).

Based on their review of the NGC database, Hussain and colleagues (2009) suggest the following criteria be followed in presentation and formulation of recommendations:

1. Identify the critical recommendations in guideline text using semantic indicators (e.g., "The Committee recommends . . ." or "Whenever X, Y, and Z occur clinicians should . . .") and formatting (e.g., bullets, enumeration, and boldface text).
2. Use consistent semantic and formatting indicators throughout the publication.
3. Group recommendations together in a summary section to facilitate their identification.
4. Do not use assertions of fact as recommendations. Recommendations must be decidable and executable.
5. Clearly and consistently assign evidence quality and recommendation strength in proximity to each recommendation, and distinguish between the distinct concepts of quality of evidence and strength of recommendation.

6. **Articulation of Recommendations**
  6.1 **Recommendations should be articulated in a standardized form detailing precisely what the recommended action is, and under what circumstances it should be performed.**
  6.2 **Strong recommendations should be worded so that compliance with the recommendation(s) can be evaluated.**

EXTERNAL REVIEW

Rationale and Participants

A limited number of experts and perspectives can be represented within a GDG; hence, development groups committed to ensuring the balance, comprehensiveness, and quality of their guidelines are wise to share drafts with a spectrum of external reviewers who include not only guideline advocates, but also individuals, specialty groups, and industries expected to be critical of the GDG's evidence characterization, recommendations, or any number of aspects of the CPG (IOM, 1992). These reviewers may be able to challenge the logic applied by the guideline panel in translating the evidence into recommendations; call attention to biases, political pressure, or other factors that may be coloring panelist judgments; provide suggestions for improving and clarifying guideline messages; and allow for debate about the guideline rationale (AGREE, 2001; Burgers et al., 2003; Cluzeau et al., 2003). Potential reviewers include

- the nation's (or world's) leading investigators responsible for conduct of key studies influencing recommendations or aware of upcoming trials relevant to the guideline topic;
- representatives from federal agencies, professional organizations, specialty societies, peer review journals, and relevant guideline panels within the United States and abroad (e.g., NICE) authoring related guidelines and/or concerned with the topic;
- representatives from advocacy organizations, community groups, and public health organizations whose constituents may be affected by the guideline; and
- representatives from health plans, Medicare, businesses and industry, pharmaceutical or device manufacturers, and health systems (e.g., Kaiser, Veterans Affairs) impacted by the guideline (Shekelle et al., 2010).

Reviewers aware of the realities of clinical practice and the administration of health systems may provide useful feedback on how easily recommendations may be adopted by clinicians and systems of care, as well as broader policy ramifications, such as deficits of providers or technology to encourage a recommendation, implications for reimbursement or medicolegal liability, impracticalities created for information systems or performance review criteria, and upcoming legislation or policies bearing on the topic. Inviting commentary from stakeholders may also encourage "buy-in," as specialty societies and other entities that have reviewed and improved guidelines are often willing to participate in guideline implementation activities (Shekelle et al., 2010).

Conduct of External Review

Guideline developers differ in processes employed for identification of relevant reviewers, collection of reviewer comments, and response to reviewer recommendations. Methods for identifying reviewers range from ad hoc procedures, such as eliciting suggestions from panel members, to more systematic methods to ensure comprehensiveness. The U.S. Preventive Services Task Force sends draft CPGs to its federal and primary care partners, as well as appropriate clinical specialties, and solicits comments on the clarity, clinical usefulness, and scientific accuracy of its recommendation statement (AHRQ, 2008). NICE employs a panel of reviewers consisting of four or five members—healthcare industry professionals, the UK National Health Service commissioners and managers, and a lay person—to review all of its CPGs. This review panel comments on the draft scope as well as draft guideline (NICE, 2009). The American College of Cardiology Foundation and American Heart Association classify peer reviewers as "official," "content," and "organizational" reviewers. Official reviewers are nominated by the partnering organizations; all other reviewers are considered content or organizational reviewers (ACCF and AHA, 2008). Reviewers who express strong unsubstantiated views are of less assistance than those who articulate a sound scientific and clinical argument for their perspectives. Panel procedures for reviewer selection should consider this when choosing harsh critics, so that their viewpoints are balanced by scientific or clinical reasoning (Shekelle et al., 2010).

Reviewers may be asked to provide general responses to the guidelines as a whole or specific recommendations, or to vote on each guideline recommendation and provide alternative recommendations if those drafted by the GDG are deemed unacceptable. Whatever the process, ultimately GDGs should provide reviewers with clear directives for their criticism, including the requirement of evidence and citations as substantiation. Reviewers should focus on the completeness of the evidence that was reviewed, the rationale for particular recommendations, and the "implementability" of recommendations. To the extent that disagreements with recommendations are due to evidence that was not considered by the CPG panel, reviewers should submit the evidence that was not considered. Organizations disagreeing with recommendations may articulate the scientific evidence and clinical reasoning that, to their thinking, justifies a different policy than that in the draft guideline. Those with slightly different recommendations can argue for adjusting the guideline to provide greater harmonization and reduce confusion for clinicians and patients. In some instances, organizations recognize the value of endorsing the new guideline, updating their own guidelines to conform with new recommendations or issuing a guideline that is jointly supported by multiple organizations and agencies.

Critics of clinical practice guidelines can fault the review process if it is perceived that criticisms submitted to the panel were ignored. To allay such concerns, it is prudent for the development group to adopt a systematic process for responding to reviewer comments. For example, the panel might develop a table capturing each commentary from every reviewer, explaining how the guideline was or was not modified accordingly, and describing the rationale for the related course of action (Rosenfeld and Shiffman, 2009). The GDG may have to rewrite recommendations and guideline text and reapprove the final document, which could delay the process. GDGs should consider the potential necessity for revisions, and an additional post review meeting, when planning the original timeline. The public availability of such information is important to transparency; some GDGs provide related postings on their websites.

Development groups' reactions to reviewer comments should be consistent with the methodology used in their recommendations' derivation. For example, if a panel accepted expert opinion as a justification for recommendations, criticism by experts that the recommendation is inappropriate or subject to public or political disfavor might be sufficient justification for recommendation revision. Conversely, if a panel's methodology insists on evidence from well-designed randomized controlled trials, neither strident expert opinions nor a lengthy bibliography of supporting cohort studies would be grounds for revising recommendations. Lastly, a brief summary of the external review process should be provided at the time of release of the draft CPG (Shekelle et al., 2010).

7. External Review
    7.1 External reviewers should comprise a full spectrum of
        relevant stakeholders, including scientific and clinical ex-
        perts, organizations (e.g., health care, specialty societies),
        agencies (e.g., federal government), patients, and repre-
        sentatives of the public.
    7.2 The authorship of external reviews submitted by individ-
        uals and/or organizations should be kept confidential un-
        less that protection has been waived by the reviewer(s).
    7.3 The GDG should consider all external reviewer com-
        ments and keep a written record of the rationale for mod-
        ifying or not modifying a CPG in response to reviewers'
        comments.
    7.4 A draft of the CPG at the external review stage or imme-
        diately following it (i.e., prior to the final draft) should
        be made available to the general public for comment.
        Reasonable notice of impending publication should be
        provided to interested public stakeholders.

UPDATING

Clinical practice guideline recommendations often require
updating, although how often and by what process are debated.
For certain clinical areas, frequent updating may be necessary given
a preponderance of new evidence affecting treatment recommendations. Johnston et al. concluded that for purposes of updating
cancer care guidance, a quarterly literature search was appropriate,
although the product of this varied across cancer guideline topical
emphases (Johnston et al., 2003).

A review process detailed on the National Comprehensive Cancer Network (NCCN) website includes a continuous institutional
review, whereby each NCCN panel member is sent the current
year's guideline for distribution to institutional experts for comment. Additionally, an annual panel review consisting of a full-day
meeting takes place every 3 years and conference calls or in-person
meetings are conducted for updates between meetings (NCCN,
2003).

However, as alluded to above, there is evidence that recurrent
updating may not be an efficient activity in all clinical areas. In
a 2002 study of updated (from 1994/95 to 1998/99) primary care
evidence-based guidelines of angina and asthma in adults, Eccles
stated,

> The fact that recommendations were not overturned and only one
> new drug treatment emerged suggests that, over the 3-year period

from initial development to updating, the evidence base for both guidelines was relatively stable. This, plus the fact that there were few financial savings to be made within the updating process, highlights the questions of how frequently the updating process should be performed and whether or not it should be performed in its entirety or only in new areas. (Eccles, 2002, p. 102)

Shekelle et al. (2001) argued there are six situations (termed the "situational" approach) that may necessitate the updating of a clinical practice guideline:

1. Changes in evidence on the existing benefits and harms of interventions
2. Changes in outcomes considered important
3. Changes in available interventions
4. Changes in evidence that current practice is optimal
5. Changes in values placed on outcomes
6. Changes in resources available for health care

Changes in values placed on outcomes often reflect societal norms. Measuring values placed on outcomes and how these change over time is complex and has not been systematically studied. When changes occur in the availability of resources for health care or the costs of interventions, a generic policy on updating is unlikely to be helpful because policy makers in disparate healthcare systems consider different factors in deciding whether services remain affordable.

Most empirical effort in this area has been directed to defining when new evidence on interventions, outcomes, and performance justifies updating guidelines. This process includes two stages: (1) identifying significant new evidence, and (2) assessing whether new evidence warrants updating. Within any individual guideline, some recommendations may be invalid while others remain current. A guideline on congestive heart failure, for example, includes 27 individual recommendations related to diagnosis (Jessup et al., 2009). How many must be invalid to require updating the entire guideline? Clearly a guideline requires updating if a majority of recommendations is out of date, with current evidence demonstrating that recommended interventions are inappropriate, ineffective, superseded by new interventions, or no longer or newly generalizable to a particular population. In other cases a single, outdated recommendation could invalidate an entire document. Typically, Eccles reported in 2002, no systematic process exists to help determine whether, and in what areas, researchers have published significant new evidence (Eccles, 2002). Judgments about whether a guideline's recommendation(s) requires updating typically are inherently subjective and reflect the clinical importance and number of invalid recommendations.

In a relatively unusual empirical exercise, Shekelle and colleagues (2001) applied the six situational criteria presented above to assessment of need for updating 17 clinical guidelines published by the Agency for Healthcare Research and Quality. They found seven guidelines were so out of date a major update was required; six guidelines required a minor update; three guidelines remained valid; and one guideline's update needs were inconclusive. The authors concluded that, as a general rule, guidelines should be reevaluated no less frequently than every 3 years. Perhaps not coincidentally, in an evaluation of the need for updating systematic reviews, Shojania and colleagues found that nearly one quarter of systematic reviews are likely to be outdated 2 years after publication (Shojania et al., 2007). Shekelle and coauthors' (2001) methods provide for a balancing of guideline updating costs and benefits from the perspective that a full redevelopment is not always appropriate.

Gartlehner and colleagues (2004) directly addressed this issue in comparing the Shekelle et al. "situational" approach to a "traditional" updating strategy (comparable to de novo guideline development) across six topics from the 1996 U.S. Preventive Services Task Force Guide to Clinical Preventive Services (USPSTF, 1996). The authors examined completeness of study identification, importance of studies missed, and resources required. Gartlehner and coauthors demonstrated that "Although the [Shekelle] approach identified fewer eligible studies than the traditional approach, none of what the studies missed was rated as important by task force members acting as liaisons to the project with respect to whether the topic required an update. On average, the [Shekelle] approach produced substantially fewer citations to review than the traditional approach. The effort involved and potential time savings depended largely on the scope of the topic." On the basis of these findings, Gartlehner and coauthors concluded that, "The [Shekelle] approach provides an efficient and acceptable method for judging whether a guideline requires updating" (Gartlehner et al., 2004, p. 399).

From the time it publishes a CPG, the ACC/AHA Guidelines Task Force requires that a research analyst and committee chair monitor significant new clinical trials and peer-reviewed literature, and compare current guideline recommendations against latest topical evidence. At the behest of the entire guideline-writing committee, a full revision of the guideline is required when at least two previous focused updates and/or new evidence suggests that a significant number of recommendations require revision. Revisions are managed as new guidelines, except for writing committee selection, where half of the previous writing committee is rotated off to allow for the inclusion of new members (ACCF and AHA, 2008).

Similar methods have been enshrined within the processes of other guideline development programs. In the United Kingdom, NICE recommends a combination of literature searching and professional opinion to inform the need for "full" or "partial" updates and describes related processes. Changes in relevant evidence as well as guideline scope (outcomes of important or available interventions) are emphasized. The assessment of update need occurs every 3 years. In the National Guideline Clearinghouse, admitted guidelines are required to have been reexamined every 5 years (NGC, 2010a).

Overall, another point to emphasize is that "Many guidelines in current use were developed before criteria were available to evaluate guideline quality. Efforts to improve quality should not be limited to frequent updates of the underlying evidence review, but should incorporate other guideline improvements during the revision process" (Clark et al., 2006, p. 166). Moreover, attempts at harmonization of guidelines from different development groups may also be an appropriate consideration at the time of updating.

8. **Updating**
    8.1 **The CPG publication date, date of pertinent systematic evidence review, and proposed date for future CPG review should be documented in the CPG.**
    8.2 **Literature should be monitored regularly following CPG publication to identify the emergence of new, potentially relevant evidence and to evaluate the continued validity of the CPG.**
    8.3 **CPGs should be updated when new evidence suggests the need for modification of clinically important recommendations. For example, a CPG should be updated if new evidence shows that a recommended intervention causes previously unknown substantial harm; that a new intervention is significantly superior to a previously recommended intervention from an efficacy or harms perspective; or that a recommendation can be applied to new populations.**

CONCLUSION

For a clinical practice guideline to be deemed trustworthy, the committee believes that adherence to the proposed development standards articulated within Chapters 4 and 5 is essential, and thus recommends the following:

> **RECOMMENDATION: TRUSTWORTHINESS OF CPG DEVELOPMENT PROCESS**
> - **To be trustworthy, a clinical practice guideline should comply with proposed standards 1–8.**
> - **Optimally, CPG developers should adhere to these proposed standards and CPG users should adopt CPGs compliant with these proposed standards.**

In total, the committee's standards reflect best practices across the entire development process and thus comprise those relevant to establishing transparency, management of conflict of interest, development team composition and process, clinical practice guideline–systematic review intersection, establishing evidence foundations for and rating strength of recommendations, articulation of recommendations, external review, and updating.

Although the committee strongly supports that CPGs comply with the eight standards proposed herein, it is also sympathetic to the time and other resource requirements the standards imply. It may not be feasible, for example, for guideline developers to immediately comply with the full body of standards, and a process of evolutionary adoption over time may be more practicable. Additionally, certain standards, such as those directed to patient and public involvement in the CPG development process and external review, may appear particularly resource intensive. The committee urges developers to comply with such standards while taking care to adopt each of their key elements (e.g., adoption of strategies to increase effective participation of patient and consumer representatives) so that efficiencies may be increased.

Finally, the committee understands that the uniqueness of guideline development contexts may seemingly preclude certain developers from fully adhering to the standards the committee has proposed. For example, certain clinical areas (e.g., rare malignant tumors) are characterized by an exceptional dearth of scientific literature and an urgent need to deliver patient care. The committee recognizes that developers in this instance may conclude they are unable to comply with Standard 4.1: "Clinical practice guideline developers should use systematic reviews that meet standards set by the Institute of Medicine's Committee on Standards for Systematic Reviews of Comparative Effectiveness Research." However, SRs that conclude there are no high-quality RCTs or observational studies on a particular clinical question would still fulfill Standard 4. In all cases, whether evidence is limited or abundant, GDGs should comply with the complementary Standard 5: "Establishing Evidence Foundations for and Rating Strength of Recommendations," by providing a summary of relevant available evidence (and evidentiary gaps), descriptions of the quality (including applicability), quantity (including completeness), and consistency of the aggregate available evidence; an explanation of the part played by values, opinion, theory, or clinical experience in deriving recommendations; a judgment regarding the level of confidence in (certainty regarding) the evidence underpinning the recommendations; and a rating of the strength of recommendations.

REFERENCES

ACCF and AHA (American College of Cardiology Foundation and American Heart Association). 2008. Methodology manual for ACCF/AHA guideline writing committees. In *Methodologies and policies from ACCF/AHA taskforce on practice guidelines*. ACCF and AHA.

AGREE (Appraisal of Guidelines for Research & Evaluation). 2001. *Appraisal of Guidelines for Research & Evaluation (AGREE) Instrument.*

AHRQ (Agency for Healthcare Research and Quality). 2008. *U.S. Preventive Services Task Force procedure manual.* AHRQ Publication No. 08-05118-EF. http://www.ahrq.gov/clinic/uspstf08/methods/procmanual.htm (accessed February 16, 2009).

Akl, E. A., N. Maroun, G. Guyatt, A. D. Oxman, P. Alonso-Coello, G. E. Vist, P. J. Devereaux, V. M. Montori, and H. J. Schünemann. 2007. Symbols were superior to numbers for presenting strength of recommendations to health care consumers: A randomized trial. *Journal of Clinical Epidemiology* 60(12):1298–1305.

Anonymous. 1979. Canadian task force on the periodic health examination: The periodic health examination. *CMAJ* 121:1193–1254.

Ansari, M. T., A. Tsertsvadze, and D. Moher. 2009. Grading quality of evidence and strength of recommendations: A perspective. *PLoS Medicine* 6(9):e1000151.

Atkins, D. 2004. Grading quality of evidence and strength of recommendations. *BMJ* 328(7454):1490.

Atkins, D., M. Eccles, S. Flottorp, G. H. Guyatt, D. Henry, S. Hill, A. Liberati, D. O'Connell, A. D. Oxman, B. Phillips, H. Schünemann, T. T. T. Edejer, G. E. Vist, and J. W. Williams, Jr. 2004. Systems for grading the quality of evidence and the strength of recommendations I: Critical appraisal of existing approaches. *BMC Health Services Research* 4(38):1–7.

Atkins, D., P. Briss, M. Eccles, S. Flottorp, G. Guyatt, R. Harbour, S. Hill, R. Jaeschke, A. Liberati, N. Magrini, J. Mason, D. O'Connell, A. Oxman, B. Phillips, H. Schünemann, T. Edejer, G. Vist, J. Williams, and The Grade Working Group. 2005. Systems for grading the quality of evidence and the strength of recommendations II: Pilot study of a new system. *BMC Health Services Research* 5(1):25.

Bogardus, S. T., Jr., E. Holmboe, and J. F. Jekel. 1999. Perils, pitfalls, and possibilities in talking about medical risk. *JAMA* 281(11):1037–1041.

Boyd, C. 2010. *CPGs for people with multimorbidities.* Presented at the IOM Committee on Standards for Developing Trustworthy Clinical Practice Guidelines meeting, on November 11, Washington, DC.

Boyd, C. M., J. Darer, C. Boult, L. P. Fried, L. Boult, and A. W. Wu. 2005. Clinical practice guidelines and quality of care for older patients with multiple comorbid diseases: Implications for pay for performance. *JAMA* 294(6):716–724.

Boyd, C. M., C. O. Weiss, J. Halter, K. C. Han, W. B. Ershler, and L. P. Fried. 2007. Framework for evaluating disease severity measures in older adults with comorbidity. *Journal of Gerontology: Series A Biologic Sciences: Medical Sciences* 62(3):286–295.

Braddock, C. H., III, K. A. Edwards, N. M. Hasenberg, T. L. Laidley, and W. Levinson. 1999. Informed decision making in outpatient practice: Time to get back to basics. *JAMA* 282(24):2313–2320.

Bruera, E., J. S. Willey, J. L. Palmer, and M. Rosales. 2002. Treatment decisions for breast carcinoma: Patient preferences and physician perceptions. *Cancer* 94(7):2076–2080.

Buller, H. R., G. Agnelli, R. D. Hull, T. M. Hyers, M. H. Prins, and G. E. Raskob. 2004. Antithrombotic therapy for venous thromboembolic disease. *Chest* 126(Suppl 3):401S–428S.

Burgers, J. S., J. V. Bailey, N. S. Klazinga, A. K. van der Bij, R. Grol, and G. Feder. 2002. Inside guidelines: Comparative analysis of recommendations and evidence in diabetes guidelines from 13 countries. *Diabetes Care* 25(11):1933–1939.

Burgers, J. S., R. P. Grol, J. O. Zaat, T. H. Spies, A. K. van der Bij, and H. G. Mokkink. 2003. Characteristics of effective clinical guidelines for general practice. *British Journal of General Practice* 53(486):15–19.

Calonge, N., and R. Harris. 2010. *United States Preventive Research Task Force (USPSTF).* Presented at IOM Committee on Standards for Developing Trustworthy Clinical Practice Guidelines, April 19, 2010. Irvine, CA.

Calonge, N., and G. Randhawa. 2004. The meaning of the U.S. Preventive Services Task Force grade I recommendation: Screening for hepatitis C virus infection. *Annals of Internal Medicine* 141(9):718–719.

Carlsen, B., and O. F. Norheim. 2008. "What lies beneath it all?"—An interview study of GPs' attitudes to the use of guidelines. *BMC Health Services Research* 8(218).

Clark, E., E. F. Donovan, and P. Schoettker. 2006. From outdated to updated, keeping clinical guidelines valid. *International Journal of Quality Health Care* 18(3): 165–166.

Cluzeau, F., J. Burgers, M. Brouwers, R. Grol, M. Mäkelä, P. Littlejohns, J. Grimshaw, C. Hunt, J. Asua, A. Bataillard, G. Browman, B. Burnand, P. Durieux, B. Fervers, R. Grilli, S. Hanna, P. Have, A. Jovell, N. Klazinga, F. Kristensen, P. B. Madsen, J. Miller, G. Ollenschläger, S. Qureshi, R. Rico-Iturrioz, J. P. Vader, and J. Zaat. 2003. Development and validation of an international appraisal instrument for assessing the quality of clinical practice guidelines: The AGREE project. *Quality and Safety in Health Care* 12(1):18–23.

Coulter, A. 2002. *The autonomous patient: Ending paternalism in medical care.* London, UK: Nuffield Trust.

Cuervo, L. G., and M. Clarke. 2003. Balancing benefits and harms in health care. *BMJ* 327(7406):65–66.

Deber, R. B., N. Kraetschmer, and J. Irvine. 1996. What role do patients wish to play in treatment decision making? *Archives of Internal Medicine* 156(13):1414–1420.

Eccles, M., N. Rousseau, and N. Freemantle. 2002. Updating evidence-based clinical guidelines. *Journal of Health Services Research and Policy* 7(2):98–103.

Eisinger, F., G. Geller, W. Burke, and N. A. Holtzman. 1999. Cultural basis for differences between U.S. and French clinical recommendations for women at increased risk of breast and ovarian cancer. *The Lancet* 353(9156):919–920.

Elson, C. O., M. Ballew, J. A. Barnard, S. J. Bernstein, I. J. Check, M. B. Cohen, S. Fazio, J. F. Johanson, N. M. Lindor, E. Montgomery, L. H. Richardson, D. Rogers, and S. Vijan. 2004. *National Institutes of Health Consensus Development Conference Statement June 28–30, 2004.* Paper presented at NIH Consensus Development Conference on Celiac Diseas, Bethesda, MD.

Ferreira, P. H., M. L. Ferreira, C. G. Maher, K. Refshauge, R. D. Herbert, and J. Latimer. 2002. Effect of applying different "levels of evidence" criteria on conclusions of Cochrane reviews of interventions for low back pain. *Journal of Clinical Epidemiology* 55(11):1126–1129.

Frosch, D. L., and R. M. Kaplan. 1999. Shared decision making in clinical medicine: Past research and future directions. *American Journal of Preventive Medicine* 17(4):285–294.

Gartlehner, G., S. L. West, K. N. Lohr, L. Kahwati, J. G. Johnson, R. P. Harris, L. Whitener, C. E. Voisin, and S. Sutton. 2004. Assessing the need to update prevention guidelines: A comparison of two methods. *International Journal for Quality in Health Care* 16(5):399–406.

Gochman, D. S. 1988. *Health behavior: Emerging research perspectives.* New York: Plenum Press.

Greenfield, S., J. Billimek, F. Pellegrini, M. Franciosi, G. De Berardis, A. Nicolucci, and S. H. Kaplan. 2009. Comorbidity affects the relationship between glycemic control and cardiovascular outcomes in diabetes: A cohort study. *Annals of Internal Medicine* 151(12):854–860.

Grol, R., J. Dalhuijsen, S. Thomas, C. Veld, G. Rutten, and H. Mokkink. 1998. Attributes of clinical guidelines that influence use of guidelines in general practice: Observational study. *BMJ* 317(7162):858–861.

Guyatt, G., D. Gutterman, M. H. Baumann, D. Addrizzo-Harris, E. M. Hylek, B. Phillips, G. Raskob, S. Z. Lewis, and H. Schünemann. 2006a. Grading strength of recommendations and quality of evidence in clinical guidelines: Report from an American College of Chest Physicians task force. *Chest* 129(1):174–181.

Guyatt, G., G. Vist, Y. Falck-Ytter, R. Kunz, N. Magrini, and H. Schünemann. 2006b. An emerging consensus on grading recommendations? *Evidence Based Medicine* 11(1):2–4.

Guyatt, G. H., A. D. Oxman, R. Kunz, Y. Falck-Ytter, G. E. Vist, A. Liberati, and H. J. Schünemann. 2008a. Going from evidence to recommendations. *BMJ* 336(7652):1049–1051.

Guyatt, G. H., A. D. Oxman, R. Kunz, G. E. Vist, Y. Falck-Ytter, H. J. Schünemann, and GRADE Working Group. 2008b. What is "quality of evidence" and why is it important to clinicians? *BMJ* 336(7651):995–998.

Hibbard, J. H. 2003. Engaging health care consumers to improve the quality of care. *Medical Care* 41(Suppl 1):I61–I70.

Hill, I. D., M. H. Dirks, G. S. Liptak, R. B. Colletti, A. Fasano, S. Guandalini, E. J. Hoffenberg, K. Horvath, J. A. Murray, M. Pivor, and E. G. Seidman. 2005. Guideline for the diagnosis and treatment of celiac disease in children: Recommendations of the North American Society for Pediatric Gastroenterology, Hepatology and Nutrition. *Journal of Pediatric Gastroenterology and Nutrition* 40(1):1–19.

Holmes, M. M., D. R. Rovner, M. L. Rothert, A. S. Elstein, G. B. Holzman, R. B. Hoppe, W. P. Metheny, and M. M. Ravitch. 1987. Women's and physicians' utilities for health outcomes in estrogen replacement therapy. *Journal of General Internal Medicine* 2(3):178–182.

Hussain, T., G. Michel, and R. N. Shiffman. 2009. The Yale guideline recommendation corpus: A representative sample of the knowledge content of guidelines. *International Journal of Medical Informatics* 78(5):354–363.

IOM (Institute of Medicine). 1992. *Guidelines for clinical practice: From development to use.* Edited by M. J. Field and K. N. Lohr. Washington, DC: National Academy Press.

Jessup, M., W. T. Abraham, D. E. Casey, A. M. Feldman, G. S. Francis, T. G. Ganiats, M. A. Konstam, D. M. Mancini, P. S. Rahko, M. A. Silver, L. W. Stevenson, and C. W. Yancy. 2009. 2009 Focused update: ACCF/AHA guidelines for the diagnosis and management of heart failure in adults: A report of the American College of Cardiology Foundation/American Heart Association task force on practice guidelines: Developed in collaboration with the International Society for Heart and Lung Transplantation. *Circulation* 119(14):1977–2016.

Johnston, M. E., M. C. Brouwers, and G. P. Browman. 2003. Keeping cancer guidelines current: Results of a comprehensive prospective literature monitoring strategy for twenty clinical practice guidelines. *International Journal of Technology Assessment in Health Care* 19(4):646–655.

Kaplan, S. H., and J. E. Ware. 1995. The patient's role in health care and quality assessment. In *Providing quality care: Future challenges*, 2nd ed., edited by N. Goldfield and D. B. Nash. Ann Arbor, MI: Health Administration Press.

Kassirer, J. P. 1994. Incorporating patients' preferences into medical decisions. *New England Journal of Medicine* 330(26):1895–1896.

Kassirer, J. P., and S. G. Pauker. 1981. The toss-up. *New England Journal of Medicine* 305(24):1467–1469.

Kavanagh, B. P. 2009. The GRADE system for rating clinical guidelines. *PLoS Medicine* 6(9):e1000094.

Krahn, M., and G. Naglie. 2008. The next step in guideline development: Incorporating patient preferences. *JAMA* 300(4):436–438.

Laine, C., and F. Davidoff. 1996. Patient-centered medicine: A professional evolution. *JAMA* 275(2):152–156.

Lomotan, E. A., G. Michel, Z. Lin, and R. N. Shiffman. 2010. How "should" we write guideline recommendations? Interpretation of deontic terminology in clinical practice guidelines: Survey of the health services community. *Quality and Safety in Health Care*. 19:509–513.

Luce, B. R., M. Drummond, B. Jonsson, P. J. Neumann, J. S. Schwartz, U. Siebert, and S. D. Sullivan. 2010. EBM, HTA, and CER: Clearing the confusion. *Milbank Quarterly* 88(2):256–276.

McNutt, R. A. 2004. Shared medical decision making: Problems, process, progress. *JAMA* 292(20):2516–2518.

Merenstein, D. 2004. Winners and losers. *JAMA* 291(1):15–16.

Michie, S., and M. Johnston. 2004. Changing clinical behaviour by making guidelines specific. *BMJ* 328:343–345.

Michie, S., J. Berentson-Shaw, S. Pilling, G. Feder, P. Dieppe, R. Raine, F. Cluzeau, P. Alderson, and S. Ellis. 2007. Turning evidence into recommendations: Protocol of a study of guideline development groups. *Implementation Science* 2:29.

NCCN (National Comprehensive Cancer Network). 2003. *About the NCCN clinical practice guidelines in oncology (NCCN Guidelines™).* http://www.nccn.org/professionals/physician_gls/about.asp (accessed June 30, 2010).

Nelson, H. D., K. Tyne, A. Naik, C. Bougatsos, B. K. Chan, and L. Humphrey. 2009. Screening for breast cancer: An update for the U.S. Preventive Services Task Force. *Annals of Internal Medicine* 151(10):727–737, W237–W742.

NGC (National Guideline Clearinghouse). 2010a. *Inclusion criteria: National Guideline Clearinghouse.* http://ngc.gov/submit/inclusion.aspx (accessed April 5, 2010).

NGC. 2010b. *National Guideline Clearinghouse.* http://www.guideline.gov/ (accessed April 7, 2010).

NICE (National Institute for Health and Clinical Excellence). 2009. *Methods for the development of NICE public health guidance*, 2nd ed. London, UK: NICE.

O'Connor, A. M., I. D. Graham, and A. Visser. 2005. Implementing shared decision making in diverse health care systems: The role of patient decision aids. *Patient Education and Counseling* 57(3):247–249.

O'Connor, A. M., C. L. Bennett, D. Stacey, M. Barry, N. F. Col, K. B. Eden, V. A. Entwistle, V. Fiset, M. Holmes-Rovner, S. Khangura, H. Llewellyn-Thomas, and D. Rovner. 2009. Decision aids for people facing health treatment or screening decisions. *Cochrane Database of Systematic Reviews* (3):CD001431.

Ogan, K., H. G. Pohl, D. Carlson, A. B. Belman, and H. G. Rushton. 2001. Parental preferences in the management of vesicoureteral reflux. *Journal of Urology* 166(1):240–243.

Oxman, A. D., H. J. Schünemann, and A. Fretheim. 2006. Improving the use of research evidence in guideline development: Reporting guidelines. *Health Research Policy and Systems* 4(1):26.

Pauker, S. G., and J. P. Kassirer. 1997. Contentious screening decisions: Does the choice matter? *New England Journal of Medicine* 336(17):1243–1244.

Pignone, M., D. Bucholtz, and R. Harris. 1999. Patient preferences for colon cancer screening. *Journal of General Internal Medicine* 14(7):432–437.

Qaseem, A., V. Snow, D. K. Owens, and P. Shekelle. 2010. The development of clinical practice guidelines and guidance statements of the American College of Physicians: Summary of methods. *Annals of Internal Medicine* 153(3):194–199.

Raine, R., C. Sanderson, A. Hutchings, S. Carter, K. Larkin, and N. Black. 2004. An experimental study of determinants of group judgments in clinical guideline development. *The Lancet* 364(9432):429–437.

Rosenfeld, R., and R. N. Shiffman. 2009. Clinical practice guideline development manual: A quality-driven approach for translating evidence into action. *Otolaryngology–Head & Neck Surgery* 140(6)(Suppl 1):1–43.

Rostom, A., J. A. Murray, and M. F. Kagnoff. 2006. American Gastroenterological Association (AGA) institute technical review on the diagnosis and management of celiac disease. *Gastroenterology* 131(6):1981–2002.

Schünemann, H. J., A. Fretheim, and A. D. Oxman. 2006a. Improving the use of research evidence in guideline development: Grading evidence and recommendations. *Health Research Policy and Systems* 4:21.

Schünemann, H. J., R. Jaeschke, D. J. Cook, W. F. Bria, A. A. El-Solh, A. Ernst, B. F. Fahy, M. K. Gould, K. L. Horan, J. A. Krishnan, C. A. Manthous, J. R. Maurer, W. T. McNicholas, A. D. Oxman, G. Rubenfeld, G. M. Turino, and G. Guyatt. 2006b. An official ATS statement: Grading the quality of evidence and strength of recommendations in ATS guidelines and recommendations. *American Journal of Respiratory and Critical Care Medicine* 174(5):605–614.

Shekelle, P., R. Kravitz, J. Beart, M. Marger, M. Wang, and M. Lee. 2000. Are nonspecific practice guidelines potentially harmful? A randomized trial of the effect of nonspecific versus specific guidelines on physician decision making. *Health Services Research* 34:1429–1448.

Shekelle, P., M. P. Eccles, J. M. Grimshaw, and S. H. Woolf. 2001. When should clinical guidelines be updated? *BMJ* 323(7305):155–157.

Shekelle, P. G., H. Schünemann, S. H. Woolf, M. Eccles, and J. Grimshaw. 2010. State of the art of CPG development and best practice standards. In *Committee on Standards for Trustworthy Clinical Practice Guidelines commissioned paper*.

Shojania, K. G., M. Sampson, M. T. Ansari, J. Ji, S. Doucette, and D. Moher. 2007. How quickly do systematic reviews go out of date? A survival analysis. *Annals of Internal Medicine* 147(4):224–233.

Shrier, I., J.-F. Boivin, R. Platt, R. Steele, J. Brophy, F. Carnevale, M. Eisenberg, A. Furlan, R. Kakuma, M. Macdonald, L. Pilote, and M. Rossignol. 2008. The interpretation of systematic reviews with meta-analyses: An objective or subjective process? *BMC Medical Informatics and Decision Making* 8(1):19.

Sox, H. C., and S. Greenfield. 2010. Quality of care—how good is good enough? *JAMA* 303(23):2403–2404.

Strull, W. M., B. Lo, and G. Charles. 1984. Do patients want to participate in medical decision making? *JAMA* 252(21):2990–2994.

Swiglo, B. A., M. H. Murad, H. J. Schünemann, R. Kunz, R. A. Vigersky, G. H. Guyatt, and V. M. Montori. 2008. A case for clarity, consistency, and helpfulness: State-of-the-art clinical practice guidelines in endocrinology using the grading of recommendations, assessment, development, and evaluation system. *Journal of Clinical Endocrinology and Metabolism* 93(3):666–673.

Teno, J. M., R. B. Hakim, W. A. Knaus, N. S. Wenger, R. S. Phillips, A. W. Wu, P. Layde, A. F. Connors, Jr., N. V. Dawson, and J. Lynn. 1995. Preferences for cardiopulmonary resuscitation: physician-patient agreement and hospital resource use. The SUPPORT Investigators. *Journal of General Internal Medicine* 10(4):179–186.

Tinetti, M. E., S. T. Bogardus, Jr., and J. V. Agostini. 2004. Potential pitfalls of disease-specific guidelines for patients with multiple conditions. *New England Journal of Medicine* 351(27):2870–2874.

Uhlig, K., A. Macleod, J. Craig, J. Lau, A. S. Levey, A. Levin, L. Moist, E. Steinberg, R. Walker, C. Wanner, N. Lameire, and G. Eknoyan. 2006. Grading evidence and recommendations for clinical practice guidelines in nephrology. A position statement from Kidney Disease: Improving Global Outcomes (KDIGO). *Kidney International* 70(12):2058–2065.

USPSTF (US Preventive Services Task Force). 1996. *Guide to Clinical Preventive Services. 2nd edn.* Alexandria, VA: International Medical Publishing.

Verkerk, K., H. Van Veenendaal, J. L. Severens, E. J. M. Hendriks, and J. S. Burgers. 2006. Considered judgement in evidence-based guideline development. *International Journal for Quality in Health Care* 18(5):365–369.

Wills, C. E., and M. Holmes-Rovner. 2003. Patient comprehension of information for shared treatment decision making: State of the art and future directions. *Patient Education and Counseling* 50(3):285–290.

Woloshin, S., L. M. Schwartz, M. Moncur, S. Gabriel, and A. N. Tosteson. 2001. Assessing values for health: Numeracy matters. *Medical Decision Making* 21(5):382–390.

Woolf, S. H. 1997. Shared decision-making: The case for letting patients decide which choice is best. *Journal of Family Practice* 45(3):205–208.

Woolf, S. H., and J. N. George. 2000. Evidence-based medicine: Interpreting studies and setting policy. *Hematology/Oncology Clinics of North America* 14(4):761–784.

Woolf, S. H. 2010. The 2009 breast cancer screening recommendations of the U.S. Preventive Services Task Force. *JAMA* 303(2):162–163.

6

Promoting Adoption of
Clinical Practice Guidelines

Abstract: Promoting uptake and use of clinical practice guidelines (CPGs) at the point of care delivery represents a final translation hurdle to move scientific findings into practice. Characteristics of the intended users and context of practice are as important as guideline attributes for promoting adoption of CPG recommendations. The committee's recommendations for individual and organizational interventions for CPG implementation are as follows: **Effective multifaceted implementation strategies targeting both individuals and healthcare systems should be employed by implementers to promote adherence to trustworthy CPGs.** Increased adoption of electronic health records and clinical decision support (CDS) will open new opportunities to rapidly move CPGs to the patient encounter. The committee recommends that guideline developers and implementers take the following actions to advance this aim. **Guideline developers should structure the format, vocabulary, and content of CPGs (e.g., specific statements of evidence, the target population) to facilitate ready implementation of electronic clinical decision support (CDS) by end-users.** CPG developers, CPG implementers, and CDS designers should collaborate in an effort to align their needs with one another. In considering legal issues affecting CPG implementation, the committee suggests clinicians will be more likely to adopt guidelines if they believe they offer malpractice litigation protection. The committee

145

*also suggests courts will be more likely to adopt guidelines that
are trustworthy and urges them, given reliance on CPGs, to use
those deemed trustworthy when available.*

INTRODUCTION

Clinical practice guidelines (CPGs) draw on synthesized research findings to set forth recommendations for state-of-the-art care. Trustworthy CPGs are critical to improving quality of care, but many CPGs are not developed for ready use by clinicians. They are typically lengthy documents of written prose with graphical displays (e.g., decision trees or flow charts) making them difficult for clinical use at the point of care delivery. Furthermore, recommendations from CPGs must be applied to patient specific data to be useful, and often, data required for a given guideline either are not available or require too much time to ascertain in a useful form during a typical patient encounter (Mansouri and Lockyer, 2007). Passive dissemination (e.g., distribution) of CPGs has little effect on practitioner behaviors and thus, active implementation (e.g., opinion leaders) efforts are required.

Even with the exponential growth in publicly available CPGs (NGC, 2010), easy access to high quality, timely CPGs is out of reach for many clinicians. Large gaps remain between recommended care and that delivered to patients. A 2003 study by McGlynn et al. of adults living in 12 metropolitan areas of the United States found participants received recommended care 54.9 percent of the time. The proportion of those receiving recommended care varied only slightly among adults in need of preventive care (54.9 percent), acute care (53.5 percent) and care for chronic conditions (56.1 percent). Yet, when McGlynn et al. (2003) inspected particular medical conditions, they noticed a substantial difference in received recommended care, ranging from 10.5 percent for alcohol dependence to 78.7 percent for senile cataract. In an observational study of 10 Dutch guidelines, Grol et al. concluded that general practitioners followed guideline recommendations in only 61 percent of relevant situations (Grol et al., 1998). Furthermore, in an analysis of 41 studies of the implementation of mental health CPGs—including depression, schizophrenia, and addiction—Bauer found that physicians adhered to guidelines only 27 percent of the time in both cross-sectional and pre-post studies and 67 percent of the time in controlled trials (Bauer, 2002; Francke et al., 2008). Of course, not all quality measures are valid and reliable, nor should all CPGs necessarily be adhered to; however, those CPGs that meet standards proposed herein should be associated with high levels of adherence.

This chapter focuses on a variety of strategies to promote adoption of CPGs. The first section describes how adoption is affected by a number and variety of factors, and presents several individual and organizational implementation strategies for developers and implementers. The second section discusses use of the electronic health record (EHR) and computer-aided decision supports to promote use of CPGs in practice. The third section discusses legal issues related to CPGs that could affect their implementation.

STRATEGIES FOR IMPLEMENTATION OF CPG RECOMMENDATIONS

Promoting uptake and use of CPGs at the point of care delivery represents a final translation hurdle to move scientific findings into practice. The field of translation research is a relatively young science, and addressing this final step of bringing research findings into the mainstream of typical practice is an important challenge (Avorn, 2010). A body of knowledge in implementation science is growing and provides an empirical base for promoting adoption of CPGs (Bradley et al., 2004b; Brooks et al., 2009; Carter et al., 2006; Chin et al., 2004; Demakis et al., 2000; Eccles and Mittman, 2006; Feldman et al., 2005; Grimshaw et al., 2004c, 2006a; Horbar et al., 2004; Hysong et al., 2006; Irwin and Ozer, 2004; Jamtvedt et al., 2006b; Jones et al., 2004; Katz et al., 2004a; Levine et al., 2004; Loeb et al., 2004; McDonald et al., 2005; Murtaugh et al., 2005; Shiffman et al., 2005; Shojania and Grimshaw, 2005; Shojania et al., 2006; Solberg et al., 2000; Solomon et al., 2001; Stafford et al., 2010; Titler et al., 2009). An emerging principle for promoting adoption of CPGs is that attributes of the CPG (e.g., ease of use, strength of the evidence) as perceived by users and stakeholders are neither stable features nor isolated determinants of adoption. Rather it is the interaction among characteristics of the CPG (e.g., specificity, clarity), the intended users (physicians, nurses, pharmacists), and a particular context of practice (e.g., inpatient, ambulatory, long-term care setting) that determines the rate and extent of adoption (Greenhalgh et al., 2005b).

A number of conceptual models have been tested and are used to guide implementation of CPG recommendations (Damschroder et al., 2009; Davies et al., 2010; Dobbins et al., 2009; Rycroft-Malone and Bucknall, 2010). The Implementation Model, illustrated in Figure 6-1, is used here as an organizing framework where the rate and extent of adoption of CPGs are influenced by the nature of the CPG (e.g.,

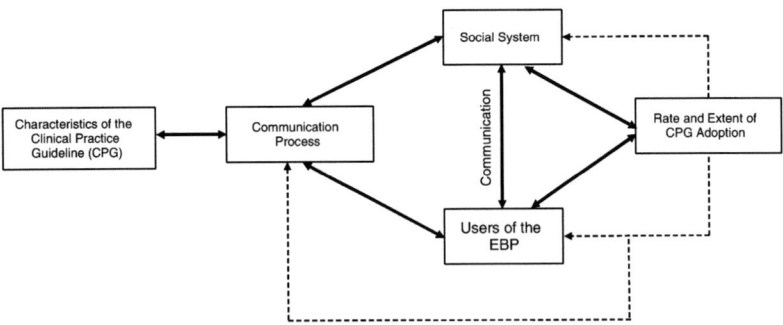

FIGURE 6-1 Implementation model.
NOTE: EBP = evidence-based practice.
SOURCE: Titler and Everett (2001).

complexity, type, and strength of the evidence) and how it is communicated (e.g., academic detailing, audit and feedback) to users of the evidence-based practice (e.g., physicians, nurses, pharmacists) of a social system/context of practice (e.g., clinic, inpatient unit, health system) (Kozel et al., 2003; Titler and Everett, 2001; Titler et al., 2009). Although discussion of implementation strategies is organized by these four areas (nature of the CPG, communication, members, context), these categories are not independent of one another.

CPG Characteristics

Characteristics of a CPG that influence the extent to which it can be implemented include clarity, specificity, strength of the evidence, perceived importance, relevance to practice, and simplicity versus complexity of the medical condition it is addressing. For example, CPGs on relatively simple healthcare practices (e.g., influenza vaccines for older adults) are more easily adopted in less time than those that are more complex (e.g., acute pain management for hospitalized older adults). To foster use of trustworthy CPGs, developers must consider organization of content, layout of key messages within the CPG, specificity of practice recommendations, and length of the CPG prose. Additionally, CPGs typically focus on one medical condition (e.g., heart failure), thereby making it challenging to use CPGs for patients with multiple comorbidities. (This topic is discussed further in Chapter 5.)

Implementation strategies that address the process of integrating essential content from CPGs to the local practice context and workflow include clinical reminders, quick reference guides, and decision aids (Balas et al., 2004; BootsMiller et al., 2004; Bradley et al., 2004b; Fung et al., 2004; Loeb et al., 2004; Wensing et al., 2006). One-page quick reference guides, depicted pictorially as flow diagrams or algorithms, are attractive from the busy provider's perspective (Baars et al., 2010; Boivin et al., 2009; Chong et al., 2009). A number of one-page quick reference guides related to prevention and treatment of cardiovascular diseases have been published (Coronel and Krantz, 2007; Krantz et al., 2005; Smith et al., 2008), though data on widespread acceptability and effectiveness warrants further study. Reminders have a small to moderate effect on adoption of CPGs when used alone or in association with other interventions, primarily regarding the use of preventive health care such as screening tests, immunizations, test ordering, and medication prescribing (Dexheimer et al., 2008; Grimshaw et al., 2004a; Shojania et al., 2009). Reminders are likely more effective for simple (e.g., ordering a lipid test [Mehler et al., 2005]) than complex actions.

Ultimately, incorporation of reminders and clinical care algorithms into electronic decision support systems holds great promise to promote use of CPGs and is discussed in further detail in the section on Electronic Interventions for CPG Implementation. Electronic decision support systems can also address adoption of recommendations from multiple CPGs in the care of individuals with multiple comorbidities.

Communication Strategies

Methods of communication and forms of communication channels influence adoption of CPGs (Greenhalgh et al., 2005b). Implementation strategies discussed in this section are education and mass media, academic detailing, and opinion leaders.

Education and Mass Media

Printed educational materials are one of the most common forms of communicating guidelines through dissemination of complete guideline documents and abridged summaries or concise reference cards. Based on an evidence review of 23 studies, the impact of printed educational materials on changing processes of care is small (median absolute increase of 4.3 percent for categorical processes to 13.6 percent for continuous processes) when compared to no intervention (Farmer et al., 2008). Given the low cost and high feasibility of printed materials, it may be reasonable to consider them as one part of a multifaceted implementation intervention, given both gaps in adoption and diversity of implementation barriers (e.g., for a brand new practice or a change in established practice).

Forsetlund summarized 81 trials on continuing medical education didactic lectures and workshops and found consistent but small effects, with a mean 6 percent absolute increase in desired clinical practices from educational meetings used alone or as a component of multifaceted interventions (Forsetlund et al., 2009). Meta-regression results suggested educational interventions were more effective when attendance was higher, when interactive sessions were mixed with didactic, and when clinical outcomes of intended actions were more serious. Education alone did not appear effective for more complex practice changes.

A review by Grilli et al. (2002) of 20 studies using interrupted time-series designs demonstrated that mass media (e.g., television, radio, newspapers, leaflets, posters, and pamphlets), targeted at the population level (providers, patients, and general public), has some effect on the use of health services for the targeted behavior (e.g., colorectal cancer screening), including providers' use. These channels of communication have an important role in influencing use of healthcare interventions; those engaged in promoting uptake of research evidence in clinical practice should consider mass media as one of the tools that may encourage use of effective services and discourage those of unproven effectiveness. However, little empirical evidence is available to guide design of mass communication messages to achieve the intended change (Grilli et al., 2002).

Opinion Leaders

An opinion leader is from the local peer group, viewed as a respected source of influence, considered by colleagues as technically competent, and trusted to judge the fit between the evidence base of practice and the local situation (Berner et al., 2003; Grimshaw et al., 2006b; Harvey et al., 2002; Soumerai et al., 1998). Opinion leadership is multifaceted and complex, with role functions varying by circumstances (e.g., nature of the CPG, clinical setting, clinician), but few successful projects to implement recommended practices in healthcare organizations have managed without the use of opinion leaders (Greenhalgh et al., 2005b; Kozel et al., 2003; Watson, 2004).

Several studies have demonstrated that opinion leaders are effective in changing behaviors of healthcare practitioners (Berner et al., 2003; Cullen, 2005; Dopson et al., 2001; Greenhalgh et al., 2005b; Irwin and Ozer, 2004; Locock et al., 2001; Redfern and Christian, 2003), especially when used in combination with academic detailing or performance feedback (discussed hereafter). A Cochrane Review summarized 12 studies engaging opinion leaders with or without other interventions (Doumit et al., 2007). Most studies focused on inpatient settings with an absolute increase of 10 percent in desired behaviors. Challenges to application of these strategies include identification of opinion leaders and high resource levels for deployment.

Academic Detailing

Academic detailing, or educational outreach, as applied to CPGs, involves interactive face-to-face education of individual practitioners in their practice setting by an educator (usually a clinician) with expertise in a particular topic (e.g., cancer pain management), and is one means of changing practice to better align with provision of CPG recommendations. Academic detailers are able to explain the research foundations of CPG recommendations and respond convincingly to specific questions, concerns or challenges that a practitioner might raise. An academic detailer also might deliver feedback on provider or team performance with respect to a selected CPG (e.g., frequency of pain assessment) or CPG-based quality measure (Avorn, 2010; O'Brien et al., 2007).

Multiple studies have demonstrated that academic detailing promotes positive changes in practice behaviors of clinical practitioners (Avorn et al., 1992; Feldman et al., 2005; Greenhalgh et al., 2005a; Hendryx et al., 1998; Horbar et al., 2004; Jones et al., 2004; Loeb et al., 2004; McDonald et al., 2005; Murtaugh et al., 2005; O'Brien et al., 2007; Solomon et al., 2001; Titler et al., 2009). In a review of 69 studies, academic detailing was found to produce a median absolute increase in desired clinical practice of 6 percent. Improvements were highly consistent for prescribing (median absolute increase of 5 percent), and varied for other types of professional performance (median absolute increase of 4 to 16 percent). A few head-to-head studies also suggest academic detailing has a slightly larger impact than audit and feedback (O'Brien et al., 2007). Academic detailing is more costly than other interventions; one analysis found that it is cost-effective (Soumerai and Avorn, 1986) while a more recent analysis concluded that it was not (Shankaran et al., 2009).

Members of Social System (CPG Users)

Intended users of a CPG must be clearly delineated to promote use of CPG recommendations at the point of care delivery. CPGs are likely to impact the practice of multiple players and types of clinicians involved in delivery of care. Those promoting adoption of a CPG must understand the work and challenges of these multiple stakeholders. Members of a social system (e.g., nurses, physicians, clerical staff) influence how quickly and widely CPGs are adopted (Greenhalgh et al., 2005b). In addition to communication strategies for implementation discussed in the previous section, implementation strategies targeted to users of a CPG include audit and feedback (A/F), performance gap assessment (PGA), and financial incentives. PGA and A/F consistently have shown positive effects on changing provider practice behavior of providers (Bradley et al., 2004b; Horbar et al., 2004; Hysong et al., 2006; Jamtvedt et al., 2006a).

Performance Gap Assessment

PGA applies performance measures to provide information and discussion of current practices relative to recommended CPG practices at the beginning of a clinical practice change (Horbar et al., 2004; Titler et al., 2009). This implementation strategy is used to engage clinicians in discussions of practice issues and formulation of steps or system-level strategies to promote alignment of their practices with CPG recommendations. Specific practice indicators selected for PGA are derived from CPG recommendations. Studies have shown improvements in performance when PGA is part of a multifaceted implementation intervention (Horbar et al., 2004; Titler et al., 2009), but use of this approach by itself is unlikely to result in improved adoption of CPG recommendations (Buetow and Roland, 1999). Yano (2008) discusses the essential nature of performance gap assessment in CPG implementation in the Veterans Affairs Quality Enhancement Research Initiative (VA QUERI) program (Yano, 2008).

Audit and Feedback

Audit and feedback is a continuous process of measuring performance (both process and outcome), aggregating data into reports, and discussing findings with practitioners (Greenhalgh et al., 2005b; Horbar et al., 2004; Jamtvedt et al., 2006a; Katz et al., 2004a,b; Titler et al., 2009). This strategy helps clinicians see how their efforts to improve care processes (e.g., pain assessment every 4 hours) and patient outcomes (e.g., lower pain intensity) are progressing. There is not clear empirical evidence for how to provide audit and feedback, although findings from several studies and systematic reviews suggest that effects may be larger when clinicians are active participants in implementing change and discussion of data audits rather than being passive recipients of feedback reports (Hysong et al., 2006; Jamtvedt et al., 2006a; Kiefe et al., 2001).

A Cochrane review compared audit and feedback uniquely or with other interventions based on 118 studies (Jamtvedt et al., 2006a). Results of audit and feedback varied substantially, with a small median effect of a 5 percent absolute increase in performance. Audit and feedback seemed most effective when baseline performance was low and feedback intensive. A meta-analysis of 19 studies demonstrated that specific suggestions for improving care, written feedback, and more frequent feedback strengthened the effect (Hysong, 2009). Qualitative studies provide some insight into use of audit and feedback (Bradley et al., 2004a; Hysong et al., 2006). One study on use of data feedback for improving treatment of acute myocardial infarction found that (1) feedback data must be perceived by physicians as important and valid; (2) the data source and timeliness of data feedback are critical to perceived validity; (3) it takes time to establish credibility of data within a hospital; (4) benchmarking improves the validity of data feedback; and (5) physician leaders can enhance the effectiveness of data feedback. The literature also supports that data feedback profiling an individual physician's practices can be effective, but may be perceived as punitive; data feedback must persist to sustain improved performance; and effectiveness of data feedback is intertwined with the organizational context, including physician leadership and organizational culture (Bradley et al., 2004a). Hysong and colleagues (2006) found that high-performing institutions provided timely, individualized, nonpunitive feedback to providers whereas low performers were more variable in their timeliness and nonpunitiveness and relied more on standardized, facility-level reports (Hysong et al., 2006). The concept of actionable feedback emerged as the core concept shared across timeliness, individualization, nonpunitiveness, and customizability.

Financial Incentives

Financial incentives have been evaluated for impact on provider performance and quality of care measures, including appropriate prescribing for specific conditions such as heart failure and appropriate delivery of preventive services (Werner and Dudley, 2009). Medicare, other insurers, and integrated health plans have begun tying reimbursement rates to targets for performance or improvement. Many "pay for performance" interventions have targeted hospitals or physician groups, in part because of the need to have sufficient numbers to measure performance reliably. Integrated health plans have

employed incentives targeting individual clinicians. Limited literature on individual-level incentives suggests generally positive effects,
targeting measures of preventive care, diabetes, asthma, and heart
failure (Christianson et al., 2008; Giuffrida et al., 1999; Greene and
Nash, 2009; Petersen et al., 2006). Petersen's review reported that five
of six studies of physician-level incentives and seven of nine studies
of group-level incentives found partial or positive effects on quality of
care process measures (e.g., cervical cancer screening, mammography,
and hemoglobin A1c testing) (Petersen et al., 2006). Obstacles associated with incentives also have been documented: physicians may try
to "game" measures by excluding certain patients; improvements
may reflect better documentation rather than practice changes; and
performance targets and payment strategies must be tailored to goals
of the incentive program and participating practices' performance
variations (Christianson et al., 2008; Werner and Dudley, 2009).

Social System/Context of Practice

Clearly, the social system or context of care delivery matters
when implementing CPGs (Anderson et al., 2005; Batalden et al.,
2003; Cummings et al., 2007; Estabrooks et al., 2008; Fleuren et
al., 2004; Fraser, 2004; Greenhalgh et al., 2005a; Kirsh et al., 2008;
Kochevar and Yano, 2006; Kothari et al., 2009; Litaker et al., 2008;
Redfern and Christian, 2003; Rubenstein and Pugh, 2006; Scott-
Findlay and Golden-Biddle, 2005; Scott et al., 2008; Stetler, 2003;
Stetler et al., 2009; Titler et al., 2009; Yano, 2008). Implementation
strategies described above are instituted within a system of care
delivery. Strategies that focus on organizational factors alter the
clinical practice environment by systematizing work processes and
involving physicians and others (e.g., nurses, physical therapists) in
guideline implementation. The underlying principle of organization
implementation strategies is creating systems of practice that make
it easier to consistently adopt guideline recommendations.

Factors within and across healthcare systems that foster use of
CPGs include overall size and complexity of the healthcare system,
infrastructure support (e.g., absorptive capacity for new knowledge;
assessing and structuring workflow), multihealth system collaboratives, and professional associations. Each is described briefly in the
following sections.

Healthcare Systems

Type (e.g., public, private) and complexity of healthcare organizations influence adoption of CPG recommendations. For example,

Vaughn et al. (2002) demonstrated that organizational resources, physician full-time equivalents per 1,000 patient visits, organizational size, and urbanicity affected use of evidence in the VA healthcare system. Aarons et al. (2009) demonstrated in a large multisite study that providers working in private organizations had more positive attitudes toward evidence-based practices and their organizations provided more support for implementing CPG recommendations (Aarons et al., 2009; Yano, 2008).

Large, mature, functionally differentiated organizations (e.g., divided into semiautonomous departments and units) that are specialized, with a focus of professional knowledge, available resources to channel into new projects, decentralized decision making, and low levels of formalization will more readily adopt innovations such as new CPG-based practices. Larger organizations are generally more innovative because size increases the likelihood that other predictors of CPG adoption will be present, such as financial and human resources and role differentiation (Greenhalgh et al., 2005a; Yano, 2008). Establishing semiautonomous teams is associated with successful implementation of CPGs, and thus should be considered in managing organizational units (Adler et al., 2003; Grumbach and Bodenheimer, 2004; Shojania et al., 2006; Shortell, 2004).

Infrastructure Support

Infrastructure support to promote use of CPG recommendations is defined in a variety of ways, but usually includes absorptive capacity, leadership, and technology infrastructure (discussed in the section on Electronic Interventions for CPG Implementation) to support application of CPG recommendations at the point of care delivery. Absorptive capacity is the knowledge and skills to enact CPG recommendations, remembering that strength of evidence alone will not promote adoption. An organization that is able to systematically identify, capture, interpret, share, reframe, and recodify new knowledge, then use it appropriately will be better able to assimilate CPG recommendations (BootsMiller et al., 2004; Ferlie et al., 2001; Stetler et al., 2009; Wensing et al., 2006). Variation in capacity for change affects sustained implementation of evidence-based preventive service delivery in community-based primary care practices (Litaker et al., 2008).

A learning culture and proactive leadership that promotes knowledge sharing are important components of building absorptive capacity for new knowledge (Estabrooks, 2003; Horbar et al., 2004; Lozano et al., 2004; Nelson et al., 2002). Components of a receptive context include strong leadership, clear strategic vision, good managerial relations, visionary staff in key positions, a climate conducive to experimentation and risk taking, and effective data capture systems. Leadership is critical in encouraging organizational members to break out of the convergent thinking and routines that are the norm in large, well-established organizations (Greenhalgh et al., 2005b; Hagedorn et al., 2006; Litaker et al., 2008; Stetler et al., 2006a; Ward et al., 2006).

An organization may be generally amenable to adopting new practices, but not ready or willing to assimilate particular CPG recommendations. Elements of system readiness include tension for change; CPG-system fit; assessment of implications, support and advocacy for a CPG; dedicated time and resources; and capacity to evaluate the impact of a CPG during and following implementation (Greenhalgh et al., 2005a; Hagedorn et al., 2006).

Structuring workflow to fit with CPG recommendations is an important component of fostering adoption. If implications of a CPG are fully assessed, anticipated, and planned, the recommendations are more likely to be adopted (Kochevar and Yano, 2006; Stetler et al., 2006b; Yano, 2008). If supporters of a specific CPG outnumber and are more strategically placed within the organizational power base than opponents, the CPG is more likely to be adopted by the organization (Bradley et al., 2004b; Hagedorn et al., 2006; Solberg, 2009).

Leadership support is important for promoting use of CPG recommendations (Cullen, 2005; Katz et al., 2004a,b; Scott-Findlay and Golden-Biddle, 2005; Solberg, 2009; Stetler et al., 2009). This support is expressed verbally and by providing necessary resources, materials, and time to fulfill assigned responsibilities. Senior leaders of health systems need to do the following tasks: (1) create an organizational mission and strategic plan that incorporates use of CPG recommendations; (2) implement staff performance expectations that include using CPG recommendations; (3) integrate the work of CPG implementation into the governance structure of the healthcare system; (4) demonstrate the value of CPGs through administrative behaviors; and (5) establish explicit expectations that leaders will create microsystems that value and support clinical inquiry (Cullen, 2005; Solberg, 2009; Titler et al., 2002).

A review of organizational interventions to implement CPGs examined five major modalities, and suggests that revision of professional roles (changing responsibilities and work of health professionals, such as expanding roles of nurses and pharmacists) improved processes of care, but questions remain regarding effects on patient outcomes. Multidisciplinary teams (collaborations of physicians, nurses, and allied health professionals) resulted in improved patient outcomes, mostly in prevalent chronic diseases. Integrated care services (e.g., disease management and case management) resulted in improved patient outcomes and cost savings. Interventions aimed at knowledge management (optimal organization of knowledge within an organization principally via use of technology to support patient care) resulted in improved adherence to CPG recommendations and patient outcomes. The last category, quality management, had the fewest studies available for analysis leading to mixed findings of effectiveness. A number of organizational interventions were not included in this review (e.g., leadership, process redesign, organizational learning), and the authors note that the lack of a widely accepted taxonomy of organizational interventions hinders examination of effectiveness across investigations (Wensing et al., 2006).

An example of an effective organizational infrastructure for implementation is detailed in Hyatt and colleagues' description of Kaiser Permanente of Southern California's diabetes guideline intervention (Hyatt et al., 2002). Kaiser's multicomponent intervention included the following:

1. Development of an electronic registry and tracking system, automatically including and updating all clinical information about all patients with diabetes and organizing them into risk levels associated with specific guidelines
2. Care management summary sheets sent to clinicians the day of a scheduled patient visit that provided organized overtime data with embedded guideline recommendations
3. Outreach letters provided to patients regarding missing tests or immunizations that serve as orders
4. Automated telephone reminders to patients
5. Summary and detailed feedback reports, termed "Physician-specific panel reports," available online and mailed to primary care physicians and diabetologists twice per year
6. Standing orders for tests, immunizations, emergency department visits, and hospital discharge
7. Pharmacist counseling
8. Care management protocols for nurses
9. Guideline-incorporated telephone patient reminders about diabetes and its care (e.g., test results and/or advice for follow-up care)

This comprehensive organizational strategy was associated with large changes in select relevant performance measures over time.

For example, microalbuminuria testing and lipid testing increased from 10 to 55 percent and 44 to 65 percent, respectively, from 1994 to 2001. For both measures, gains were relatively modest in the years immediately after the guidelines were released, but accelerated in 1998 when implementation strategies were enacted, such as patient outreach letters and computer-generated, physician-specific panel reports. Across all other outcome measures (i.e., lipid control, lipid medication use, and HbA1c control) over time, improvements were not detected, with the exception of hospitalization rates, which can be a proxy for morbidity (Hyatt et al., 2002). Although specific intervention strategies might have benefitted from organizational size, most have been implemented in much smaller clinic settings without electronic technology (Solberg et al., 2006). Leader and staff commitment to implementing change was a major contribution in success.

An organizational implementation strategy receiving more recent attention is tailored interventions to overcome barriers to change (Baker et al., 2010; Hagedorn et al., 2006; Kochevar and Yano, 2006). This type of intervention focuses on assessing needs regarding factors contributing to gaps between current practices and CPG recommendations; discussions regarding behaviors and/or system mechanisms requiring change; discussions about organizational units, and persons appropriate for inclusion; and identification of ways to facilitate change. This information is then used in tailoring an intervention for the setting that will promote use of specified CPG recommendations. Based on a recent systematic review of 26 studies, effectiveness of tailored implementation interventions is modest, and shows wide variation across studies (Baker et al., 2010). The tailored implementation approach has not yet been developed to the point where there is wide agreement about design and components of the constituent elements (Baker et al., 2010). There is insufficient empirical understanding of how to link barriers and facilitators of change to effective interventions (Baker et al., 2010; Wallin, 2009).

Collaboratives

Collaborations across health systems are another mechanism for implementation of CPGs (Graham et al., 2009). The work of the Institute for Clinical Systems Improvement (ICSI) is an illustrative example. ICSI was formed in 1993 in Minnesota to encourage cooperative development of evidence-based clinical guidelines by HealthPartners, Mayo Clinic, and Park Nicollet Health Services, and shortly moved to a CPG implementation focus, based largely on organizational change strategies (Allen, 2008; Farley et al., 2003). ICSI today is composed of 57 medical groups representing about 85 percent of Minnesota physicians (ICSI, 2010).

ICSI developed an organizational strategy to implement one of its earliest CPGs for simple urinary tract infections (UTIs) in women. ICSI recommended treating uncomplicated cystitis in females ages 18–64 with selected antibiotics for 3 days in the absence of a urine culture. The existing practice was to treat for 10 days, after confirming infection with urine culture results that requiring several days to obtain results. This guideline did not specify who should perform the recommendation, so several medical groups delegated UTI cases to a registered nurse (RN) to handle by telephone. Explicit guideline recommendations directed the RN to rule out more complex cases, and triage them to a physician. O'Connor et al. (1996) studied this approach in 5 clinics, identifying 441 guideline-eligible patients, and found the adoption of a 3-day course of treatment increased from 28 to 52 percent and urine culture rates dropped from 70 to 37 percent. There was no evidence of clinical harm in guideline-treated cases, and cost of care declined by 35 percent per case. Notably, improved guideline adherence was only found for cases managed by nurses. Although RNs treated patients with cystitis symptoms, physician visits occurred if a patient insisted, or if appointment secretaries failed to elicit symptoms. O'Connor and colleagues found no significant change in the use of 3-day treatment or urine cultures when cystitis patients were managed by physicians (O'Connor et al., 1996).

Professional Associations

Guideline implementation is facilitated by many professional associations. For example, the American College of Cardiology developed the Guidelines Applied in Practice (GAP) project in 2000, starting with its guideline for management of patients with acute myocardial infarction (ACC, 2010). Like most large-scale implementation efforts, GAP focuses on specific organizational strategies, facilitated by a tool kit that includes a template for orders, a critical pathway, patient information, a discharge form, chart stickers, performance charts, and a pocket guide. The GAP quality improvement project measured implementation of improvement strategies in 10 acute care hospitals in southeast Michigan. Mehta and colleagues found adherence to key treatments increased in administration of aspirin (81 percent vs. 87 percent; $P = .02$), and beta-blockers (65 percent vs. 74 percent; $P = .04$) at admission, and use of aspirin (84 percent vs. 92 percent; $P = .002$) and smoking cessation counseling (53 percent vs. 65 percent; P = .02) at discharge. The authors observed insignificant, but, favorable trends toward adherence to treatment goals for remaining indicators (Mehta et al., 2002). GAP's counterpart, the American Heart Association's Get with the Guidelines (GWTG), is based on a similar tool kit containing order sets, clinical pathways, web-based patient management tools, decision support tools, registries, regional workshops, teleconferences, and patient education aids (AHA, 2010). Fonarow et al.'s (2010) evaluation of GWTG programming from 2003 to 2009 in 1,256 hospitals concluded that ischemic stroke treatment rates improved significantly over time for ischemic stroke patients, based on selected performance measures. Improvements were realized in all age groups, narrowing age-related treatment gaps.

In summary, multiple organizational factors influence implementation of CPG recommendations. While allowance for alternatives to CPG recommendations is necessary given patient variation and preferences as well as contrasting guideline implementation processes across clinical topics and actions, implementation strategies at the organizational level are critical.

Multifaceted Interventions

Multifaceted implementation strategies are needed to promote use of research evidence in clinical and administrative healthcare decision making (Bertoni et al., 2009; Feldman et al., 2005; Greenhalgh et al., 2005b; Katz et al., 2004a,b; Murtaugh et al., 2005; Nieva et al., 2005; Rubenstein and Pugh, 2006; Solberg et al., 2000; Titler et al., 2009). Grimshaw's 2004 review of implementation interventions included 61 studies comparing various combinations of interventions to a control, most frequently printed materials or educational meetings (Grimshaw et al., 2004b). More intensive educational efforts (including outreach) appeared to be more effective than simple, and the addition of reminders to educational interventions was more effective than educational measures alone. The Leeds Castle international roundtable and several other recent syntheses of systematic reviews are complementary in concluding that multifaceted implementation interventions are more effective than single modalities (Francke et al., 2008; Grimshaw et al., 2001, 2003; Gross, 2000; Gross et al., 2001; Prior et al., 2008). Given this evidence asserting the relative effectiveness of multifaceted intervention strategies and their dependence on organizations, it seems that implementation of CPGs requires multifaceted strategies including both individual and organizational strategies (Sales et al., 2010). Fundamentally, for trustworthy guidelines to affect quality of care and patient outcomes, they must be implemented; hence, the committee offers the following recommendation:

RECOMMENDATION: INDIVIDUAL AND ORGANIZATIONAL INTERVENTIONS FOR CPG IMPLEMENTATION

Effective multifaceted implementation strategies targeting all relevant populations affected by CPGs should be employed by implementers to promote adherence to trustworthy CPGs.

ELECTRONIC INTERVENTIONS FOR CPG IMPLEMENTATION

Data and Systems' Challenges

The federal government's recent appropriation of $19 billion to promoting adoption and use of health information technology and particularly electronic health records in the 2009 stimulus bill (Blumenthal, 2009), combined with the growing number of large, integrated delivery systems (e.g., Geisinger, GroupHealth Cooperative of Puget Sound, Kaiser) adopting multifunctional health information systems, has convinced many health policy professionals that guidelines must become electronically compatible to have any hope for influencing future practice. The following sections explore the current state of electronic clinical decision support (CDS) and directions for moving the digital application of CPGs forward.

Computer-aided clinical decision support, often based on translation of CPGs, should facilitate a more personalized and timely form of guideline-based care. Diagnostic decision support, preventive care reminders, disease management or protocols for bundles of reminders, and drug dosing and prescribing protocols are all examples of interactive, point-of-care CDS (Garg et al., 2005). Interactive, point-of-care CDS relies on inputting structured patient data, which then are processed by knowledge-based rules, or statistical algorithms, to generate output in support of a clinical decision (Berg, 1997; Berner, 2009). Empirical support for guideline-based CDS interventions is mixed. Positive results include a 1999 evaluation of EHR-generated physician reminders to follow post-fracture osteoporosis guidelines at a Pacific Northwest health maintenance organization. At 6 months post-fracture, 51.9 percent of patients of physicians exposed to the electronic reminder intervention received CPG-recommended Bone

Mass Density (BMD) measurement or osteoporosis medication, compared to 5.9 percent of patients of physician controls. The study also evaluated use of patient educational mailings in addition to the EHR physician advice, but found no statistical difference relative to provider EHR advice alone (Feldstein et al., 2006).

Another successful CDS intervention involved an Internet-based decision-support system for applying American Thoracic Society and Centers for Disease Control and Prevention Guidelines for Tuberculosis preventive therapy. The web tool offered patient-tailored recommendations based on patient-specific input data supplied by physicians. A randomized controlled trial (RCT) including general internal medicine residents found that 95.8 percent who had access to the web tool correctly applied recommended therapy compared with 56.6 percent of the group with access to only written resources (Dayton et al., 2000). Furthermore, a 2006 RCT evaluating AsthmaCritic, a guideline-based critiquing system in 32 Dutch general practices, found the system altered (to more closely follow asthma and chronic obstructive pulmonary disorder guidelines) the way physicians monitored and, to a lesser extent, treated their patients (Kuilboer et al., 2006).

In 2007, Kaiser Permanente's Southern California Region developed the Proactive Office Encounter (POE) program to improve consistency of preventive care and quality of care for chronic conditions. The POE sought to engage staff in both primary care and specialty departments to assist physicians by using standard work flows and electronic tools to identify gaps in patient care. POE was more comprehensive and successful than earlier attempts, such as Care Management Summary Sheets (mentioned earlier in this chapter), to address preventive and chronic care needs, "Since its inception, POE has contributed to sharp improvement in the Southern California Region's clinical quality performance, including double digit improvements in colorectal cancer screening, advice to quit smoking, and blood pressure control" (Kanter et al., 2010).

A 2008 Cochrane review evaluated 26 comparisons to assess whether computerized advice on drug dosing has beneficial effects on provider prescribing and dosing of drugs (Durieux et al., 2008). Findings showed that the computerized advice for drug dosage (1) increases the initial dose of drug and tends to increase serum concentrations; (2) leads to more rapid therapeutic control; (3) decreases hospital length of stay; and (4) decreases toxic drug levels, but has no effect on adverse reactions. A Cochrane review of 28 studies reporting 32 comparisons of on-screen, point-of-care computer reminders found that computerized reminders achieved small to modest improvements (< 10 percent) in provider behaviors. No specific reminder or contextual features were significantly associated with magnitude of effect (Shojania et al., 2010).

Reporting of a small number of additional individual CDS interventions offers contrasting results. A randomized trial of electronic clinical reminders to improve diabetes and coronary artery disease (CAD) care among primary care physicians resulted in limited effectiveness. Although reminders increased odds that participants followed recommended diabetes and CAD care, adherence to quality measures remained low and significant variability in practice persisted (Sequist et al., 2005). A 2004 German evaluation of a guideline-based computerized educational tool found no significant difference in guideline knowledge between physician groups with and without access to the tool (Butzlaff et al., 2004). And, an English 2002 evaluation of the use of a CDS to aid implementation of CPGs for the management of asthma and angina by primary care practitioners, found that CDS had no significant effect on consultation rates, process of care measures (including prescribing), or any patient reported outcomes for either condition (Eccles et al., 2002).

Explaining and Enhancing the State of the Art

An emergent literature sheds some light on possible underlying explanations for CDS successes and failures, and carries implications for enhancing the state of the art. Wright et al. offer a taxonomy for interactive, point-of-care CDS composed of four functional features: (1) *triggers* that cause decision support rules to be invoked (e.g., prescribing a drug); (2) *input data* elements used by a rule to make patient inferences (e.g., medication orders); (3) *interventions*, or the possible actions a decision support module can take (e.g., displaying a relevant medication guideline); and (4) *offered choices*, or the options available to a decision support user when a rule is invoked (e.g., change a medication order) (Wright et al., 2007). Table 6-1 elaborates on Wright's functional features across several examples of guideline-based CDS.

Problems arise with Wright's framework in real-world situations. CDS needs to be complemented by easily accessible patient input data, largely EHR, to be of value to clinicians and patients. A recent study estimated that less than 10 percent of U.S. hospitals have a basic EHR (ability to record patient demographic and health data; manage prescription order entry, laboratory and imaging results) and less than 2 percent have a comprehensive EHR (increased order entry management and CDS capabilities). In the

TABLE 6-1 CDS Types and Features

		CDS Features	
CDS Type	Goal of CDS	CDS Specificity	Trigger
Osteoporosis CDS	Deliver patient-specific guideline advice to primary care physician via Electronic Health Record (EHR) message	Generic	Search of electronic databases for patients meeting criteria for increased osteoporosis risk
		Highly tailored	
Academic information platform for CPG use in practice	Improve guideline-recommended osteoporosis care using EHR reminders	Generic	Physician volition (i.e., no EHR-based trigger)
Internet-based decision support for tuberculosis therapy	Improve physician knowledge of guidelines	Generic	Physician volition (i.e., no EHR-based trigger)
Clinical reminders for diabetes, coronary heart disease	Improve quality of care for diabetes and heart disease using EHR reminders	Generic	—
		Highly tailored	Physician opens medical record
Asthma-Critic	Provide patient-specific asthma treatment feedback using EHR data	Generic	—
		Highly tailored	Automatic when record is open and asthma-specific data are entered

SOURCE: Jones et al. (2010).

Input Data	Intervention	Offered Choices
	Tailored inbox message in EHR that links to patient record	Inbox message lists internal and external guideline resources that provide detailed information on osteoporosis evaluation and management
Demographic and diagnostic information from the EHR used to identify patients requiring management		
None	Availability of web-based or CD-ROM–based access to text of guidelines for dementia, Chronic Heart Failure, Urinary Track Infection, and colorectal carcinoma	None; guidelines are read-only
Physician-provided data on patient characteristics and clinical reaction to diagnostic test	Web-based implementation of hierarchical decision tree for administering preventive therapy	Guideline-based recommendations for treatment
—	—	Care recommendation; reminders were actionable, but did not require acknowledgment or link to intervention
EHR data (lab, radiology results, problem list, medication list, allergy list)	Reminders list in the EHR in the context of other patient data	—
—	—	—
Physician-entered data on diagnosis and treatment	On-screen, patient-specific comments presented to physician, tailored to current clinical situation	Physician presented with "critiquing comments" related to treatment decisions; can drill down to view guidelines to understand reason for comment

outpatient setting, a national survey placed the estimate at 17 and 4 percent for basic and comprehensive EHR, respectively (DesRoches et al., 2008). Theoretically, a great volume of input data is available directly from patients. However, collection of patient-reported data (PRD) in routine practice has been limited by operational challenges (Jones et al., 2007). The emergence of web-based technologies hopefully will allow for greater capture and real-time use of structured PRD. Yet even when EHR systems are in place, input data may be poorly represented (e.g., U.S. Preventive Services Task Force gonorrhea guideline requirement for sexual activity assessment). Fundamentally, PRD will not be useful in translation of CPGs to practice unless data are captured in valid, reliable, and actionable form.

Furthermore, devising appropriate guideline-based CDS interventions poses other obstacles due to treatment diversity. For example, Geisinger health system has developed an EHR-based CDS model ("eDiabetes") for expert treatment guidance and management of HbA1c in diabetes. Four input variables are used to identify patient-specific treatment advice from 93 therapeutic alternatives. Notably, each additional input variable increases veracity of output and specificity of advice offered, but exponentially inflates the size and complexity of the CDS database (Miller et al., 2001).

All in all, the current state of CDS is far from ideal, largely because data necessary to support Wright's four functional features are not easily obtainable, or systems lack sophistication to handle them. Where guidelines have been applied, CDS interventions usually are idiosyncratic to a given healthcare setting. Initial implementation of an EHR is followed, often rapidly, by naïve attempts to implement rudimentary forms of CDS (e.g., alerts of potential drug–drug interactions). Many providers find these alerts interruptive, unhelpful, and unsatisfying, often termed "alert fatigue" by the literature (Sittig et al., 2009a; Wright et al., 2009). More robust forms of CDS require translation of "knowledge" (e.g., as embodied by guidelines) to a structured, computer-ready form before use in an EHR CDS protocol. Implementation of these CDS types is even more daunting. Lack of accepted standards for clinical vocabularies, CDS formats, clinical workflow applications, and clinical and patient-reported data further limit electronic use of CPGs.

Furthermore, despite numerous attempts, there is no universally accepted means of translating guidelines into CDS-related protocols. A number of guideline representation approaches, allowing for translation of CPG knowledge to a structured form prior to use in an EHR CDS protocol, are actively being developed; a few (e.g., Arden Syntax, the Guideline Interchange Format, Guideline Elements Model) have been accepted into routine use by different organizations (e.g., American Society for Testing and Materials [ASTM], Health Level-7), but this is not indicative of use in practice outside of research settings (Open Clinical, 2010).

Generalizability Challenges

Increased adoption of EHRs and CDS will offer unique opportunities to rapidly move clinical knowledge from the scientific literature to the patient encounter. Earlier we discussed many data and systems-driven challenges inherent to CDS and its application to guidelines implementation. As alluded to above, there is yet another realm in which substantial advances are required before CDS-based implementation may be realized: standardization and codification of CPGs for uniform adoption across the diversity of care settings.

In an effort to derive generalizable principles for CPG implementation via CDS, the CDS Consortium (CDSC), funded by the Agency for Healthcare Research and Quality, has studied CDS practices at five institutions (Partners HealthCare) in Boston, Wishard Health System/Regenstrief Institute and Roudebush VA Medical Center in Indianapolis, the Mid-Valley Independent Physicians Association in Salem, Oregon, and the University of Medicine and Dentistry of New Jersey in New Brunswick, New Jersey with both commercially developed and internally developed EHR and CDS systems. From this effort arose guidance for enhancement of CDS-driven CPG implementation founded on locally extant knowledge and systems that were applicable to the universe of clinical practice environments. Overall, CDSC emphasizes that to be more actionable in a digital environment, CPG structure (format, lexicon, and content) should facilitate simple and efficient adoption by health systems organizations. Specifically, CPGs will be of greater use if they are structured to identify clinical and administrative data triggers according to Wright's model (i.e., define relevant patient subgroup triggers and/or input data, intervention options, and offered choices) and guide physicians and patients in making optimal, evidence-based decisions. Furthermore, guideline developers should minimize the ambiguity of their recommendations to facilitate incorporation in a computer-executable form. Whenever possible, guidelines should state explicitly when particular CDS rules apply in a clinical context. For example, allowing rules to be "turned off" when not warranted will assist in reducing "alert fatigue."

CDS protocols need to accommodate needs of end-users, the designation of appropriate personnel, and insertion points in the clinical workflow. Physicians are trained to complete cognitively demanding tasks, process complex information, and make judgments in the face of uncertainty. Accordingly, they may not be effective or efficient in performing rudimentary tasks better suited for less skilled staff or complete automation. Where strong evidence indicates when and for whom a care process or treatment should be implemented (e.g., pneumovax in older patients), it may be sensible to prompt the clinical action 100 percent of the time (Dexter et al., 2001). For example, all Type II diabetics without a recent HbA1c should have this laboratory test completed at appropriate intervals, but neither the decision nor the completion of the test requires physician involvement. Thus, where strength of CPG recommendations is high, related actions can be implemented easily (e.g., management of hypertension, hyperlipidemia, etc.), and when risks are low, as much care oversight as possible should be shifted to nonphysicians, within limits of common sense. Where risk of confusion and of making the "wrong decision" increase (e.g., as decision complexity increases), decision support tools may become increasingly important for providers involved in care processes at all levels. Further detailed advice extending from CDSC's research is provided in Table 6-2.

If clinical guideline developers adopt this counsel, the CDSC believes a greater number of healthcare organizations could develop and implement basic CDS features necessary to transfer clinical knowledge from the literature to point of care and begin to transform radically both the quality and safety of the current health system (Sittig et al., 2009b).

Over the next several years, the CDSC anticipates new insights respecting CDS–CPG interrelationships applicable to the universe of clinical practice, extending from a number of demonstration projects, including

1. examination of more than 50 different CDS intervention types to elucidate factors important to their integration within existing Electronic Medical Records (EMR) systems;
2. development of a service-oriented approach to creating CDS interventions that can be used across existing EHR systems; and
3. formulation of a "starter set" of CDS interventions to be shared among members of the CDS consortium (Sittig et al., 2009b).

TABLE 6-2 CDSC Guidance for CPG Development Activities

Number	Recommendation	Description	Rationale
1	Identify standard data triggers	Guidelines should explicitly identify clinical or administrative data required to initiate any of the electronic Clinical Decision support (CDS) interventions included in the guideline	Required data need to be captured and stored in structured and coded fields so they can be used by CDS systems
1.1	Review access to existing input data	Commonly available input data for use by CDS logic (e.g., for alerts) include laboratory test results, patient demographics, and the problem list; CPGs should specify only coded data types that are currently or soon will be available in certified EHRs	Input data that are not available in certified Electronic Health Records (EHRs) will result in guidelines that cannot be incorporated in a computable manner within EHRs
2	Work on increasing clarity and internal consistency of all clinical logic included in guidelines	CPGs should minimize the ambiguity of their recommendations (e.g., include threshold values for blood pressure rather than stating "if the patient's blood pressure is high then. . . ")	Logic in CPGs must be able to be incorporated in a computer-executable form
3	Suggest appropriate personnel and best insertion points in the clinical workflow for CDS interventions to be delivered	CPGs should specify how the EHR can route recommended actions to the appropriate person or role, at the right time and in the right place, based on logic included with the CDS intervention	Increase CDS utility, efficiency, and integration with clinic workflows

continued

TABLE 6-2 Continued

Number	Recommendation	Description	Rationale
4	Guidelines should facilitate selective filtering or tailoring of rules	Specify explicitly when particular rules either apply or don't apply in the rule's logic description	Allow rules to be turned off when they do not apply to a clinical context (e.g., specific practices, physicians, specialties, or clinical situations)
5	Guidelines should support the Health Level (HL7) Infobutton standard	Specific definitions of items such as clinical problems, medications, and laboratory tests should be clearly defined using standardized data types	Allow EHRs to link to specific sections of a guideline and provide context-sensitive explanations
6	Composition of guideline development groups	CPG development groups/committees should include well-trained and experienced clinical informaticians	CPGs will be easier to transform into computer-executable forms

SOURCE: Jones et al. (2010).

The committee recommends the following for advancing electronic methods for CPG implementation:

RECOMMENDATION: ELECTRONIC INTERVENTIONS FOR CPG IMPLEMENTATION
- Guideline developers should structure the format, vocabulary, and content of CPGs (e.g., specific statements of evidence, the target population) to facilitate ready implementation of computer-aided clinical decision support (CDS) by end-users.
- CPG developers, CPG implementers, and CDS designers should collaborate in an effort to align their needs with one another.

DECISION ANALYTIC MODELING AND CPG IMPLEMENTATION

A frontier of evidence-based medicine is decision analytic modeling in health care alternatives' assessment. Through discussions with leaders in the field, David Eddy and Wiley Chan, the committee explored potential applications of decision analysis to development and implementation of CPGs. The International Society for Pharmacoeconomics and Outcomes Research (ISPOR) Health Sciences Committee Taskforce on Decision Analytic Modeling wrote, "The purpose of modeling is to structure evidence on clinical and economic outcomes in a form that can help to inform decisions about clinical practices and healthcare resource allocations. Models synthesize evidence on health consequences and costs from many different sources, including data from clinical trials, observational studies, insurance claim databases, case registries, public health statistics, and preference surveys" (Weinstein et al., 2003, pp. 9–10). Though the ISPOR Taskforce found model-based evaluations to be a valuable resource for health care decision-makers, they cautioned that models are to be taken as aides to decision-making rather than scientific fact. They also advocated the continual assessment of models against real scientific data, and encouraged modelers to firmly communicate that their conclusions are always conditional and based on assumptions and secondary data. Hence, any flaws in the original studies will necessarily transfer to the model's evaluations (Weinstein et al., 2003). Although the field is currently fraught with controversy, the committee acknowledges it as exciting and potentially promising, however, decided the state of the art is not ready for direct comment.

LEGAL ISSUES AFFECTING CPG IMPLEMENTATION

Medical malpractice is a pervasive issue in health care, one that is both influenced by the use of CPGs and could influence future use of CPGs. Product liability suits and disputes over what is or what should be covered by insurance policies and how to interpret "medical necessity" can also involve CPGs. The following section discusses some of the legal issues related to use or nonuse of guidelines.

All physicians are affected by medical malpractice, whether they have been sued by a patient or not, through insurance premiums they pay. Although the costs of malpractice and defensive medicine are difficult to calculate, and estimates in the past have varied depending on study methods, the most recent study of the U.S. medical liability system estimates costs of $55.6 billion in 2008 dollars, including the cost of defensive medicine (Mello, 2001). Because total health spending was $2.3 trillion, malpractice is an estimated 2.4 percent of the healthcare dollar. Data for estimating the cost of defensive medicine were extremely limited and the authors relied heavily on older studies, assumptions, and extrapolations to conservatively estimate a total of $45.6 billion in hospital, physician, and clinic services. Another study of defensive medicine (Thomas et al., 2010) based an estimate of defensive medicine costs and potential savings from tort reform on an analysis of 400 million paid medical and pharmaceutical claims from CIGNA HealthCare from 2004 to 2006 from cases in selected specialties. The authors concluded that "the magnitude of savings that could be realized [from a 10 percent reduction in malpractice premiums] is small, accounting for less than 1 percent of all medical care costs in every specialty" (Thomas et al., 2010, p. 1582).

In addition to costing the health system, medical liability is a cost and concern for most physicians. Defensive medicine is also a cost and quality concern of health insurers and policy makers. In 2009 a national survey mailed to a random sample of 2,416 eligible physicians drawn from the American Medical Association's Physician Master File in primary care, nonsurgical (medical), surgical, and other specialties produced a 50 percent response rate. Of the respondents, 91 percent agreed that "Doctors order more tests and procedures than patients need to protect themselves against malpractice suits" and 90.7 percent agreed that "Unnecessary use of diagnostic tests will not decrease without protections for physicians against unwarranted malpractice suits" (Bishop et al., 2010, p. 1081). The authors interpret their findings to "suggest that proposals to promote cost-effective care, such as the promulgation of guidelines from a national comparative effectiveness center, could be limited by physicians' fears of malpractice unless such protections are ensured. Malpractice reforms should focus on ways of offering assurance to physicians that they will have protection against malpractice if they competently practice the standard of care" (Bishop et al., 2010, pp. 1081–1082). Another recent study, based on a 2008 Health Tracking Survey of 4,720 physicians with a 62 percent response rate by the Center for Health System Change, highlights the need for that assurance. The survey asked physicians about their level of concern about malpractice litigation and whether they used some defensive practices (Carrier et al., 2010). The authors compared those data to specialty and state liability environments and found that physicians had high levels of concern about risks of malpractice cases across specialty, fee-for-service, or health maintenance practice settings, and geographic areas. A high level of concern was expressed by the physicians surveyed, even if they were in relatively low-risk malpractice environments.

It has been suggested that CPGs could be used as a "liability shield" to define a national standard of care, rather than local customary practice, and protect physicians who follow it. Alternatively, CPGs could be used as a "liability sword" against physicians who commit errors of misuse, underuse, or overuse with resultant complications, when not following the appropriate CPG (Rosoff, 2001). The evidentiary acceptability of CPGs is an issue; expert witnesses can introduce CPGs as legal evidence; direct introduction of written CPGs is limited by hearsay rules. Another limiting factor is that most malpractice litigation occurs in state courts, not federal ones. Currently most states permit defendants to escape liability if their procedure reflects customary care, even if it is not necessarily optimal care (Avraham and Sage, 2010). CPGs attempting to establish a new standard of practice might reflect latest evidence, but not the lagging customary care in the community. Thus, CPGs might not be fully used by the courts. That might also be attributed to uncertainty about what CPGs represent. According to Mello, "judicial and academic statements of what CPGs are meant to represent are characterized by confusion and overgeneralization. There exists little agreement as to whether CPGs represent a minimum baseline, a not-yet-attained ideal, or a customary practice that lies somewhere in between these two extremes" (Mello, 2001, p. 19). In fact, courts seldom even acknowledge the distinction between evidence-based and consensus-based CPGs (Avraham and Sage, 2010).

Because information on specifically how the courts and lawyers use CPGs is limited, authors recently have updated a 1995 study surveying case law (Hyams et al., 1995). The original study identified 37 published cases involving CPGs. Of these cases, 28 used CPGs successfully, 22 as swords (inculpatory), and 6 as shields (exculpatory). The Avraham and Sage (2010) update reviewed judicial decisions published between January 2000 and March 2010 and found that courts continue to use guidelines only occasionally and largely conservatively. Of 28 new cases found with parties employing guidelines in some form, 16 (57 percent) involved use by plaintiffs (as "swords"), compared to 78 percent in the Hyams et al. study, and 12 (43 percent) involved use by defendants (as "shields"), compared to 22 percent in the Hyams et al. study (Avraham and Sage, 2010), The success rates of users of guidelines were lower than in the Hyams report.

Avraham and Sage (2010) also cite historical experiments related to malpractice reform and guideline use in Maine, Florida, and Minnesota[1] during the 1990s (Florida Agency for Health Care Administration, 1998; LeCraw, 2007). Although the structure of each project differed and the link of guidelines to malpractice protection also varied, none of the projects showed a substantial positive impact on physician practice behavior and professional liability claims, settlement costs, or malpractice premiums, or they failed before an impact could be recorded (Avraham and Sage, 2010).

Overall, the application of CPGs to medical malpractice have had varying practical influence. And from a larger policy view, reliance upon CPGs in medical malpractice implies potential advantages and disadvantages, respectively, including enhanced efficiency in establishment of the standard of care; and the inordinate authority of CPGs in physician decision making discretion (LeCraw, 2007). Further, some CPG proponents worry that if courts use guidelines as standards of care in malpractice suits, CPG developers may be more reluctant to write strong clinical recommendations (and instead water down recommendations with weasel words and disclaimers) for fear of their legal repercussions. Yet, given an emergent trend to apply CPGs in the courts, the notion of trustworthiness may be increasingly relevant to that setting. However, mandating courts to rely on CPGs or some other enforcement mechanism is well beyond the scope of this committee and would be more appropriately considered in the context of major malpractice reform.

---

[1]State of Minnesota, 1995. *Minnesota Care Act of 1992*, Chapter 549 (HF No. 2800).

REFERENCES

Aarons, G. A., D. H. Sommerfeld, and C. M. Walrath-Greene. 2009. Evidence-based practice implementation: The impact of public versus private sector organization type on organizational support, provider attitudes, and adoption of evidence-based practice. *Implementation Science* 4:83.

ACC (American College of Cardiology). 2010. *CardioSource.* http://www.cardio source.org/ (accessed July 8, 2010).

Adler, P. S., S.-W. Kwon, and J. M. K. Singer. 2003. The "six-west" problem: Professionals and the intraorganizational diffusion of innovations, with particular reference to the case of hospitals. In *Working paper 3–15.* Los Angeles, CA: Marshall School of Business, University of Southern California.

AHA (American Heart Association). 2010. *GWTG supporting guidelines.* http://www. americanheart.org/presenter.jhtml?identifier=3043013 (accessed July 8, 2010).

Allen, J. 2008. Crossing the quality chasm: Taking the lead as ICSI turns 15. *Minnesota Physician* XXII(2)(1):12–13.

Anderson, R. A., B. F. Crabtree, D. J. Steele, and R. R. McDaniel, Jr. 2005. Case study research: The view from complexity science. *Quality Health Research* 15(5): 669–685.

Avorn, J. 2010. Transforming trial results into practice change: The final translational hurdle: Comment on "Impact of the ALLHAT/JNC7 Dissemination Project on thiazide-type diuretic use." *Archives of Internal Medicine* 170(10):858–860.

Avorn, J., S. B. Soumerai, D. E. Everitt, D. Ross-Degnan, M. H. Beers, D. Sherman, S. R. Salem-Schatz, and D. Fields. 1992. A randomized trial of a program to reduce the use of psychoactive drugs in nursing homes. *New England Journal of Medicine* 327(3):168–173.

Avraham, R., and W. M. Sage. 2010. Legal models for assuring quality of CPGs. In *Committee on Standards for Trustworthy Clinical Practice Guidelines commissioned paper.*

Baars, J. E., T. Markus, E. J. Kuipers, and C. J. van der Woude. 2010. Patients' preferences regarding shared decision-making in the treatment of inflammatory bowel disease: Results from a patient-empowerment study. *Digestion* 81(2):113–119.

Baker, R., J. Camosso-Stefinovic, C. Gillies, E. J. Shaw, F. Cheater, S. Flottorp, and N. Robertson. 2010. Tailored interventions to overcome identified barriers to change: Effects on professional practice and health care outcomes. *Cochrane Database of Systematic Reviews* 3:CD005470.

Balas, E. A., S. Krishna, R. A. Kretschmer, T. R. Cheek, D. F. Lobach, and S. A. Boren. 2004. Computerized knowledge management in diabetes care. *Medical Care* 42(6):610–621.

Batalden, P. B., E. C. Nelson, W. H. Edwards, M. M. Godfrey, and J. J. Mohr. 2003. Microsystems in health care: Developing small clinical units to attain peak performance. *Joint Commission of the Journal of Quality and Safety* 29(11):575–585.

Bauer, M. S. 2002. A review of quantitative studies of adherence to mental health clinical practice guidelines. *Harvard Review of Psychiatry* 10(3):138–153.

Berg, M. 1997. *Rationalizing medical work: Decision-support techniques and medical practices.* Cambridge, MA: MIT Press.

Berner, E. S. 2009. *Clinical decision support systems: State of the art.* Rockville, MD: Agency for Healthcare Research and Quality.

Berner, E. S., C. S. Baker, E. Funkhouser, G. R. Heudebert, J. J. Allison, C. A. Fargason, Jr., Q. Li, S. D. Person, and C. I. Kiefe. 2003. Do local opinion leaders augment hospital quality improvement efforts? A randomized trial to promote adherence to unstable angina guidelines. *Medical Care* 41(3):420–431.

Bertoni, A. G., D. E. Bonds, H. Chen, P. Hogan, L. Crago, E. Rosenberger, A. H. Barham, C. R. Clinch, and D. C. Goff, Jr. 2009. Impact of a multifaceted intervention on cholesterol management in primary care practices: Guideline adherence for heart health randomized trial. *Archives of Internal Medicine* 169(7):678–686.

Bishop, T. F., A. D. Federman, and S. Keyhani. 2010. Physicians' views on defensive medicine: A national survey. *Archives of Internal Medicine* 170(12):1081–1083.

Blumenthal, D. 2009. Stimulating the adoption of health information technology. *New England Journal of Medicine* 360(15):1477–1479.

Boivin, A., J. Green, J. van der Meulen, F. Legare, and E. Nolte. 2009. Why consider patients' preferences?: A discourse analysis of clinical practice guideline developers. *Medical Care* 47(8):908–915.

BootsMiller, B. J., J. W. Yankey, S. D. Flach, M. M. Ward, T. E. Vaughn, K. F. Welke, and B. N. Doebbeling. 2004. Classifying the effectiveness of Veterans Affairs guideline implementation approaches. *American Journal of Medical Quality* 19(6):248–254.

Bradley, E. H., E. S. Holmboe, J. A. Mattera, S. A. Roumanis, M. J. Radford, and H. M. Krumholz. 2004a. Data feedback efforts in quality improvement: lessons learned from U.S. hospitals. *Quality and Safety in Health Care* 13(1):26–31.

Bradley, E. H., M. Schlesinger, T. R. Webster, D. Baker, and S. K. Inouye. 2004b. Translating research into clinical practice: Making change happen. *Journal of the American Geriatrics Society* 52(11):1875–1882.

Brooks, J. M., M. G. Titler, G. Ardery, and K. Herr. 2009. Effect of evidence-based acute pain management practices on inpatient costs. *Health Services Research* 44(1):245–263.

Buetow, S. A., and M. Roland. 1999. Clinical governance: Bridging the gap between managerial and clinical approaches to quality of care. *Quality Health Care* 8(3):184–190.

Butzlaff, M., H. Vollmar, B. Floer, N. Koneczny, J. Isfort, and S. Lange. 2004. Learning with computerized guidelines in general practice?: A randomized controlled trial. *Family Practice* 21(2):183–188.

Carrier, E. R., J. D. Reschovsky, M. M. Mello, R. C. Mayrell, and D. Katz. 2010. Physicians' fears of malpractice lawsuits are not assuaged by tort reforms. *Health Affairs* 29(9):1585–1592.

Carter, B. L., A. Hartz, G. Bergus, J. D. Dawson, W. R. Doucette, J. J. Stewart, and Y. Xu. 2006. Relationship between physician knowledge of hypertension and blood pressure control. *Journal of Clinical Hypertension (Greenwich)* 8(7):481–486.

Chin, M. H., S. Cook, M. L. Drum, L. Jin, M. Guillen, C. A. Humikowski, J. Koppert, J. F. Harrison, S. Lippold, and C. T. Schaefer. 2004. Improving diabetes care in midwest community health centers with the health disparities collaborative. *Diabetes Care* 27(1):2–8.

Chong, C. A., I. J. Chen, G. Naglie, and M. D. Krahn. 2009. How well do guidelines incorporate evidence on patient preferences? *Journal of General Internal Medicine* 24(8):977–982.

Christianson, J. B., S. Leatherman, and K. Sutherland. 2008. Lessons from evaluations of purchaser Pay-for-Performance programs: A review of the evidence. *Medical Care Research Review* 65(6 Suppl):5S–35S.

Coronel, S., and M. J. Krantz. 2007. Medical therapy for symptomatic heart failure: A contemporary treatment algorithm. *Critical Pathways in Cardiology: A Journal of Evidence-Based Medicine* 6(1):15–17.

Cullen, L. 2005. Evidence-based practice: Strategies for nursing leaders. In *Leadership and nursing care management*, 3rd ed., edited by D. Huber. Philadelphia, PA: Elsevier. Pp. 461–478.

Cummings, G. G., C. A. Estabrooks, W. K. Midodzi, L. Wallin, and L. Hayduk. 2007. Influence of organizational characteristics and context on research utilization. *Nursing Research* 56(4 Suppl):S24–S39.

Damschroder, L., D. Aron, R. Keith, S. Kirsh, J. Alexander, and J. Lowery. 2009. Fostering implementation of health services research findings into practice: A consolidated framework for advancing implementation science. *Implementation Science* 4(1):50.

Davies, P., A. Walker, and J. Grimshaw. 2010. A systematic review of the use of theory in the design of guideline dissemination and implementation strategies and interpretation of the results of rigorous evaluations. *Implementation Science* 5(1):14.

Dayton, C. S., J. Scott Ferguson, D. B. Hornick, and M. W. Peterson. 2000. Evaluation of an Internet-based decision-support system for applying the ATS/CDC guidelines for tuberculosis preventive therapy. *Medical Decision Making* 20(1):1–6.

Demakis, J. G., L. McQueen, K. W. Kizer, and J. R. Feussner. 2000. Quality Enhancement Research Initiative (QUERI): A collaboration between research and clinical practice. *Medical Care* 38(6 Suppl 1):I17–I25.

DesRoches, C. M., E. G. Campbell, S. R. Rao, K. Donelan, T. G. Ferris, A. Jha, R. Kaushal, D. E. Levy, S. Rosenbaum, A. E. Shields, and D. Blumenthal. 2008. Electronic health records in ambulatory care—A national survey of physicians. *New England Journal of Medicine* 359(1):50–60.

Dexheimer, J. W., T. R. Talbot, D. L. Sanders, S. T. Rosenbloom, and D. Aronsky. 2008. Prompting clinicians about preventive care measures: A systematic review of randomized controlled trials. *Journal of the American Medical Informatics Association* 15(3):311–320.

Dexter, P. R., S. Perkins, J. M. Overhage, K. Maharry, R. B. Kohler, and C. J. McDonald. 2001. A computerized reminder system to increase the use of preventive care for hospitalized patients. *New England Journal of Medicine* 345(13):965–970.

Dobbins, M., S. E. Hanna, D. Ciliska, S. Manske, R. Cameron, S. L. Mercer, L. O'Mara, K. DeCorby, and P. Robeson. 2009. A randomized controlled trial evaluating the impact of knowledge translation and exchange strategies. *Implementation Science* 4:61.

Dopson, S., L. Locock, D. Chambers, and J. Gabbay. 2001. Implementation of evidence-based medicine: Evaluation of the Promoting Action on Clinical Effectiveness programme. *Journal of Health Services Research and Policy* 6(1):23–31.

Doumit, G., M. Gattellari, J. Grimshaw, and M. A. O'Brien. 2007. Local opinion leaders: Effects on professional practice and health care outcomes. *Cochrane Database of Systematic Reviews* (1):CD000125.

Durieux, P., L. Trinquart, I. Colombet, J. Nies, R. Walton, A. Rajeswaran, M. Rege Walther, E. Harvey, and B. Burnand. 2008. Computerized advice on drug dosage to improve prescribing practice. *Cochrane Database of Systematic Reviews* (3):CD002894.

Eccles, M. P., and B. S. Mittman. 2006. Welcome to implementation science. *Implementation Science* 1:7:1–6.

Eccles, M., E. McColl, N. Steen, N. Rousseau, J. Grimshaw, and D. Parkin. 2002. Effect of computerised evidence-based guidelines on management of asthma and angina in adults in primary care: Cluster randomised controlled trial. *BMJ* 325:941–948.

Estabrooks, C. A. 2003. Translating research into practice: Implications for organizations and administrators. *Canadian Journal of Nursing Research* 35(3):53–68.

Estabrooks, C. A., L. Derksen, C. Winther, J. N. Lavis, S. D. Scott, L. Wallin, and J. Profetto-McGrath. 2008. The intellectual structure and substance of the knowledge utilization field: A longitudinal author co-citation analysis, 1945 to 2004. *Implementation Science* 3:49.

Farley, D. O., M. C. Haims, D. J. Keyser, S. S. Olmsted, S. V. Curry, and M. Sorbero. 2003. *Regional health quality improvement coalitions: Lessons across the life cycle.* Santa Monica, CA: RAND Health.

Farmer, A. P., F. Legare, L. Turcot, J. Grimshaw, E. Harvey, J. L. McGowan, and F. Wolf. 2008. Printed educational materials: Effects on professional practice and health care outcomes. *Cochrane Database of Systematic Reviews* (3):CD004398.

Feldman, P. H., C. M. Murtaugh, L. E. Pezzin, M. V. McDonald, and T. R. Peng. 2005. Just-in-time evidence-based e-mail "reminders" in home health care: Impact on patient outcomes. *Health Services Research* 40(3):865–885.

Feldstein, A., P. J. Elmer, D. H. Smith, M. Herson, E. Orwoll, C. Chen, M. Aickin, and M. C. Swain. 2006. Electronic medical record reminder improves osteoporosis management after a fracture: A randomized, controlled trial. *Journal of the American Geriatrics Society* 54(3):450–457.

Ferlie, E., J. Gabbay, L. Fitzgerald, L. Locock, and S. Dopson. 2001. Evidence-based medicine and organisational change: An overview of some recent qualitative research. In *Organisational behavior and organisational studies in health care: Reflections on the future*, edited by L. Ashburner. Basingstoke: Palgrave.

Fleuren, M., K. Wiefferink, and T. Paulussen. 2004. Determinants of innovation within health care organizations: Literature review and Delphi study. *International Journal of Quality Health Care* 16(2):107–123.

Florida Agency for Health Care Administration 1998. *Practice guidelines as affirmative defense: The Cesarean Demonstration Project Report.*

Fonarow, G. C., M. J. Reeves, X. Zhao, D. M. Olson, E. E. Smith, J. L. Saver, and L. H. Schwamm. 2010. Age-related differences in characteristics, performance measures, treatment trends, and outcomes in patients with ischemic stroke. *Circulation* 121(7):879–891.

Forsetlund, L., A. Bjorndal, A. Rashidian, G. Jamtvedt, M. A. O'Brien, F. Wolf, D. Davis, J. Odgaard-Jensen, and A. D. Oxman. 2009. Continuing education meetings and workshops: Effects on professional practice and health care outcomes. *Cochrane Database of Systematic Reviews* (2):CD003030.

Francke, A. L., M. C. Smit, A. J. de Veer, and P. Mistiaen. 2008. Factors influencing the implementation of clinical guidelines for health care professionals: A systematic meta-review. *BMC Medical Informatics and Decision Making* 8:38.

Fraser, I. 2004. Organizational research with impact: Working backwards. *Worldviews Evidence Based Nursing* 1(Suppl 1):S52–S59.

Fung, C. H., J. N. Woods, S. M. Asch, P. Glassman, and B. N. Doebbeling. 2004. Variation in implementation and use of computerized clinical reminders in an integrated healthcare system. *American Journal of Managed Care* 10(11 Pt 2):878–885.

Garg, A. X., N. K. J. Adhikari, H. McDonald, M. P. Rosas-Arellano, P. J. Devereaux, J. Beyene, J. Sam, and R. B. Haynes. 2005. Effects of computerized clinical decision support systems on practitioner performance and patient outcomes: A systematic review. *JAMA* 293(10):1223–1238.

Giuffrida, A., H. Gravelle, and M. Roland. 1999. Measuring quality of care with routine data: Avoiding confusion between performance indicators and health outcomes. *BMJ* 319(7202):94–98.

Graham, I. D., J. Tetroe, and M. Gagnon. 2009. Lost in translation: Just lost or beginning to find our way? *Annals of Emergency Medicine* 54(2):313–314; discussion 314.

Greene, S. E., and D. B. Nash. 2009. Pay for Performance: An overview of the literature. *American Journal of Medical Quality* 24(2):140–163.

Greenhalgh, T., A. Collard, and N. Begum. 2005a. Sharing stories: Complex intervention for diabetes education in minority ethnic groups who do not speak English. *BMJ* 330(7492):628.

Greenhalgh, T., G. Robert, P. Bate, F. Macfarlane, and O. Kyriakidou. 2005b. *Diffusion of innovations in health service organisations: A systematic literature review.* Malden, MA: Blackwell Publishing Ltd.

Grilli, R., C. Ramsay, and S. Minozzi. 2002. Mass media interventions: Effects on health services utilisation. *Cochrane Database of Systematic Reviews* (1):CD000389.

Grimshaw, J. M., L. Shirran, R. Thomas, G. Mowatt, C. Fraser, L. Bero, R. Grilli, E. Harvey, A. Oxman, and M. A. O'Brien. 2001. Changing provider behavior: An overview of systematic reviews of interventions. *Medical Care* 39(8 Suppl 2): II2–II45.

Grimshaw, J., L. M. McAuley, L. A. Bero, R. Grilli, A. D. Oxman, C. Ramsay, L. Vale, and M. Zwarenstein. 2003. Systematic reviews of the effectiveness of quality improvement strategies and programmes. *Quality and Safety in Health Care* 12(4):298–303.

Grimshaw, J., M. Eccles, and J. Tetroe. 2004a. Implementing clinical guidelines: Current evidence and future implications. *The Journal of Continuing Education in the Health Professions* 24(Suppl 1):S31–S37.

Grimshaw, J., R. Thomas, G. MacLennan, C. Fraser, C. Ramsay, L. Vale, P. Whitty, M. Eccles, L. Matowe, L. Shirran, M. Wensing, R. Dijkstra, and C. Donaldson. 2004b. Effectiveness and efficiency of guideline dissemination and implementation strategies. *Health Technology Assessment* 8(6):1–72.

Grimshaw, J. M., R. E. Thomas, G. MacLennan, C. Fraser, C. R. Ramsay, L. Vale, P. Whitty, M. P. Eccles, L. Matowe, L. Shirran, M. Wensing, R. Dijkstra, and C. Donaldson. 2004c. Effectiveness and efficiency of guideline dissemination and implementation strategies. *Health Technology Assessment* 8(6):iii–iv, 1–72.

Grimshaw, J., M. Eccles, R. Thomas, G. MacLennan, C. Ramsay, C. Fraser, and L. Vale. 2006a. Toward evidence-based quality improvement. *Journal of General Internal Medicine* 1(Suppl 2):S14–S20.

Grimshaw, J. M., M. P. Eccles, J. Greener, G. Maclennan, T. Ibbotson, J. P. Kahan, and F. Sullivan. 2006b. Is the involvement of opinion leaders in the implementation of research findings a feasible strategy? *Implementation Science* 1:3.

Grol, R., J. Dalhuijsen, S. Thomas, C. Veld, G. Rutten, and H. Mokkink. 1998. Attributes of clinical guidelines that influence use of guidelines in general practice: Observational study. *BMJ* 317(7162):858–861.

Gross, P. A. 2000. Implementing Evidence-Based Recommendations for Health Care: A Roundtable Comparing European and American Experiences. *Joint Commission Journal on Quality and Patient Safety* 26:547–553.

Gross, P. A., S. Greenfield, S. Cretin, J. Ferguson, J. Grimshaw, R. Grol, N. Klazinga, W. Lorenz, G. S. Meyer, C. Riccobono, S. C. Schoenbaum, P. Schyve, and C. Shaw. 2001. Optimal methods for guideline implementation: Conclusions from Leeds Castle meeting. *Medical Care* 39(8 Suppl 2):II85–II92.

Grumbach, K., and T. Bodenheimer. 2004. Can health care teams improve primary care practice? *JAMA* 291(10):1246–1251.

Hagedorn, H., M. Hogan, J. Smith, C. Bowman, G. Curran, D. Espadas, B. Kimmel, L. Kochevar, M. Legro, and A. Sales. 2006. Lessons learned about implementing research evidence into clinical practice. *Journal of General Internal Medicine* 21(0):S21–S24.

Harvey, G., A. Loftus-Hills, J. Rycroft-Malone, A. Titchen, A. Kitson, B. McCormack, and K. Seers. 2002. Getting evidence into practice: The role and function of facilitation. *Journal of Advanced Nursing* 37(6):577–588.

Hendryx, M. S., J. F. Fieselmann, M. J. Bock, D. S. Wakefield, C. M. Helms, and S. E. Bentler. 1998. Outreach education to improve quality of rural ICU care. Results of a randomized trial. *American Journal of Respiratory and Critical Care Medicine* 158(2):418–423.

Horbar, J. D., R. F. Soll, G. Suresh, J. Buzas, M. B. Bracken, P. E. Plsek. 2004. Evidence-based surfactant therapy for preterm infants. In *Final progress report to AHRQ*. Burlington: University of Vermont.

Hyams, A. L., J. A. Brandenburg, S. R. Lipsitz, D. W. Shapiro, and T. A. Brennan. 1995. Practice guidelines and malpractice litigation: A two-way street. *Annals of Internal Medicine* 122(6):450–455.

Hyatt, J. D., R. P. Benton, and S. F. Derose. 2002. A multifaceted model for implementing clinical practice guidelines across the continuum of care. *Journal of Clinical Outcomes Management* 9(4):199–206.

Hysong, S. J. 2009. Meta-analysis: Audit and feedback features impact effectiveness on care quality. *Medical Care* 47(3):356–363.

Hysong, S., R. Best, and J. Pugh. 2006. Audit and feedback and clinical practice guideline adherence: Making feedback actionable. *Implementation Science* 1(1):9.

ICSI (Institute for Clinical Systems Improvement). 2010. *ICSI history*. http://www.icsi.org/about/icsi_history/ (accessed July 8, 2010).

Irwin, C., and E. M. Ozer. 2004. Implementing adolescent preventive guidelines. In *Final progress report to AHRQ*. San Francisco: University of California–San Francisco Division of Adolescent Medicine.

Jamtvedt, G., J. M. Young, D. T. Kristoffersen, M. A. O'Brien, and A. D. Oxman. 2006a. Audit and feedback: Effects on professional practice and health care outcomes. *Cochrane Database of Systematic Reviews* (2):CD000259.

Jamtvedt, G., J. M. Young, D. T. Kristoffersen, M. A. O'Brien, and A. D. Oxman. 2006b. Does telling people what they have been doing change what they do? A systematic review of the effects of audit and feedback. *Quality and Safety in Health Care* 15(6):433–436.

Jones, K. R., R. Fink, C. Vojir, G. Pepper, E. Hutt, L. Clark, J. Scott, R. Martinez, D. Vincent, and B. K. Mellis. 2004. Translation research in long-term care: Improving pain management in nursing homes. *Worldviews Evidence Based Nursing* 1(Suppl 1):S13–S20.

Jones, J., C. Snyder, and A. Wu. 2007. Issues in the design of Internet-based systems for collecting patient-reported outcomes. *Quality of Life Research* 16(8):1407–1417.

Jones, J. B., W. F. Stewart, J. Darer, and D. F. Sittig. 2010. Beyond the threshold: Real time use of evidence in practice. In *Committee on Standards for Trustworthy Clinical Practice Guidelines commissioned paper*.

Kanter, M., O. Martinez, G. Lindsay, K. Andrews, and C. Denver. 2010. Proactive office encounter: A systematic approach to preventive and chronic care at every patient encounter. *The Permanente Journal* 14(3):38–43.

Katz, D. A., R. B. Brown, D. R. Muehlenbruch, M. C. Fiore, and T. B. Baker. 2004a. Implementing guidelines for smoking cessation: Comparing the efforts of nurses and medical assistants. *American Journal of Preventive Medicine* 27(5):411–416.

Katz, D. A., D. R. Muehlenbruch, R. L. Brown, M. C. Fiore, and T. B. Baker. 2004b. Effectiveness of implementing the Agency for Healthcare Research and Quality smoking cessation clinical practice guideline: A randomized, controlled trial. *Journal of National Cancer Institute* 96(8):594–603.

Kiefe, C. I., J. J. Allison, O. D. Williams, S. D. Person, M. T. Weaver, and N. W. Weissman. 2001. Improving quality improvement using achievable benchmarks for physician feedback: A randomized controlled trial. *JAMA* 285(22):2871–2879.

Kirsh, S. R., R. H. Lawrence, and D. C. Aron. 2008. Tailoring an intervention to the context and system redesign related to the intervention: A case study of implementing shared medical appointments for diabetes. *Implementation Science* 3:34.

Kochevar, L. K., and E. M. Yano. 2006. Understanding health care organization needs and context. Beyond performance gaps. *Journal of General Internal Medicine* 21(Suppl 2):S25–S29.

Kothari, A., N. Edwards, N. Hamel, and M. Judd. 2009. Is research working for you? Validating a tool to examine the capacity of health organizations to use research. *Implementation Science* 4:46.

Kozel, C. T., W. M. Kane, E. M. Rogers, J. E. Brandon, M. T. Hatcher, M. J. Hammes, and R. E. Operhall. 2003. Exploring health promotion agenda-setting in New Mexico: Reshaping health promotion leadership. *Promoting Education* 10(4):171–177, 198, 209.

Krantz, M. J., S. Cornel, and W. R. Hiatt. 2005. Use of ankle brachial index screening for selecting patients for antiplatelet drug therapy. *Pharmacotherapy* 25(12):1826–1828.

Kuilboer, M. M., M. A. van Wijk, M. Mosseveld, E. van der Does, J. C. de Jongste, S. E. Overbeek, B. Ponsioen, and J. van der Lei. 2006. Computed critiquing integrated into daily clinical practice affects physicians' behavior: A randomized clinical trial with AsthmaCritic. *Methods of Information in Medicine* 45(5):431–437.

LeCraw, L. L. 2007. Use of clinical practice guidelines in medical malpractice litigation. *Oncology Practice* (3):254.

Levine, R. S., B. A. Husaini, N. Briggs, V. Cain, T. Cantrell, C. Craun.. 2004. Translating prevention research into practice. In *Final progress report to AHRQ.* Nashville: Meharry Medical College/Tennessee State University.

Litaker, D., M. Ruhe, S. Weyer, and K. Stange. 2008. Association of intervention outcomes with practice capacity for change: Subgroup analysis from a group randomized trial. *Implementation Science* 3(1):25.

Locock, L., S. Dopson, D. Chambers, and J. Gabbay. 2001. Understanding the role of opinion leaders in improving clinical effectiveness. *Social Science and Medicine* 53(6):745–757.

Loeb, M., K. Brazil, A. McGeer, K. Stevenson, S. D. Walter, L. Lohfeld. 2004. Optimizing antibiotic use in long term care. In *Final progress report to AHRQ.* Hamilton, Ontario, Canada: McMaster University.

Lozano, P., J. A. Finkelstein, V. J. Carey, E. H. Wagner, T. S. Inui, A. L. Fuhlbrigge, S. B. Soumerai, S. D. Sullivan, S. T. Weiss, and K. B. Weiss. 2004. A multisite randomized trial of the effects of physician education and organizational change in chronic-asthma care: Health outcomes of the Pediatric Asthma Care Patient Outcomes Research Team II Study. *Archives of Pediatric Adolescent Medicine* 158(9):875–883.

Mansouri, M., and J. Lockyer. 2007. A meta-analysis of continuing medical education effectiveness. *Journal of Continuing Education in the Health Professions* 27(1):6–15.

McDonald, M. V., L. E. Pezzin, P. H. Feldman, C. M. Murtaugh, and T. R. Peng. 2005. Can just-in-time, evidence-based "reminders" improve pain management among home health care nurses and their patients? *Journal of Pain Symptom Management* 29(5):474–488.

McGlynn, E. A., S. M. Asch, J. Adams, J. Keesey, J. Hicks, A. DeCristofaro, and E. A. Kerr. 2003. The quality of health care delivered to adults in the United States. *New England Journal of Medicine* 348(26):2635–2645.

Mehler, P. S., M. J. Krantz, R. A. Lundgren, R. O. Estacio, T. D. MacKenzie, L. Petralia, and W. R. Hiatt. 2005. Bridging the quality gap in diabetic hyperlipidemia: A practice-based intervention. *American Journal of Medicine* 118(12):1414.

Mehta, R. H., C. K. Montoye, M. Gallogly, P. Baker, A. Blount, J. Faul, C. Roychoudhury, S. Borzak, S. Fox, M. Franklin, M. Freundl, E. Kline-Rogers, T. LaLonde, M. Orza, R. Parrish, M. Satwicz, M. J. Smith, P. Sobotka, S. Winston, A. A. Riba, and K. A. Eagle. 2002. Improving quality of care for acute myocardial infarction: The Guidelines Applied in Practice (GAP) initiative. *JAMA* 287(10):1269–1276.

Mello, M. M. 2001. Of swords and shields: The role of clinical practice guidelines in medical practice litigation. *University of Pennsylvania Law Review* 149 U. Pa. L. Rev. 645.

Miller, P. L., S. J. Frawley, and F. G. Sayward. 2001. Maintaining and incrementally revalidating a computer-based clinical guideline: A case study. *Journal of Biomedical Informatics* 34(2):99–111.

Murtaugh, C. M., L. E. Pezzin, M. V. McDonald, P. H. Feldman, and T. R. Peng. 2005. Just-in-time evidence-based e-mail "reminders" in home health care: Impact on nurse practices. *Health Services Research* 40(3):849–864.

Nelson, E. C., P. B. Batalden, T. P. Huber, J. J. Mohr, M. M. Godfrey, L. A. Headrick, and J. H. Wasson. 2002. Microsystems in health care: Learning from high-performing front-line clinical units. *Joint Commission Journal of Quality Improvement* 28(9):472–493.

NGC (National Guideline Clearinghouse). 2010. *National Guideline Clearinghouse.* http://www.guideline.gov/ (accessed April 7, 2010).

Nieva, V., R. Murphy, N. Ridley, N. Donaldson, J. Combes, P. Mitchell. 2005. *From science to service: A framework for the transfer of patient safety research into practice, advanced in patient safety: From research to implementation.* Rockville, MD: Agency for Healthcare Research and Quality.

O'Brien, M. A., S. Rogers, G. Jamtvedt, A. D. Oxman, J. Odgaard-Jensen, D. T. Kristoffersen, L. Forsetlund, D. Bainbridge, N. Freemantle, D. A. Davis, R. B. Haynes, and E. L. Harvey. 2007. Educational outreach visits: Effects on professional practice and health care outcomes. *Cochrane Database of Systematic Reviewvs* (4):CD000409.

O'Connor, P. J., L. I. Solberg, J. Christianson, G. Amundson, and G. Mosser. 1996. Mechanism of action and impact of a cystitis clinical practice guideline on outcomes and costs of care in an HMO. *Joint Commission Journal of Quality Improvement* 22(10):673–682.

Open Clinical. 2010. *Guideline modeling methods summaries.* http://www.openclinical. org/gmmsummaries.html (accessed July 8 2010).

Petersen, L. A., L. D. Woodard, T. Urech, C. Daw, and S. Sookanan. 2006. Does pay-for-performance improve the quality of health care? *Annals of Internal Medicine* 145(4):265–272.

Prior, M., M. Guerin, and K. Grimmer-Somers. 2008. The effectiveness of clinical guideline implementation strategies—A synthesis of systematic review findings. *Journal of Evaluation in Clinical Practice* 14(5):888–897.

Redfern, S., and S. Christian. 2003. Achieving change in health care practice. *Journal of Evaluation in Clinical Practice* 9(2):225–238.

Rosoff, A. J. 2001. Evidence-based medicine and the law: The courts confront clinical practice guidelines. *Journal of Health Politics, Policy & Law* 26(2):327–368.

Rubenstein, L. V., and J. Pugh. 2006. Strategies for promoting organizational and practice change by advancing implementation research. *Journal of General Internal Medicine* 21 (Suppl 2):S58–S64.

Rycroft-Malone, J., and T. Bucknall. 2010. *Models and frameworks for implementing evidence-based practice: Linking evidence to action.* Evidence-based Nursing Series. Chichester, West Sussex, UK, and Ames, IA: Wiley-Blackwell.

Sales, A., D. Atkins, M. J. Krantz, and L. Solberg. 2010. Issues in implementation of trusted clinical practice guidelines. In *Committee on Standards for Developing Trustworthy Clinical Practice Guidelines commissioned paper.*

Scott, S. D., R. C. Plotnikoff, N. Karunamuni, R. Bize, and W. Rodgers. 2008. Factors influencing the adoption of an innovation: An examination of the uptake of the Canadian Heart Health Kit (HHK). *Implementation Science* 3:41.

Scott-Findlay, S., and K. Golden-Biddle. 2005. Understanding how organizational culture shapes research use. *Journal of Nursing Administration* 35(7–8):359–365.

Sequist, T. D., T. K. Gandhi, A. S. Karson, J. M. Fiskio, D. Bugbee, M. Sperling, E. F. Cook, E. J. Orav, D. G. Fairchild, and D. W. Bates. 2005. A randomized trial of electronic clinical reminders to improve quality of care for diabetes and coronary artery disease. *Journal of the American Medical Informatics Association* 12(4):431–437.

Shankaran, V., T. H. Luu, N. Nonzee, E. Richey, J. M. McKoy, J. Graff Zivin, A. Ashford, R. Lantigua, H. Frucht, M. Scoppettone, C. L. Bennett, and S. Sheinfeld Gorin. 2009. Costs and cost effectiveness of a health care provider-directed intervention to promote colorectal cancer screening. *Journal of Clinical Oncology* 27(32):5370–5375.

Shiffman, R., J. Dixon, C. Brandt, A. Essaihi, A. Hsiao, G. Michel, and R. O'Connell. 2005. The guideline implementability appraisal (glia): Development of an instrument to identify obstacles to guideline implementation. *BMC Medical Informatics and Decision Making* 5(1):23.

Shojania, K. G., and J. M. Grimshaw. 2005. Evidence-based quality improvement: The state of the science. *Health Affairs* 24(1):138–150.

Shojania, K. G., S. R. Ranji, K. M. McDonald, J. M. Grimshaw, V. Sundaram, R. J. Rushakoff, and D. K. Owens. 2006. Effects of quality improvement strategies for Type 2 diabetes on glycemic control: A meta-regression analysis. *JAMA* 296(4):427–440.

Shojania, K. G., A. Jennings, A. Mayhew, C. R. Ramsay, M. P. Eccles, and J. Grimshaw. 2009. The effects of on-screen, point of care computer reminders on processes and outcomes of care. *Cochrane Database of Systematic Reviews* (3):CD001096.

Shojania, K. G., A. Jennings, A. Mayhew, C. Ramsay, M. Eccles, and J. Grimshaw. 2010. Effect of point-of-care computer reminders on physician behaviour: A systematic review. *Canadian Medical Association Journal* 182(5):E216–E225.

Shortell, S. M. 2004. Increasing value: A research agenda for addressing the managerial and organizational challenges facing health care delivery in the United States. *Medical Care Research Reviews* 61(3 Suppl):12S–30S.

Sittig, D., A. Wright, J. S. Ash, and B. Middleton. 2009a. A set of preliminary standards recommended for achieving a national repository of clinical decision support interventions. *AMIA Annual Symposium Proceedings 2009*: 614–618.

Sittig, D. F., A. Wright, J. S. Ash, and B. Middleton. 2009b. *A set of preliminary standards recommended for achieving a national repository of clinical decision support interventions.* Paper presented at AMIA 2009 Symposium, San Francisco, CA.

Smith, C. S., M. G. Harbrecht, S. M. Coronel, and M. J. Krantz. 2008. State consensus guideline for the prevention of cardiovascular disease in primary care settings. *Critical Pathways in Cardiology: A Journal of Evidence-Based Medicine* 7:122–125.

Solberg, L. 2009. Lessons for non-VA care delivery systems from the U.S. Department of Veterans Affairs Quality Enhancement Research Initiative: QUERI Series. *Implementation Science* 4(1):9.

Solberg, L. I., M. L. Brekke, C. J. Fazio, J. Fowles, D. N. Jacobsen, T. E. Kottke, G. Mosser, P. J. O'Connor, K. A. Ohnsorg, and S. J. Rolnick. 2000. Lessons from experienced guideline implementers: Attend to many factors and use multiple strategies. *Joint Commission Journal of Quality Improvement* 26(4):171–188.

Solberg, L. I., M. C. Hroscikoski, J. M. Sperl-Hillen, P. G. Harper, and B. F. Crabtree. 2006. Transforming medical care: Case study of an exemplary, small medical group. *Annals of Family Medicine* 4(2):109–116.

Solomon, D. H., L. Van Houten, R. J. Glynn, L. Baden, K. Curtis, H. Schrager, and J. Avorn. 2001. Academic detailing to improve use of broad-spectrum antibiotics at an academic medical center. *Archives of Internal Medicine* 161(15):1897–1902.

Soumerai, S. B., and J. Avorn. 1986. Economic and policy analysis of university-based drug "detailing." *Medical Care* 24(4):313–331.

Soumerai, S. B., T. J. McLaughlin, J. H. Gurwitz, E. Guadagnoli, P. J. Hauptman, C. Borbas, N. Morris, B. McLaughlin, X. Gao, D. J. Willison, R. Asinger, and F. Gobel. 1998. Effect of local medical opinion leaders on quality of care for acute myocardial infarction: A randomized controlled trial. *JAMA* 279(17):1358–1363.

Stafford, R. S., L. K. Bartholomew, W. C. Cushman, J. A. Cutler, B. R. Davis, G. Dawson, P. T. Einhorn, C. D. Furberg, L. B. Piller, S. L. Pressel, and P. K. Whelton. 2010. Impact of the ALLHAT/JNC7 Dissemination Project on thiazide-type diuretic use. *Archives of Internal Medicine* 170(10):851–858.

Stetler, C. B. 2003. Role of the organization in translating research into evidence-based practice. *Outcomes Management* 7(3):97–103; quiz 104–105.

Stetler, C. B., M. W. Legro, J. Rycroft-Malone, C. Bowman, G. Curran, M. Guihan, H. Hagedorn, S. Pineros, and C. M. Wallace. 2006a. Role of "external facilitation" in implementation of research findings: A qualitative evaluation of facilitation experiences in the Veterans Health Administration. *Implementation Science* 1:23.

Stetler, C. B., M. W. Legro, C. M. Wallace, C. Bowman, M. Guihan, H. Hagedorn, B. Kimmel, N. D. Sharp, and J. L. Smith. 2006b. The role of formative evaluation in implementation research and the QUERI experience. *Journal of General Internal Medicine* 21(Suppl 2):S1–S8.

Stetler, C. B., J. A. Ritchie, J. Rycroft-Malone, A. A. Schultz, and M. P. Charns. 2009. Institutionalizing evidence-based practice: An organizational case study using a model of strategic change. *Implementation Science* 4:78.

Thomas, J. W., E. C. Ziller, and D. A. Thayer. 2010. Low costs of defensive medicine, small savings from tort reform. *Health Affairs* 29(9):1578–1584.

Titler, M. G., and L. Q. Everett. 2001. Translating research into practice. Considerations for critical care investigators. *Critical Care Nursing Clinics of North America* 13(4):587–604.

Titler, M. G., L. Cullen, and G. Ardery. 2002. Evidence-based practice: An administrative perspective. *Reflections Nursing Leadership* 28(2):26–27, 45, 46.

Titler, M. G., K. Herr, J. M. Brooks, X. J. Xie, G. Ardery, M. L. Schilling, J. L. Marsh, L. Q. Everett, and W. R. Clarke. 2009. Translating research into practice intervention improves management of acute pain in older hip fracture patients. *Health Services Research* 44(1):264–287.

Vaughn, T. E., K. D. McCoy, B. J. BootsMiller, R. F. Woolson, B. Sorofman, T. Tripp-Reimer, J. Perlin, and B. N. Doebbeling. 2002. Organizational predictors of adherence to ambulatory care screening guidelines. *Medical Care* 40(12):1172–1185.

Wallin, L. 2009. Knowledge translation and implementation research in nursing. *International Journal of Nursing Studies* 46(4):576–587.

Ward, M. M., T. C. Evans, A. J. Spies, L. L. Roberts, and D. S. Wakefield. 2006. National Quality Forum 30 safe practices: Priority and progress in Iowa hospitals. *American Journal of Medical Quality* 21(2):101–108.

Watson, N. M. 2004. Advancing quality of urinary incontinence evaluation and treatment in nursing homes through translational research. *Worldviews Evidence Based Nursing* 1(Suppl 1):S21–S25.

Weinstein, M. C., B. O'Brien, J. Hornberger, J. Jackson, M. Johannesson, C. McCabe, and B. R. Luce. 2003. Principles of good practice for decision analytic modeling in health-care evaluation: Report of the ISPOR Task Force on Good Research Practices—Modeling Studies. *Value Health* 6(1):9–17.

Wensing, M., H. Wollersheim, and R. Grol. 2006. Organizational interventions to implement improvements in patient care: A structured review of reviews. *Implementation Science* 1:2.

Werner, R. M., and R. A. Dudley. 2009. Making the "Pay" matter in Pay-For-Performance: Implications for payment strategies. *Health Affairs* 28(5):1498–1508.

Wright, A., H. Goldberg, T. Hongsermeier, and B. Middleton. 2007. A description and functional taxonomy of rule-based decision support content at a large integrated delivery network. *Journal of the American Medical Informatics Association* 14(4):489–496.

Wright, A., D. F. Sittig, J. S. Ash, S. Sharma, J. E. Pang, and B. Middleton. 2009. Clinical decision support capabilities of commercially-available clinical information systems. *Journal of the American Medical Informatics Association* 16(5):637–644.

Yano, E. M. 2008. The role of organizational research in implementing evidence-based practice: QUERI Series. *Implementation Science* 3:29.

7

Development, Identification, and Evaluation of Trustworthy Clinical Practice Guidelines

Abstract: In this final chapter, the committee discusses national policy issues related to clinical practice guidelines (CPGs), addressing questions of who should develop and fund CPGs and how those that are trustworthy should be identified. Furthermore, the committee discusses approaches to harmonization, dissemination (particularly the role of the National Guideline Clearinghouse [NGC]), and evaluation of guidelines. Currently a diverse group of organizations develop CPGs; the committee supports their efforts, but acknowledges the associated challenges in promoting and identifying adherence to standards. **The committee recommends that the Secretary of Health and Human Services establish a public–private mechanism to examine, at the request of developer organizations, the procedures they use to produce guidelines and certify, organizations whose processes meet those standards, for a limited period of time.** *The committee urges* **the Agency for Healthcare Research and Quality (AHRQ) to examine the causes of inconsistent existing CPGs and prioritize them for harmonization.** *Finally, the committee urges that* **AHRQ continue to provide a clearinghouse function, through the NGC, but require higher standards for guideline inclusion and efficient identification of guidelines from certified organizations. AHRQ also should be involved in evaluation of the proposed standards, their effect on the quality of guidelines, and ultimately on patient care.**

INTRODUCTION

Previous chapters discussed standards for trustworthy guidelines, explored methods for their development and implementation, and put forth committee recommendations. In this final chapter, the committee discusses national policy questions related to clinical practice guidelines (CPGs), such as who should develop guidelines; how CPGs that meet the proposed standards should be identified; whether there is a continuing need for the National Guideline Clearinghouse (NGC); whether there should be a process to harmonize related CPGs and identify recommendations for quality measures; and how proposed standards and impact of standards-based CPGs should be pilot-tested and evaluated. Finally, the committee makes recommendations regarding the identification and certification of trustworthy CPGs, research on harmonization of inconsistent CPGs, and evaluation of the proposed standards and the impact of trustworthy clinical practice guidelines on healthcare and patient outcomes.

WHO SHOULD DEVELOP GUIDELINES?

Researchers have raised the possibility of centralizing development of CPGs in one federal organization (Shaneyfelt and Centor, 2009). The potential benefits from this arrangement could include reduced bias, a reduction in multiple CPGs on the same topic, and improved guidance for future research. A single organization that develops CPGs based on the proposed standards and provides assurance that all CPGs meet the standards would be efficient. Although the Agency for Healthcare Research and Quality (AHRQ) performed a guideline development function early in its history, it was not the sole producer of CPGs during that period. It was a politically difficult function for a public agency subject to congressional appropriations, and the agency has not attempted to reestablish that activity.

Throughout its study, the committee has recognized the many public and private organizations participating in clinical practice guideline development. The Institute of Medicine report, *Knowing What Works*, concluded that a pluralistic approach to guideline development, while not without problems, was desirable (IOM, 2008). This committee recognizes value in a diverse community of developers and the unique relationships each has with its constituency, relevant experts, practitioners, and funding sources. Many organizations have made major investments in technical staff and other resources devoted to CPG development (Coates, 2010). In addition, many have earned public trust for their efforts. Organizations may have one or more goals in creating a guideline: education of members and the public on a care topic, reductions in unjustified practice variations, meeting members' demands for guidance, or assuring a role for a specialty in treatment of a particular condition or procedure.

The committee sees greater value in having a variety of organizations developing CPGs than in limiting all development to a single agency. With multiple developers, however, there is likely to be a continuing problem of multiple CPGs on the same topic (see discussion of harmonization below). Given the diversity of organizations developing CPGs and their differing needs, the committee recognizes both the desirability and hazards of proposing standards and priorities.

Furthermore, given the large number of development organizations and their differing capabilities, some may attempt to meet IOM standards, but fail in achieving all of them. It could still be difficult for guideline users to recognize which CPGs are trustworthy. (The committee addresses this problem of identifying trustworthy CPGs below.)

Current CPG development generally is financed by each organization creating a guideline. At times two or more organizations jointly develop a CPG, pooling their staff and financial resources. At other times development funds may originate from interested commercial parties (McClure, 2010). The committee believes potential for conflicts of interest are great when funding for CPG development or for the supporting organization comes from stakeholders, particularly the pharmaceutical and device industries or specialty societies, which might benefit or whose members might gain from guideline recommendations. The committee also recognizes that the proposed standards are likely to add to costs of development for some organizations, and may force other small groups to exit the guidelines business.

Because members of a guideline development group usually serve as volunteers, a major expense in production is often the systematic review (SR). The IOM Committee on the Development of Standards for Systematic Reviews of Comparative Effectiveness Research, in its related study, recommends that all SRs conducted by research organizations under contract to the Department of Health and Human Services (HHS) or the Patient-Centered Outcomes Research Institute (PCORI) agree to standards set by that committee. Given the funding for comparative effectiveness research by PCORI, the number of federally supported SRs is likely to increase significantly. Completed, high-quality SRs presumably would then be available free (or at cost for printing) to the general public as well as to organizations wishing to develop related guidelines.

The IOM committee on CPGs hopes this SR recommendation will be implemented quickly. Nonetheless, the committee recognizes that substantial costs will remain for CPG developers. Many organizations testifying before the committee stressed the need for additional funds to produce high-quality CPGs (Fochtmann, 2010; Kelly-Thomas, 2010).

To further enhance guideline development, additional steps should be taken. Clinical topics that are of interest to limited populations, such as rare but treatable diseases, may need practice guidelines. There may be no disease group or clinical specialty society with the resources to develop such CPGs. Outside funding assistance could spur the development of such needed guidelines. The committee urges organizations desiring to produce such guidelines to coordinate their efforts with other, related organizations so they may pool their resources. This could also strengthen their efforts to seek financial assistance from foundations, government agencies, and other nonconflicted sources. In addition, HHS should promote the identification of best practices in CPG development, guided by the proposed standards herein, and should assist in the training of individuals in the specific technical skills needed in the CPG process. Importantly, HHS should assist in the training of patient and consumer representatives to participate in this process.

SHOULD THERE BE A PROCESS TO IDENTIFY CPGS THAT MEET THE PROPOSED TRUSTWORTHY STANDARDS?

With nearly 2,700 guidelines in the National Guideline Clearinghouse, numerous additional commercial guidelines, and an unknown number of others in existence, many addressing identical topics, users often face challenges in identification of guidelines based on high-quality development methods. The NGC provides a standardized summary of each CPG posting, describing its development methodology and evidence base, and providing a link to the full guideline, but the NGC makes no quality judgment. ECRI, the NGC contractor, has identified 25 medical conditions characterized by conflicting guidelines in the clearinghouse. For guidelines on closely related topics, NGC has described differences and similarities, absent individual CPG quality assessment. Reviewing substantively relevant CPGs and determining the one of highest quality for a condition is a daunting task for clinicians, and conducting such assessments independently is inefficient for them. Often clinicians look to specialty societies or professional organizations for guidelines, or their practice organizations may develop their own CPGs or adopt a commercial suite of CPGs and encourage or expect their clinicians to follow them. Fundamentally, however, it is now nearly impossible for all stakeholders to be confident of CPG quality.

What would it mean if guidelines' developers and users had a mechanism to immediately identify high-quality, evidence-based CPGs, which could be considered trustworthy? Users could make better clinical decisions based on the best available scientific evidence. If such high-quality CPGs were publicly identified and recognized, more developer organizations would be likely to strive for such recognition and improve their development procedures to meet standards.

Linking such identification to regulatory procedures, insurance coverage, payment systems, or quality measures is not within the committee's scope, but an official identification or certification of trustworthy CPGs is a goal. No organization or process in the United States currently distinguishes trustworthy CPGs.

The committee believes that some guideline developers will readily embrace the eight standards in this report and adapt their development process to create CPGs that are trustworthy. However, not all developers will be able or willing to do that. Thus, the committee believes it is essential that its proposed standards be accompanied by creation of a mechanism to identify guidelines that meet development standards. Such identification will serve three purposes.

It will

- promote wider adoption of quality standards by developers because CPGs publicly identified as trustworthy, with a "seal of approval," will have an advantage;
- provide users of CPGs with an easy guide to identify trustworthy ones; and
- promote adoption of trustworthy CPGs.

A process could (1) identify each guideline to see if it meets specified standards, (2) certify organizations producing guidelines that comply with quality standards, or (3) acknowledge standards compliance for each guideline production process prior to development of the guideline. The selection of any of these options has practical implications for costs, work volume, and reliability of the designation.

Identification of Individual Trustworthy CPGs

A process could be set up to review individual CPGs, assessing whether they meet standards, and labeling as "trustworthy" those that do. The process might be similar to that used by ECRI for the NGC, but would require more data to support in-depth assessment, including conflict of interest (COI) review. Creating a more transparent process is also desirable. Given the large number of CPGs and CPG updates in the clearinghouse and the new ones produced regularly, thorough inspection of each would be a very resource-intensive task. A priority-setting procedure might be useful to identify CPGs that should take precedence for review. Eventually existing CPGs will undergo an update or be withdrawn from the NGC. The updates and new CPGs will more likely be developed according to the proposed standards. If the future number of new CPGs is smaller, the identification of trustworthy CPGs may be less onerous. But if availability of medical evidence continues to expand and the development of CPGs continues to increase, the task will remain large.

Certification of Organizations with Trustworthy CPG Development Procedures

Alternatively, one could review organizations developing CPGs and their production procedures, certifying adherence to quality development standards. In that case, guidelines issued over a specified time period by certified organizations might be considered trustworthy. If an organization did not maintain proper procedures throughout the certified period, its guidelines could be challenged and certification withdrawn, if justified.

The National Institute for Health and Clinical Excellence (NICE), an independent organization offering guidance on health promotion and disease prevention and treatment in the United Kingdom, takes the organizational certification approach. National Health Service (NHS) Evidence, a part of NICE, reviews procedures that applicant organizations use to produce various types of guidance and provides an identifiable mark to be placed on future CPGs of those organizations meeting accreditation requirements and agreeing to maintain the approved processes during a 3-year accreditation period. The mark may be applied to any type of guidance for which the organization has been approved. NHS Evidence may review organizational procedures at any point during the accreditation period and, if noncompliance with accreditation requirements is detected, withdraw accreditation and the accompanying mark (NHS, 2009).

NHS Evidence has a sequential application and review process, including (1) internal review of organizational procedures, using published criteria based on the Appraisal of Guidelines Research and Evaluation (AGREE) instrument (discussed in Chapter 3) and selected recent guidance documents, (2) elicitation of external expert opinions of the staff's review, (3) draft decision by the Advisory Committee posted on the web, (4) public consultation and comment on the draft decision, (5) final decision by the Advisory Committee, taking into account public comments, and (6) publication of the certification decision. The process is detailed on the web; related forms, manual, and additional information are available there to promote transparency and public involvement. Because NICE accreditation began in June 2009, evaluation of its process and impact is limited. However, the time from application to final decision typically should require 6–8 months. Compared to the CPG environment in the United States, which has a few hundred independent developers (the NGC includes more than 280 separate organizations developing CPGs), NICE contracts with a relatively small number of organizations to produce various guidance forms, including clinical practice guidelines (NHS, 2009). Because some U.S. CPG developers currently do not have documented, standardized procedures, and a large number have not developed many CPGs, all developers are unlikely to seek certification through such a process.

Identification of the Development Process for Each CPG

This alternative would involve assessment of the proposed development process for each planned CPG, rather than review of the organizational process, as described above. This approach provides protection against organizational failure to maintain quality procedures over time. It would require additional review effort, compared to the preceding organizational approach, if organizations produce multiple CPGs during the accreditation period. It offers an advantage over individual CPG review because it may be conducted mainly at the beginning and during the development process rather than at the end. This should minimize delays in identifying trustworthy CPGs after release, although a brief evaluation of the final draft would be necessary to ensure the developer was in procedural compliance. This approach would have an additional advantage if it induced more developers to formalize their process before creating a CPG.

Committee Endorsement

The committee believes the second option, certification of an organization for a period of time based on its generic development procedures, would be the most efficient approach to identifying trustworthy CPGs.

Because the focus of the committee was on the development of standards, not the creation of a certifying body, it has not researched and prescribed all the details for such a mechanism to accomplish the functions recommended above. The committee favors a mechanism that includes participation by individuals from public and private institutions because guideline users in federal and state governments, professional associations, industry, and patient organizations have a strong interest in improving the quality of CPGs. Drawing on existing institutions for the authority and support the certifying body will need should speed its creation. At the same time, creation of the public–private certifying body would alert CPG developers of the new standards, encourage them to adopt the standards, and build on existing capacities.

Because the certification process will entail significant costs, the committee believes the Secretary of HHS should develop a way to fund this certification mechanism by drawing on the resources of interested stakeholders without biasing its decision making or the public's perception that such a bias exists. The committee stresses that this certifying mechanism would not endorse particular drugs or treatment options for medical conditions. Nor would it make clinical decisions about the guidelines it reviews. It would merely certify the organizations' guideline development process and identify the CPGs that result from that process as trustworthy.

Without specifying the details of such a public–private mechanism, the committee notes that the healthcare world has several examples of such organizations. The committee suggests they be examined to determine whether any might be appropriate to assume the task or identify strengths of their structures that might be incorporated in such a mechanism. Examples include the following:

- National Guideline Clearinghouse: As mentioned in Chapter 2, AHRQ, in partnership with the American Medical Association and America's Health Insurance Plans (then the American Association of Health Plans) created the NGC as a public web resource, funded federally, and managed privately through a contract with ECRI (NGC, 2010).
- National Quality Forum (NQF): The Forum, a private nonprofit organization, was created in 1999 by a coalition of

public and private leaders in healthcare to promote health-care safety and quality improvement and to endorse quality measures based on a national consensus for use in public reporting. It is governed by a board with a full range of private stakeholders as well as the directors of AHRQ, Centers for Medicare & Medicaid Services (CMS), and National Institutes of Health. Funding comes from government, including a substantial contract with CMS on performance measurement from the *Medicare Improvements for Patients and Providers Act*, and various private foundations, industry, and annual membership dues (NQF, 2010).

- National Committee for Quality Assurance (NCQA): NCQA, a private non-profit organization founded in 1990, develops and applies HEDIS: Healthcare Effectiveness Data and Information Set measures to 90 percent of the nation's health plans. NCQA also has programs dedicated to the accreditation, certification, recognition and distinction of health plans, disease management organizations, medical home models and other organizations working in health management and improvement. An independent board of directors generally comprising representatives from employers, physicians, public policy experts, consumer groups, and health systems governs the organization. NCQA employs COI disclosure and conflict management policies for its Board and expert panels. Funding comes from many donors and sponsors including health plans, banks, professional medical societies, healthcare foundations, medical centers and others (NCQA, 2011).

- Patient-Centered Outcomes Research Institute: A new quasi-public/private nonprofit body was created under the *Patient Protection and Affordable Care Act*, Sec. 6301, called PCORI. Established and funded by Congress, it sits outside of government and is directed by a board that includes representatives of federal and state agencies as well as academicians, researchers, consumers, patients, and other experts. Because PCORI funding originates from Medicare Trust Funds, rather than industry, risk of COI is limited and funds are more protected and steady than those requiring annual appropriations or private fundraising.[1]

---

[1]*The Patient Protection and Affordable Care Act*, Public Law 111-148, § 6301, 111th Cong. (March 23, 2010).

- National Institute for Health and Clinical Excellence: The governments of England and Wales fund NICE to provide evidence-based advice to the NHS and the public on health promotion and treatment. (See discussion in Chapter 2.) It is an independent body that works in consultation with public- and private-sector experts and a council of the public. NICE supports a private, professional network of guideline developers through contracts with England's Royal Colleges of Medicine and Surgery and with academic research centers. NICE also includes NHS Evidence, a web-based service that performs a structured review of guideline developers seeking accreditation and that recommends action to NICE (NICE, 2010).

IS THERE A CONTINUING NEED FOR A GUIDELINE CLEARINGHOUSE?

Knowledge of the existence of a CPG is prerequisite to adoption by clinicians and health plans. Having an accessible, centralized repository for viewing all publicly available, good-quality CPGs developed in the United States and by some international organizations is helpful to potential users. Without such a collection, there would be greater burden on guideline developers to publicize CPG availability and there might be reduced application of their products.

The National Guideline Clearinghouse has served as a public, accessible repository of CPGs for a number of years and has an established role in the promulgation of new and updated guidelines. NGC reviews each CPG submitted to assure compliance with the clearinghouse's minimal standards, and requests additional information if needed. The NGC recognizes that the products listed within are of widely varying quality (Coates, 2010). The committee has heard testimony that the NGC performs a public service, but does not set sufficiently high standards to assure users that poor-quality guidelines are not admitted (Coates, 2010). Given the mixed quality of clearinghouse contents, its large volume is also problematic.

AHRQ and ECRI could take several steps to differentiate between trustworthy guidelines and others and non-CPG guidance to increase clearinghouse utility. The committee understands that, when there are no trustworthy CPGs on a topic, clinicians may need to rely on guidance of more limited quality. The steps are as follows:

- To be a constructive resource, the NGC should eliminate CPGs for which trustworthiness cannot be determined, and identify the trustworthiness of those retained. As a central repository for all CPGs, the committee does not believe the NGC should be restricted to listing only those CPGs identified as trustworthy. However, the NGC's contribution may be of questionable value when listing guidelines providing too little information for an informed reader to judge quality and trustworthiness. Additionally, "Not stated" should not be an acceptable response to items in the NGC's structured abstract form (upon which acceptance to the NGC depends) and should disqualify a CPG for NGC inclusion.
- Items that have not included a thorough SR of the relevant scientific evidence base should be excluded from the NGC. AHRQ may consider storing rejected guidelines in a public inventory of excluded guidelines within the NGC, so that stakeholders may identify any possible guideline of interest and understand why the NGC may not regard it as acceptable. Findings of no scientific evidence resulting from an SR should not preclude listing of the CPG in the NGC.
- The NGC should prominently identify guidelines originating from CPG developers certified by the designated mechanism as trustworthy (if such a process is implemented).
- CPGs from an organization that requested and failed review by the certifying mechanism should also be identified in a special category, with standards met and shortcomings specified.
- Forms of guidance currently in the NGC or considered for future inclusion that do not meet IOM CPG definitional requirements or clearly do not adhere to trustworthy CPG standards should receive a different guidance label and be included in a separate, non-CPG category within the NGC.
- AHRQ and the NGC should produce more Guideline Syntheses of topically similar CPGs. These syntheses highlight the importance of coordination among various organizations developing CPGs on similar topics, may highlight potential areas for harmonization, and offer assistance to CPG users.
- The proposed standards will require additional NGC effort as current NGC abstraction does not require review of development process data adequate to meet the requirements of the proposed standards. On the other hand, coordination with the public–private certification process might expedite NGC abstraction.

Based on the preceding discussion, the NGC clearly provides a useful function for both guidelines developers and users. However, the committee believes it could do much more. Its policy of broad inclusion has led to a bewildering number of CPGs and other forms of clinical guidance of widely varying quality. Potential users of CPGs need more clarity about choices. The committee does not believe the NGC should restrict listings to CPGs identified as trustworthy. However, it should eliminate from public listings the weakest CPGs, based on their development process, as well as those CPGs that provide too little information for an informed reader to be able to judge their quality. Remaining CPGs should be distinguished from other forms of clinical guidance. Finally, the National Guideline Clearinghouse needs to be funded at a sufficient level for it to improve the quality, timeliness, and trustworthiness of its CPGs and other products.

SHOULD THERE BE A PROCESS TO HARMONIZE RELATED CPGS?

Once awareness and adoption of the proposed IOM standards for CPGs generally have been achieved, the committee believes the need for a special process to harmonize CPGs will be reduced. Increased transparency and encouragement of all developers to discuss why they believe their recommendations are similar or different from those of others would make harmonization a more conscious part of development. In addition, the NGC, when comparing similar CPGs in Guideline Syntheses, might also contrast recommendations contained in each to identify sources of convergence or areas lacking harmony. The standards are likely to reduce current and future levels of guideline duplication for several reasons:

- The total number of CPGs produced may be smaller because some organizations will be unable to meet the standards. Those organizations either will choose not to produce inferior guidelines or choose to use existing trustworthy CPGs if the topic is closely related to what they need.
- As current CPGs become outdated, developers might choose not to update if they cannot meet the new standards. They may also look to partner with other organizations concerned with the same issues, and pool resources and expertise to meet the standards.

- Proposed Standard 3 concerning CPG development team composition calls for representation of a wide range of interests and perspectives. This should encourage collaboration among guideline development organizations and likely result in representative members from organizations having CPGs with overlapping recommendations. Their participation in the development of a new, related CPG should help minimize conflicting recommendations.
- Proposed Standard 8 requires annual, ongoing monitoring of new, potentially relevant evidence. It also requires updating of extant CPGs when new evidence indicates a modification of guideline recommendations. Both of these activities help ensure that earlier guidelines are accounted for as future CPGs are developed.
- If the NGC adopts higher standards for clearinghouse admission, fewer CPGs will be accessible and probably somewhat fewer will require harmonization now and in the future because some CPGs that do not meet NGC standards will not be widely circulated.

Whether or not commercial guideline developers choose to follow the proposed standards, to the extent they rely on existing CPGs from reputable developers, and to the extent there would be fewer CPGs in need of harmonization, commercial guidelines would contribute to the convergence toward existing, higher quality CPGs, rather than to a proliferation of poorer quality CPGs.

If a new, separate process were proposed to encourage CPG harmonization, it would require some authority and have a significant job tackling existing, duplicative guidelines, and also an endless job if the development standards were ineffective in reducing production of duplicative guidelines. The committee recognizes that, although future need for harmonization should be reduced, conflicting recommendations in CPGs may remain. Because the committee does not assume that all remaining duplication and conflicting recommendations are necessarily bad, AHRQ and the NGC should examine the causes of remaining multiple inconsistent CPGs and prioritize them for harmonization if considered necessary. Particular attention to harmonization should be paid when the oldest CPG on a topic is due for updating.

SHOULD THERE BE A PROCESS TO IDENTIFY WHICH RECOMMENDATIONS SHOULD BE CONSIDERED FOR QUALITY MEASURES?

Clinical Practice Guidelines have had, and are expected to have, an important influence on development of physician and hospital performance measures, especially when CPGs conform to development methods such as those recommended herein. The data gathered from use of such measures have provided consumers with valuable information on the quality of different health care providers. The committee recognizes that healthcare quality measures are developed by many different organizations for various purposes and audiences. Some measure developers and users may work for proprietary interests and prefer keeping measures confidential; others submit measures to the NQF for approval and dissemination and to a web-based clearinghouse, the National Quality Measures Clearinghouse (NQMC). Although some CPG developers also develop related quality measures and promote their use, typically those actions have not been within the purview of guideline development to produce performance measures. In fact, performing both functions might create conflicting interests. For example, a CPG might recommend the latest state-of-the-art treatment, but the Guideline Development Group (GDG) might consider it unfair or inappropriate for use as a quality measure, if the measure could be used in a pay-for-performance scheme. Measures developers, however, often rely on CPG recommendations and the related scientific evidence base. Because the NQMC is closely linked to the NGC, users of either clearinghouse can readily find related measures and CPGs.

As reflected in the NQMC, quality measures can assist in evaluating aspects of the process of care, care outcomes, access to care, and the patient's care experience. The evidence base for a measure posted in the NQMC can be minimal—at least "one or more research studies published in a National Library of Medicine indexed, peer-reviewed journal, a[n] SR of the clinical literature, a CPG or other peer-reviewed synthesis of the clinical evidence, or a formal consensus procedure involving expert clinicians and clinical researchers," and evidence from patients for measures of patient experience, as well as documentation concerning use of the measure (NQMC, 2010).

Because rating the strength of recommendations will occur in the development process of all CPGs adhering to the IOM's recommended standards, the committee concludes that no additional processes are needed to identify recommendations of sufficient strength for quality measurement. The committee urges all developers of CPG-related measures to employ only CPGs identified as trustworthy (as defined herein) when available. Only recommendations conceived in accordance with development standards, such as those proposed herein, should be transformed into quality measures.

HOW SHOULD CPG DEVELOPMENT AND IMPLEMENTATION PROCESSES AND IMPACT BE EVALUATED?

The proposed standards have not yet been evaluated by CPG developers and users. Without evaluation of the recommended guideline development process and interventions to promote CPG implementation, it will not be known whether the standards give rise to development of unbiased, scientifically valid, and trustworthy CPGs, or whether implementation of IOM standards-based CPGs gives rise to improved health outcomes. The committee believes answering questions related is important, such as,

- What are strengths and weaknesses in the current execution of standards and how might the standards be revised before broad distribution (e.g., what is the optimal model of GDG-SR relationship, what is the optimal method of involving consumers, etc.)?
- Are the IOM guideline development standards valid and reliable?
- Are the development standards being adopted?
- Is adoption increasing stakeholders' confidence in CPGs?
- Is adoption of the proposed standards enhancing the quality of the development of CPGs?
- Are CPGs developed on the basis of the proposed standards more likely to be adopted?
- Which interventions to promote adoption of CPGs are most effective, for which audiences, and for what types of clinical interventions?
- Do CPGs developed on the basis of the proposed standards for trustworthy guidelines improve healthcare and patient outcomes?
- What is the impact of the NGC?

Research to answer such questions is consistent with the mission of AHRQ. Hence, the committee believes that AHRQ should direct a portion of its research funds to investigations of, and methods for studying, the impact of the proposed standards, and CPGs.

It is important to emphasize that understanding the feasibility of the proposed standards should be supported by pilot testing. Ultimately, the interest is in identifying strengths and weaknesses in the current execution of standards with the aim of revising and enhancing them in advance of final production, full distribution and promotion (Szklo and Nieto, 2007).

Given the growth expected in the next decade in clinical research, comparative effectiveness studies, and systematic reviews, the availability of trustworthy CPGs will become even more critical in assisting clinicians and patients in their treatment considerations. The recommendations below should help to improve the quality of CPGs available for their use.

RECOMMENDATION: DEVELOPMENT, IDENTIFICATION, AND EVALUATION OF TRUSTWORTHY CPGS

- The Secretary of HHS should establish a public–private mechanism to examine, at the request of developer organizations, the procedures they use to produce their clinical practice guidelines and to certify whether these organizations' CPG development procedures comply with standards for trustworthy CPGs.
- AHRQ should take the following actions:
  - Require the NGC to provide a clear indication of the extent to which the clinical practice guidelines it receives adhere to standards for trustworthiness.
  - Conduct research on the causes of inconsistent CPGs, and strategies to encourage their harmonization.
  - Assess the strengths and weaknesses of proposed IOM standards by pilot-test; estimate the validity and reliability of proposed standards; evaluate the effectiveness of interventions to encourage standards' implementation; and evaluate the effects of standards on CPG development, healthcare quality, and patient outcomes.

REFERENCES

Coates, V. 2010. *National Guidelines Clearinghouse NGC/ECRI Institute*. Presented at the IOM Committee on Developing Standards for Trustworthy Clinical Practice Guidelines meeting, January 11, 2010, Washington, DC.

Fochtmann, L. 2010. *American Psychiatric Association*. Presented at the IOM Committee on Standards for Developing Trustworthy Clinical Practice Guidelines meeting, January 11, 2010, Washington, DC.

IOM (Institute of Medicine). 2008. *Knowing what works in healthcare: A roadmap for the nation*. Edited by J. Eden, B. Wheatley, B. McNeil, and H. Sox. Washington, DC: The National Academies Press.

Kelly-Thomas, K. 2010. *National Association of Pediatric Nurse Practitioners*. Presented at the IOM Committee on Standards for Developing Trustworthy Clinical Practice Guidelines meeting, January 11, 2010, Washington, DC.

McClure, J. 2010. *National Comprehensive Cancer Network (NCCN)*. Presented at IOM Committee on Standards for Developing Trustworthy Clinical Practice Guidelines meeting on January 11, 2010, Washington, DC.

NCQA (National Committee for Quality Assurance). 2011. *About NCQA*. http://www.ncqa.org/tabid/675/Default.aspx (accessed February 2, 2011).

NGC (National Guideline Clearinghouse). 2010. *National Guideline Clearinghouse*. http://www.guideline.gov/ (accessed April 7, 2010).

NHS (National Health Service). 2009. Process manual for accrediting producers of guidance and recommendations for practice: A guide for producers and stakeholders: National Institute for Health and Clinical Excellence.

NICE (National Institute for Health and Clinical Excellence). 2010. *Homepage*. http://www.nice.org.uk/ (accessed March 7, 2010).

NQF (The National Quality Forum). 2010. *About NQF*. http://www.qualityforum.org/About_NQF/About_NQF.aspx (accessed October 8, 2010).

NQMC (National Quality Measures Clearinghouse). 2010. *National Quality Measures Clearinghouse: Inclusion criteria*. http://www.qualitymeasures.ahrq.gov/about/inclusion.aspx (accessed July 16, 2010).

Shaneyfelt, T. M., and R. M. Centor. 2009. Reassessment of clinical practice guidelines: Go gently into that good night. *JAMA* 301(8):868–869.

Szklo, M., and F. J. Nieto. 2007. *Epidemiology: Beyond the basics. 2nd ed*. Sudbury, Massachusetts: Jones and Bartlett Publishers.

Appendix A

Abbreviations and Acronyms

AAN	American Academy of Neurology
AANN	American Association of Neuroscience Nurses
ACC	American College of Cardiology
ACCF	American College of Cardiology Foundation
ACCP	American College of Chest Physicians
ACP	American College of Physicians
ACR	American College of Radiology
ACS	American Cancer Society
A/F	audit and feedback
AGA	American Gastroenterology Association
AGO	Attorney General's Office
AGREE	Appraisal of Guidelines Research and Evaluation instrument
AGS	American Geriatrics Society
AHA	American Heart Association
AHCPR	Agency for Health Care Policy and Research
AHIP	America's Health Insurance Plans
AHRQ	Agency for Healthcare Research and Quality
AMA	American Medical Association
ARRA	*American Recovery and Reinvestment Act*
ASCO	American Society for Clinical Oncology
ATS	American Thoracic Society
BCBS	Blue Cross Blue Shield
BMD	bone mineral density

CAD	coronary artery disease
CADTH	Canadian Agency for Drugs and Technology in Health
CDC	Centers for Disease Control and Prevention
CDS	computer-aided decision support
CDSC	CDS Consortium
CEBM	Centre for Evidence-Based Medicine
CER	comparative effectiveness research
CHF	chronic heart failure
CMS	Centers for Medicare & Medicaid Services
CMSS	Council of Medical Specialty Societies
COGS	Conference on Guideline Standardization
COI	conflict of interest
COMPUS	Canadian Optimal Medication Prescribing and Utilization Service
COPD	chronic obstructive pulmonary disease
CPG	clinical practice guideline
DoD	Department of Defense
EBM	evidence-based medicine
EHR	electronic health record
EPC	evidence-based practice center
ESC	European Society of Cardiology
FAO	Food and Agriculture Organization
FTE	full-time equivalent
GAP	Guidelines Applied in Practice
GDG	Guideline Development Group
GEM	Guideline Elements Model
GIN	Guidelines International Network
GLIF	Guideline Interchange Format
GRADE	Grading of Recommendations, Assessment, Development, and Evaluation
GWTG	American Heart Association's Get with the Guidelines
HHS	Department of Health and Human Services
HIT	health information technology
ICSI	Institute for Clinical Systems Improvement
IDSA	Infectious Diseases Society of America

| IOM | Institute of Medicine |
| INQRI | Interdisciplinary Nursing Quality Research Initiative |

KFF	Kaiser Family Foundation
KDIGO	Kidney Disease: Improving Global Outcomes
KDOQI	Kidney Disease Outcomes Quality Initiative
KWW	*Knowing What Works in Health Care*

MeSH	medical subject headings
MIPPA	*Medicare Improvements for Patients and Providers Act*
MMWR	*Morbidity and Mortality Weekly Report*
MSTF	U.S. Multi-Society Task Force on Colorectal Cancer

NCCN	National Comprehensive Cancer Network
NEJM	*New England Journal of Medicine*
NGC	National Guideline Clearinghouse
NGT	Nominal Group Technique
NHS	National Health System (UK)
NICE	National Institute for Health and Clinical Excellence (UK)
NIH	National Institutes of Health
NINR	National Institute of Nursing Research
NKF	National Kidney Foundation
NQF	National Quality Forum
NSAIDs	nonsteroidal anti-inflammatory drugs
NTIS	National Technical Information Service
NZGG	New Zealand Guidelines Group

PCORI	Patient-Centered Outcomes Research Institute
PGA	performance gap assessment
PRD	patient-reported data

| QIO | quality improvement organization |

| RCT | randomized controlled trial |
| REM | risk evaluation and management plan |

SCCM	Society for Critical Care Medicine
SIGN	Scottish Intercollegiate Guidelines Network
SORT	Strength of Recommendation Taxonomy
SR	systematic review

USPSTF   U.S. Preventive Services Task Force

VA   Veterans Administration

WHO   World Health Organization

Appendix B

Workshop Agenda and Questions to Panelists

January 11, 2010

Keck Center of The National Academies
500 Fifth Street, N.W., Room 100
Washington, DC

8:30 am   **PUBLIC FORUM**
Ethan Basch, American Society of Clinical Oncology
Christopher Bever, Chair, Quality Measures and
   Reporting, American Academy of Neurology
Terrie Cowley, President and Cofounder, The
   Temporomandibular Joint and Muscle Disorders
   Association
Steven Findlay, Senior Health Policy Analyst,
   Consumers Union
Merrill Goozner, Editor and Publisher, *Health Tech
   Review*/GoozNews.com
David Paul Harries, International Spine Intervention
   Society
Belinda Ireland, Senior Epidemiologist, BJC HealthCare
Norman Kahn, Executive Vice President and Chief
   Executive Officer, Council of
Medical Specialty Societies Lisa Mojer-Torres, Chair,
   Citizens' Advisory Council for the Division of
   Addiction Services, State of New Jersey (via
   telephone)

Katherine Nordal, Executive Director for Professional
     Practice, American Psychological Association
Jennifer Padberg, Vice President of Clinical Affairs,
     Infectious Diseases Society of America
William Rich, Medical Director of Health Policy,
     American Academy of Ophthalmology
Richard Rosenfeld, Guideline Development Task Force,
     American Academy of Otolaryngology–Head and
     Neck Surgery
Kathleen Sazama, President, Society for the
     Advancement of Blood Management
Aryeh Shander, President-Elect, Society for the
     Advancement of Blood Management
Christopher Wolfkiel, Director of Practice Guidelines,
     American College of Occupational and
     Environmental Medicine
Diana Zuckerman, President, National Research Center
     for Women & Families
Moderated by Dr. Sheldon Greenfield

COMMITTEE Q&A

10:05   **PANELS BEGIN**

10:05   *Panel One: Clinical Practice Guideline (CPG) Developers I*
          Alice Jacobs, M.D., American College of Cardiology and
               American Heart Association (ACC/AHA)
          Joan McClure, M.D., National Comprehensive Cancer
               Network
          Katrin Uhlig, M.D., M.S., National Kidney Foundation
          Jim Schibanoff, M.D., Milliman Care Guidelines
          Michael Bettmann, M.D., American College of
               Radiology
          Moderated by Dr. Sheldon Greenfield

11:30   *Panel Two: CPG Developers II*
          Ted Ganiats, M.D., Family Physician
          Sandra Zelman Lewis, Ph.D., American College of
               Chest Physicians
          Laura Fochtmann, M.D., American Psychiatric
               Association
          Vincenza Snow, M.D., American College of Physicians

William G. Adams, M.D., FAAP, American Academy of
   Pediatrics
Moderated by Dr. Sheldon Greenfield

12:50–1:20 pm   BREAK

1:20   *Panel Three: Government CPG Developers and Other*
            Government-Sponsored CPG Initiatives
            Vivian Coates, M.B.A., National Guidelines
               Clearinghouse/ECRI Institute
            David Atkins, M.D., M.P.H., Veterans Administration
            Nita L. Seibel, M.D., National Cancer Institute
            Denise Simons-Morton, M.D., Ph.D., National Heart,
               Lung, and Blood Institute
            Moderated by Dr. Earl Steinberg

2:45   *Panel Four: Organizational CPG Consumers*
            Marguerite Koster, M.A., M.F.T., Kaiser Permanente
               Southern California
            Kent Bottles, M.D., Institute for Clinical Systems
               Improvement
            Louis B. Jacques, M.D., Centers for Medicare &
               Medicaid Services
            Richard Kahn, Ph.D., Former Chief Scientific and
               Medical Officer of the American Diabetes Association
            Elizabeth Mort, M.D., M.P.H., Vice President, Quality
               and Safety, Massachusetts General Hospital and
               Massachusetts General Physicians Organization
            Moderated by Dr. Earl Steinberg

4:10   *Panel Five: Clinician and Patient CPG Consumers*
            Cynthia Boyd, M.D., M.P.H., Physician Expert in Multi-
               morbidity, Johns Hopkins Department of Medicine
            Arleen Brown, M.D., Ph.D., Physician Expert in Health
               Disparities, UCLA Internal Medicine
            Karen Kelly-Thomas, Ph.D., R.N., CAE, FAAN, National
               Association of Pediatric Nurse Practitioners
            Joyce Dubow, AARP
            Zobeida Bonilla, Ph.D., Our Bodies Ourselves
            Moderated by Dr. Earl Steinberg

5:30   Adjourn

Questions for the Panelists

- What do you believe are the biggest challenges clinical practice guidelines developers/users face today? For example:
  - o What do you do when the scientific evidence is absent or poor?
  - o How do you reconcile disagreements in evidence interpretation among guidelines?
  - o How do guidelines accommodate subgroups (e.g., older populations or persons with multimorbidities) whose treatment outcomes may differ from the average patient?
  - o Are there other challenges you believe are important?

- What topics and/or processes do you think the committee should consider in deriving quality standards for clinical practice guidelines? For example:
  - o What should the composition of CPG development panels, in particular the balance of methodologists, topical experts, and consumers, look like?
  - o What methods might be developed for determining which recommendations among those in a guideline should be applied to quality measures or electronic medical record decision prompts?
  - o Is there an available assessment tool that adequately rates both the level of the scientific evidence and strength of clinical recommendations that should be used as standard practice in guideline development?
  - o What administrative (e.g., accreditation) or legal approaches might improve the quality of clinical practice guidelines?
  - o What explicit approaches might harmonize guideline developers and increase guidelines convergence?
  - o What types of strategies might promote greater use of guidelines?
  - o Are there other characteristics of guideline standards you think are important for the committee to consider?

Appendix C

Clinical Practice Guideline
Appraisal Tools

TABLE C-1 Examples of Tools for Measuring the Quality of Clinical Practice Guidelines Development

Tool/Authors	Purpose	Tool

A Provisional Instrument for Assessing Clinical Practice Guidelines
 	
IOM (1992)
	To provide an explicit method for examining the soundness of clinical practice guidelines (CPGs) and to encourage their systematic development. The committee developed this instrument to be used as an education tool, a self-assessment tool, or a means of judging guidelines before their adoption.	Each of the tool's seven attributes subsumes a number of dimensions. Each dimension is assigned a "yes/no" score (the dimension is or is not represented in the guideline). If yes, an associated rating of satisfactory, conditionally satisfactory, or unsatisfactory (degree to which the dimension is satisfied) is given. If the dimension is not represented (i.e., "no" response), then a judgment of whether the omission is unimportant, minor, or major is made. If most responses to the questions are "satisfactory" (or "unimportant omissions"), one might reasonably conclude that such a guideline would be sufficient for most clinical situations. Alternatively, if most responses were unsatisfactory (or major omissions), one would probably argue that the guideline needed to be revised before it could be used effectively.
		
		The seven attributes include
		
		1. Clinical applicability
		  a. The guideline document describes the patient populations to which the guidelines are meant to apply.
		  b. The guideline document discusses complex clinical problems for the population(s) covered by the guidelines.
		  c. The guideline document gives a rationale for excluding patient population(s).
		2. Clinical flexibility
		  a. The guideline document provides specific information about situations in which clinical exceptions might be made in applying the guidelines.

b. The guideline document provides specific information about nonclinical situations in which exceptions might be made in applying the guidelines.

c. The guideline document discusses the role of patient preferences as they relate to healthcare decisions in the particular case that the guidelines cover.

d. The guideline document describes how patient preferences were taken into account during the guideline development process.

3. **Reliability/reproducibility**

a. The guidelines were subjected to independent review by experts or outside panels.

b. The guideline document explains the lack of independent review.

c. The guidelines were pretested in some manner.

4. **Validity: Definition and evaluation questions**

a. The guideline document specifically describes the method(s) used to collect (i.e., identify and retrieve) the scientific evidence on which recommendations are based.

b. The guideline document gives adequate references or citations to the sources of information used in developing the guidelines.

c. The guideline document discusses in general terms the strength of the scientific evidence on which recommendations are based.

d. The guideline document explicitly rates the strength of evidence.

continued

TABLE C-1 Continued

Tool/Authors	Purpose	Tool
		e. If a formal method of synthesis is used to combine the scientific evidence quantitatively or otherwise to develop summary outcome measures that reflect the strength of the scientific evidence, then the guideline document explicitly describes the method.
		f. Given that a formal method of synthesis is used to combine the scientific evidence quantitatively or otherwise to develop summary outcome measures, the guideline document explicitly reports the results of that synthesis.
		g. If formal expert or group judgment techniques are used to reach professional consensus, then the guideline document explicitly describes the techniques.
		h. Given that expert or group judgment method(s) are used to reach professional consensus, the guideline document explicitly gives information about the strength of professional consensus.
		i. The guideline document provides a qualitative description of the health benefits that are expected from a specific health practice.
		j. The guideline document provides a qualitative description of the potential harms or risks that may occur as a result of a specific health practice.
		k. The guideline document provides quantitative information or estimates about the health benefits to be expected as a result of a specific health practice.

l. The guideline document projects health benefits or outcomes in terms of additional life expectancy or similar measures, such as Quality-Adjusted Life Years (QUALYs).

m. The guideline document provides a quantitative description of the potential harms or risks that may occur as a result of a specific health practice.

n. The guideline document provides a qualitative description of the health costs or expenditures that are expected from a specific health practice.

o. The guideline document provides a quantitative description of the health costs or expenditures that are expected from a specific health practice.

p. If health benefits are projected in terms of additional life expectancy or similar measures, such as QUALYs, then the cost per unit of each identified benefit is estimated.

q. Generally, the estimates of the benefits, harms, and costs are consistent with the strength of the evidence presented in the guideline document.

r. The guideline document explicitly discusses the strength of the scientific evidence on which each major recommendation is based.

s. Each major recommendation is consistent with the estimated benefits, harms, and costs of the service or intervention (and thus with the strength of evidence).

t. The guideline document identifies other sets of guidelines that deal with the same clinical condition, technology, or topic.

u. The guideline document identifies possible conflicts among existing guidelines and the reasons for them.

continued

TABLE C-1 Continued

Tool/Authors	Purpose	Tool
		5. Clarity a. The guidelines describe the health condition to be prevented, detected, or treated in unambiguous terms. b. The guidelines describe the options for management of the health condition (i.e., the health practice and its alternatives) in unambiguous terms. c. If the guidelines give major recommendations, each is written in unambiguous terms. d. Recommendations are comprehensive, insofar as the evidence permits, and recommendations that might be expected are given. e. Recommendations are consistent (do not conflict with each other). f. The guideline document uses clear headings, indexes, lists, flow charts, or other devices to identify major topics discussed. g. The guideline document has a summary or abstract that accurately reflects the methods, content, and recommendations of the entire document. h. Each user of the guideline document can easily find each major recommendation. **6. Scheduled review** a. The guideline document gives a specific date for the scheduled review, gives other information concerning the procedure by which a scheduled review might be done, or gives a sunset or expiration date.

7. **Multidisciplinary process**

a. Persons with appropriate clinical and methodological disciplines participated in developing the guideline document—that is, a multidisciplinary approach was followed.

b. The guideline document explicitly notes any potential biases and/or conflicts of interests of the panel members, or states that biases and conflicts of interest were discussed among panel members or otherwise taken into account.

c. Overall, potential biases and/or conflicts of interest appear to be adequately balanced or otherwise accounted for in the guideline development process.

The guideline process describes the methods used to solicit views of interested parties not on the guidelines development panel and to present those views to the members of the panel.

AGREE consists of 23 key items organized in 6 domains. Each domain is intended to capture a separate dimension of guideline quality. Each item is rated on a 4-point Likert scale ranging from 4 (strongly agree) to 1 (strongly disagree). Domain scores are calculated by summing up all the scores of the individual items in a domain and by standardizing the total as a percentage of the maximum possible score for that domain. The six domain scores are independent and should not be aggregated into a single quality score; there is no threshold score that separates a "good" from a "not good" guideline. However, there is a section at the end for an overall assessment of the guideline, with a series of options (strongly recommend, recommend, would not recommend, and unsure).

continued

Appraisal of Guidelines for Research & Evaluation (AGREE)

Cluzeau, F.A., J. Burgers and an international group of researchers from 13 countries.

AGREE (2001)

To assess the quality of CPGs: how well a guideline is developed and reported. It does not assess the clinical content or quality of evidence of the recommendations.

TABLE C-1 Continued

Tool/Authors	Purpose	Tool
AGREE II Brouwers et al. (2010)		AGREE II represents an update of the original tool to improve its usability and methodological properties, namely its validity and reliability. AGREE II also includes 2 final overall assessment items that require the appraiser to make overall judgments of the practice guideline and consider how they rated the 23 items. AGREE II contains the same six domains as the original AGREE; changes to individual attributes of the domains are highlighted below in italics.

Scope and purpose

1. The overall objective(s) of the guideline is (are) specifically described.
2. The clinical question(s) covered by the guideline is (are) specifically described. *AGREE II: The health question(s) covered by the guideline is (are) specifically described.*
3. The patients to whom the guideline is meant to apply are specifically described. *AGREE II: The population (patients, public, etc.) to whom the guideline is meant to apply is specifically described.*

Stakeholder involvement

4. The guideline development group includes individuals from all the relevant professional groups.
5. The patients' views and preferences have been sought. *AGREE II: The views and preferences of the target population (patients, public, etc.) have been sought.*
6. The target users of the guideline are clearly defined.
7. The guideline has been piloted among target users. *AGREE II: Deleted item. Incorporated into user guide description of item 19.*

Rigor of development

8. Systematic methods were used to search for evidence.
   AGREE II: No change. Renumber to 7.
9. The criteria for selecting the evidence are clearly described.
   AGREE II: No change. Renumber to 8.
   a. *AGREE II: New item number 9. The strengths and limitations of the body of evidence are clearly described.*
10. The methods used for formulating the recommendations are clearly described.
11. The health benefits, side effects, and risks have been considered in formulating the recommendations.
12. There is an explicit link between recommendations and the supporting evidence.
13. The guideline has been externally reviewed by experts prior to its publication.
14. A procedure for updating the guideline is provided.

Clarity and presentation

15. The recommendations are specific and unambiguous.
16. The different options for management of the condition are clearly presented. *AGREE II: The different options for management of the condition or health issue are clearly presented.*
17. Key recommendations are easily identifiable.
18. The guideline is supported with tools for application.
   AGREE II: The guideline provides advice and/or tools on how the recommendations can be put into practice. Domain changes from clarity of presentation to applicability, and renumbered to 19.

continued

TABLE C-1 Continued

Tool/Authors	Purpose	Tool
		Applicability
		19. The potential organizational barriers in applying the recommendations have been discussed. *AGREE II: The guideline describes facilitators and barriers to its implementation. Change in order from 19 to 18.*
		20. The potential cost implications of applying the recommendations have been considered. *AGREE II: The potential resource implications of applying the recommendations have been considered.*
		21. The guideline presents key review criteria for monitoring and/or audit purposes. *AGREE II: The guideline presents monitoring and/or auditing criteria.*
		Editorial independence
		22. The guideline is editorially independent from the funding body. *AGREE II: The views of the functioning body have not influenced the content of the guideline.*
		Conflicts of interest of guideline development members have been recorded. *AGREE II: Competing interests of guideline development group members have been recorded and addressed.*
Cluzeau's "Appraisal Instrument" Cluzeau et al. (1999)	A critical appraisal instrument that assesses whether guideline developers have minimized biases inherent in creating guidelines and addresses requirements for effective dissemination and implementation.	A checklist containing 37 items categorized into 3 conceptual dimensions: rigor of development (validity and reproducibility), context and content (reliability, applicability, flexibility, and clarity), and application (implementation, dissemination, and monitoring strategies). The specific questions are answered yes, no, or unsure, which are then given values of 1, 0, and 0 respectively.

A guideline dimension score is obtained by calculating the mean of the appraiser's scores, and is then expressed as a percentage of the maximum possible score for that dimension in order to compare scores across the three dimensions. There is also a global qualitative assessment of the guidelines, with the options (strongly recommended, recommended, and not recommended) as a measure for overall quality.

Dimension one: Rigor of development process

1. Is the agency responsible for the development of the guidelines clearly identified?

2. Was external funding or other support received for developing the guidelines?

3. If external funding or support was received, is there evidence that potential biases of the funding body(ies) were taken into account?

4. Is there a description of the individuals (e.g., professionals, interest groups—including patients) who were involved in the guideline development group?

5. If so, did the group contain representatives of all key disciplines?

6. Is there a description of the sources of information used to select the evidence on which the recommendations are based?

7. If so, are the sources of information adequate?

8. Is there a description of the method(s) used to interpret and assess the strength of evidence?

continued

TABLE C-1 Continued

Tool/Authors	Purpose	Tool
		9. If so, is (are) the method(s) for rating the evidence adequate?
		10. Is there a description of the methods used to formulate the recommendations?
		11. If so, are the methods satisfactory?
		12. Is there an indication of how the views of interested parties not on the panel were taken into account?
		13. Is there an explicit link between the major recommendations and the level of supporting evidence?
		14. Were the guidelines independently reviewed prior to publication/release?
		15. If so, is explicit information given about the methods and how the comments were addressed?
		16. Were the guidelines piloted?
		17. If so, is explicit information given about the methods used and the results adopted?
		18. Is a date mentioned for reviewing or updating the guidelines?
		19. Is the body responsible for the reviewing and updating clearly indentified?
		20. Overall, have the potential biases of guideline development been adequately addressed?
		Dimension two: Context and content
		1. Are the reasons for developing the guidelines clearly stated?
		2. Are the objectives of the guidelines clearly defined?

3. Is there a satisfactory description of the patients to which the guidelines are meant to apply?

4. Is there a description of the circumstances (clinical or nonclinical) in which exceptions might be made in using the guidelines?

5. Is there an explicit statement of how the patient's preferences should be taken into account in applying the guidelines?

6. Do the guidelines describe the condition to be detected, treated, or prevented in unambiguous terms?

7. Are the different possible options for the management of the condition clearly stated in the guidelines?

8. Are the recommendations clearly presented?

9. Is there an adequate description of the health benefits that are likely to be gained from the recommended management?

10. Is there an adequate description of the potential harms or risks that may occur as a result of the recommended management?

11. Is there an estimate of the costs or expenditures likely to incur from the recommended management?

12. Are the recommendations supported by the estimated benefits, harms, and costs of the intervention?

Dimension three: Application of guidelines

13. Does the guideline document suggest possible methods for dissemination and implementation?

14. (National guidelines only) Does the guideline document identify key elements that need to be considered by local guideline groups?

continued

TABLE C-1 Continued

Tool/Authors	Purpose	Tool
		15. Does the guideline document specify criteria for monitoring compliance? 16. Does the guideline document identify clear standards or targets? 17. Does the guideline document define measureable outcomes that can be monitored?
Hayward et al.'s "Structured Abstracts of CPGs" Hayward et al. (1993)	A structured format for abstracts of articles describing CPGs to help readers assess the applicability, importance, and validity of any guideline.	The instrument includes eight topics essential to CPG developmental reporting. **Format for structured abstracts of CPGs** 1. Objective: The primary objective of the guideline, including health problem and the targeted patients, providers, and settings. 2. Options: The clinical practice options considered in formulating the guideline. 3. Outcomes: Significant health and economic outcomes considered in comparing alternative practices. 4. Evidence: How and when evidence was gathered, selected, and synthesized. 5. Values: Disclosure of how values were assigned to potential outcomes of practice options and who participated in the process. 6. Benefits, harms, and costs: The type and magnitude of benefits, harms, and costs expected for patients from guideline implementation.

7. Recommendations: Summary of key recommendations.
8. Validation: Report of any external review, comparison with other guidelines, or clinical testing of guideline use.

Sponsors: Disclosure of the persons who developed, funded, or endorsed the guideline.

The 25-item instrument uses a yes or no format to measure adherence to three broadly grouped quality criteria. A guideline's score reflects the total number of standards it satisfies, that is, "yes" responses (0–25).

Standards of guidelines development and format

1. Purpose of the guideline is specified.
2. Rationale and importance of the guideline are explained.
3. The participants in the guideline development process and their areas of expertise are specified.
4. Targeted health problem or technology is clearly defined.
5. Targeted patient population is specified.
6. Intended audience or users of the guideline are specified.
7. The principal preventive, diagnostic, or therapeutic options available to clinicians and patients are specified.
8. The health outcomes are specified.
9. The method by which the guideline underwent external review is specified.
10. An expiration date or date of scheduled review is specified.

Shaneyfelt's "Methodological Standards"

Shaneyfelt et al. (1999)

A tool to assess methodological quality of the development and reporting of clinical practice guidelines in the peer-reviewed medical literature.

continued

TABLE C-1 Continued

Tool/Authors	Purpose	Tool
		Standards of evidence identification and summary
		11. Method of identifying scientific evidence is specified.
		12. The time period from which evidence is reviewed is specified.
		13. The evidence used is identified by citation and referenced.
		14. Method of data extractions is specified.
		15. Method for grading or classifying the scientific evidence is specified.
		16. Formal methods of combining evidence or expert opinion are used and described.
		17. Benefits and harms of specific health practices are specified.
		18. Benefits and harms are quantified.
		19. The effect on healthcare costs from specific health practices is specified.
		20. Costs are quantified.
		Standards on the formulation of recommendations
		21. The role of value judgments used by the guideline developers in making recommendations is discussed.
		22. The role of patient preferences is discussed.
		23. Recommendations are specific and apply to the stated goals of the guideline.
		24. Recommendations are graded according to the strength of the evidence.
		Flexibility in the recommendations is specified.

SOURCES: AGREE (2001); Brouwers et al. (2010); Cluzeau et al. (1999); Hayward et al. (1993); IOM (1992); Shaneyfelt et al. (1999).

REFERENCES

AGREE. 2001. Appraisal of guidelines for research & evaluation (AGREE) instrument.

Brouwers, M. C., M. E. Kho, G. P. Browman, J. S. Burgers, F. Cluzeau, G. Feder, B. Fervers, I. D. Graham, S. E. Hanna, J. Makarski, and for the AGREE Next Steps Consortium. 2010. Development of the AGREE II, part 2: Assessment of validity of items and tools to support application. *CMAJ* 182(10):E472–E478.

Cluzeau, F. A., P. Littlejohns, J. M. Grimshaw, G. Feder, and S. E. Moran. 1999. Development and application of a generic methodology to assess the quality of clinical guidelines. *International Journal for Quality in Health Care* 11(1):21–28.

Hayward, R. S. A., M. C. Wilson, S. R. Tunis, E. B. Bass, H. R. Rubin, and R. B. Haynes. 1993. More informative abstracts of articles describing clinical practice guidelines. *Annals of Internal Medicine* 118(9):731–737.

IOM (Institute of Medicine). 1992. *Guidelines for clinical practice: From development to use.* Edited by M. J. Field and K. N. Lohr. Washington, DC: National Academy Press.

Shaneyfelt, T., M. Mayo-Smith, and J. Rothwangl. 1999. Are guidelines following guidelines? The methodological quality of clinical practice guidelines in the peer-reviewed medical literature. *JAMA* 281:1900–1905.

Appendix D

Systems for Rating the Strength of Evidence and Clinical Recommendations

TABLE D-1 Selected Approaches to Rating Strength of Evidence and Clinical Recommendations

System	Focus/ Audience	Systems for Rating Evidence Quality
International Approaches		
Grading of Recommendations Assessment, Development, and Evaluation (GRADE) Working Group (2009) A voluntary, international, collaboration	**Focus:** Diagnosis and therapy **Audience:** Guideline developers	**Grades of evidence** Randomized trial: High Observational study: Low Any other evidence: Very low **Decrease grade if** limitations in study quality, important inconsistency of results, uncertainty about the directness of the evidence, imprecise or sparse data, and high risk of reporting bias. **Increase grade if** a very strong association, evidence of a dose–response gradient, presence of all plausible residual confounding would have reduced the observed effect.

System for Rating Clinical Recommendations' Strength

Strong: Desirable effects clearly outweigh the undesirable effects, or clearly do not. Quality of evidence is high and other considerations support a strong recommendation.

Weak: Trade-offs are less certain—either because of low-quality evidence or because evidence suggests that desirable and undesirable effects are closely balanced. The quality of evidence is high and other considerations support a weak recommendation.

Based on:
- Quality of evidence.
- Uncertainty about the balance between desirable and undesirable effects.
- Uncertainty or variability in values or preferences.
- Uncertainty about whether the intervention represents a wise use of resources.

NOTE: Many organizations claim to use GRADE, but modify the system in the application of translating evidence into clinical recommendations or guidelines.

continued

TABLE D-1 Continued

System	Focus/ Audience	Systems for Rating Evidence Quality
Centre for Evidence-Based Medicine (CEBM) (2009) One of several UK centers with the aim of promoting evidence-based health care	**Focus:** Prevention, diagnosis, prognosis, therapy, differential diagnosis/ symptom prevalence, and economic and decision analyses	CEBM is currently working on updating its level of evidence rankings and providing further rationale for them, tentatively due to become available in January 2010. This approach has different evidence rating system depending on the type of healthcare intervention. For example, the following rating system is used for therapy interventions:
	Audience: Doctors, clinicians, teachers, and others	**Level 1a:** Systematic review (SR) of randomized controlled trials (RCTs) with homogeneity.[a] **Level 1b:** Individual RCT with narrow confidence interval. **Level 1c:** All or none case series.[b] **Level 2a:** SR with homogeneity of cohort studies. **Level 2b:** Individual cohort studies (including quality RCT; e.g., <80% follow-up). **Level 2c:** Outcomes research, ecological studies.[c] **Level 3a:** SR with homogeneity of case control studies. **Level 3b:** Individual case control study. **Level 4:** Case series (and poor-quality cohort and case control studies[d]). **Level 5:** Expert opinion without explicitly critical appraisal, or based on physiology, bench research, or "first principles."

System for Rating Clinical Recommendations' Strength

A: Consistent level 1 studies.

B: Consistent level 2 or 3 studies *or* extrapolations[e] from level 1 studies.

C: Level 4 studies *or* extrapolations from level 2 or 3 studies.

D: Level 5 evidence *or* troublingly inconsistent or inconclusive studies of any level.

continued

TABLE D-1 Continued

System	Focus/ Audience	Systems for Rating Evidence Quality
Scottish Intercollegiate Guidelines Network (SIGN) (2009)	**Focus:** All healthcare interventions **Audience:** National Health Service in Scotland	**Levels of evidence** 1++ High-quality meta-analyses, systematic reviews of RCTs, or RCTs with a very low risk of bias. 1+ Well-conducted meta-analyses, systematic reviews, or RCTs with a low risk of bias. 1– Meta-analyses, systematic reviews, or RCTs with a high risk of bias. 2++ High-quality systematic reviews of case control or cohort studies. ___ High-quality case control or cohort studies with a very low risk of confounding or bias and a high probability that the relationship is causal. 2+ Well-conducted case control or cohort studies with a low risk of confounding or bias and a moderate probability that the relationship is causal. 2– Case control or cohort studies with a high risk of confounding or bias and a significant risk that the relationship is not causal. 3 Non-analytic studies, such as case reports, case series. 4 Expert opinion.
New Zealand Guidelines Group (NZGG) (2007) Independent, not-for-profit	**Focus:** Screening, diagnosis, prognosis, and therapy **Audience:** Clinical practitioners, policy makers, and consumers	The body of evidence is the sum of the evidence of all the individual studies and the quality ratings of each study. **Good evidence:** From studies of strong design for answering the question addressed. **Fair evidence:** Reasonable evidence, but there may be minimal inconsistency, or uncertainty. **Expert opinion:** For some outcomes, trials or studies cannot be or have not been performed and practice is informed only by expert opinion.

System for Rating Clinical Recommendations' Strength

Guidelines are developed based on judgment on the consistency, clinical relevance, and external validity of the whole body of evidence.

A: At least one meta-analysis, systematic review, or RCT rated as 1++, and directly applicable to the target population; *or* a body of evidence consisting principally of studies rated as 1+, directly applicable to the target population, and demonstrating overall consistency of results.

B: A body of evidence including studies rated as 2++, directly applicable to the target population, and demonstrating overall consistency of results; *or* extrapolated evidence from studies rated as 1++ or 1+.

C: A body of evidence including studies rated as 2+, directly applicable to the target population and demonstrating overall consistency of results; *or* extrapolated evidence from studies rated as 2++.

D: Evidence level 3 or 4; *or* extrapolated evidence from studies rated as 2+.

Good practice points: Occasionally, guideline development groups find that there is an important practical point that they wish to emphasize, but for which there is not, nor is there likely to be, any research evidence. This typically will be where some aspect of treatment is regarded as such sound clinical practice that nobody is likely to question it. These are shown in the guideline as Good Practice Points, and are marked with a green check.

The grade of the recommendation is based on consideration of
- The design and quality of individual studies that have been identified.
- Quantity, consistency, applicability, and clinical impact of the body of evidence that is applicable to the guidelines question.
- The consensus of a guideline development team.

A: The recommendation is supported by GOOD evidence.

B: The recommendation is supported by FAIR.

C: The recommendation is supported by EXPERT opinion (published) only.

I: Evidence to make a recommendation is INSUFFICIENT.

continued

TABLE D-1 Continued

System	Focus/ Audience	Systems for Rating Evidence Quality
The Canadian Hypertension Education Program (2007) A Canadian volunteer, non-profit organization	**Focus:** Diagnosis and therapy related to hypertension **Audience:** Canadian Diabetes Association, Canadian Society of Nephrology, Canadian Coalition for High Blood Pressure Prevention and Control, The College of Family Physicians of Canada, Heart and Stroke Foundation of Canada, and Public Health Agency of Canada	**Uses flow charts to assess the evidence according to study methodology:** **A:** RCT with blinded assessment of outcomes, intention-to-treat analysis, adequate follow-up, and sufficient sample size to detect a clinically important difference with power >80%. **B:** Adequate subgroup analysis: Analysis was a priori, performed within an adequate RCT and one of only a few tested, and there was sufficient sample size within the examined subgroup to detect a clinically important difference. **C:** Systematic review or meta-analysis: Comparison arms are derived from head-to-head comparisons within the same RCT. **D:** Observational study or systematic review in which the comparison arms are derived from different placebo-controlled RCTs and then extrapolations are made across RCTs.

System for Rating Clinical Recommendations' Strength

A: The recommendation is supported by a-, b-, or c-level evidence. Clinically important outcomes and the study population is representative of the population in the recommendation.

B: The recommendation is supported by a-, b-, or c-level evidence. Clinically important or validated surrogate outcomes.

C: The recommendation is supported by a-, b-, c-, or d-level evidence. For levels a, b, and c evidence, the outcome is an unvalidated surrogate for clinically important outcomes. For level d evidence, there must be a clinically important outcome and study population representative of the recommendation population, or an outcome-validated surrogate, or results that are extrapolated from study population to real population.

D: Outcome is an unvalidated surrogate for clinically important population, or the applicability of the study is irrelevant.

continued

TABLE D-1 Continued

System	Focus/ Audience	Systems for Rating Evidence Quality
U.S. Approaches		
Institute for Clinical Systems Improvement (ICSI) (2003)	**Focus:** Prevention, diagnosis, or management of a given symptom, disease, or condition for individual patients under normal circumstances	**Primary reports of new data collection:** **A:** RCT. **B:** Cohort study. **C:** Nonrandomized trial with concurrent or historical controls, case control study, study of sensitivity and specificity of a diagnostic test, population-based descriptive study. **D:** Cross-sectional study, case series, or case report.
Collaborative of 57 medical groups in Minnesota		
	Audience: Minnesota healthcare providers and payers	

System for Rating Clinical Recommendations' Strength

Grade I: Good evidence
The evidence consists of results from studies of strong design for answering the question addressed. The results are both clinically important and consistent with minor exceptions at most. The results are free of any significant doubts about generalizability, bias, and flaws in research design. Studies with negative results have sufficiently large samples to have adequate statistical power.

Grade II: Fair evidence
The evidence consists of results from studies of strong design for answering the question addressed, but there is some uncertainty attached to the conclusion because of inconsistencies among the results from the studies or because of minor doubts about generalizability, bias, research design flaws, or adequacy of sample size. Alternatively, the evidence consists solely of results from weaker designs for the question addressed, but the results have been confirmed in separate studies and are consistent with minor exceptions at most.

Grade III: Limited evidence
The evidence consists of results from studies of strong design for answering the question addressed, but there is substantial uncertainty attached to the conclusion because of inconsistencies among the results from different studies or because of serious doubts about generalizability, bias, research design flaws, or adequacy of sample size. Alternatively, the evidence consists solely of results from a limited number of studies of weak design for answering the question addressed.

Grade not assignable: No evidence is available that directly supports or refutes the conclusion.

continued

TABLE D-1 Continued

System	Focus/ Audience	Systems for Rating Evidence Quality
Strength of Recommendation Taxonomy (SORT) (2004) Developed by the editors of *American Family Physician, Family Medicine, The Journal of Family Practice, Journal of the American Board of Family Practice,* and *BMJ-USA*	**Focus:** Prevention, screening, diagnosis, prognosis, and therapy **Audience:** Guideline developers, family practice, and other primary care providers	**Level 1:** Good-quality, patient-oriented evidence: • Diagnosis: Validated clinical decision rule,[f] SR/meta-analysis of high-quality studies, high-quality diagnostic cohort study. • Treatment, prevention, or screening: SR/meta-analysis of RCTs with consistent findings, high-quality individual randomized controlled all-or-none study. • Prognosis: SR/meta-analysis of good-quality cohort studies, prospective cohort study with good follow-up. **Level 2:** Limited-quality, patient-oriented evidence:[g] • Diagnosis: Unvalidated clinical decision rule, SR/meta-analysis of lower quality studies or studies with inconsistent findings, lower quality diagnostic cohort study or diagnostic case control study. • Treatment, prevention, or screening: SR/meta-analysis of lower quality clinical trials or studies with inconsistent findings, lower quality clinical trial, cohort study, case control study. • Prognosis: SR/meta-analysis of lower quality cohort studies or with inconsistent results, retrospective cohort study or prospective cohort study with poor follow-up, case control study, case series. **Level 3:** Other evidence: Consensus guidelines, extrapolations from bench research, usual practice, opinion, disease-oriented evidence (intermediate or physiologic outcomes only), or case series for studies of diagnosis, treatment, prevention or screening.

System for Rating Clinical Recommendations' Strength

A: Consistent and good-quality, patient-oriented evidence.* (Level 1)

B: Inconsistent or limited-quality, patient-oriented evidence.* (Level 2)

C: Consensus, usual practice, opinion, disease-oriented evidence,* or case series for studies of diagnosis, treatment, prevention, or screening. (Level 3)

continued

TABLE D-1 Continued

System	Focus/ Audience	Systems for Rating Evidence Quality
U.S. Preventive Services Task Force (USPSTF) (2008)	**Focus:** Prevention **Audience:** Guideline developers and users	**High:** The available evidence usually includes consistent results from well-designed, well-conducted studies in representative primary care populations. These studies assess the effects of the preventive service on health outcomes. This conclusion is therefore unlikely to be strongly affected by the results of future studies. **Moderate:** The available evidence is sufficient to determine the effects of the preventive service on health outcomes, but confidence in the estimate is constrained by factors such as • The number, size, or quality of individual studies. • Inconsistency of findings across individual studies. • Limited generalizability of findings to routine primary care practice. • Lack of coherence in the chain of evidence. As more information becomes available, the magnitude or direction of the observed effect could change, and this change may be large enough to alter the conclusion. **Low:** The available evidence is insufficient to assess effects on health outcomes. Evidence is insufficient because of • The limited number or size of studies. • Important flaws in study design or methods. • Inconsistency of findings across individual studies. • Gaps in the chain of evidence. • Findings not generalizable to routine primary care practice. • Lack of information on important health outcomes. More information may allow estimation of effects on health outcomes.

System for Rating Clinical Recommendations' Strength

A: The USPSTF recommends the service. There is high certainty that the net benefit is substantial. Offer or provide this service.

B: The USPSTF recommends the service. There is high certainty that the net benefit is moderate or there is moderate certainty that the net benefit is moderate to substantial. Offer or provide this service.

C: The USPSTF recommends against routinely providing the service. There may be considerations that support providing the service in an individual patient. There is at least moderate certainty that the net benefit is small. Offer or provide this service only if other considerations support the offering or providing the service in an individual patient.

D: The USPSTF recommends against the service. There is moderate or high certainty that the service has no net benefit or that the harms outweigh the benefits. Discourage the use of this service.

I statement: The USPSTF concludes that the current evidence is insufficient to assess the balance of benefits and harms of the service. Evidence is lacking, of poor quality, or conflicting, and the balance of benefits and harms cannot be determined. Read the clinical considerations section of USPSTF Recommendation Statement. If the service is offered, patients should understand the uncertainty about the balance of benefits and harms.

continued

TABLE D-1 Continued

System	Focus/Audience	Systems for Rating Evidence Quality
Professional Societies		
American College of Cardiology Foundation/American Heart Association (ACCF/AHA) (2009)	**Focus:** Prevention, diagnosis, or management of heart diseases or conditions **Audience:** Healthcare providers	**A:** Data derived from multiple randomized clinical trials or meta-analyses. **B:** Data derived from a single randomized trial, or non-randomized studies. **C:** Consensus opinion of experts, case studies, or standard of care.
American Academy of Pediatrics (AAP) (2004)	**Focus:** Pediatric guidelines for all healthcare interventions **Audience:** Guideline developers, implementers, and users	**A:** Well-designed, randomized controlled trials or diagnostic studies on relevant populations. **B:** RCTs or diagnostics studies with minor limitations; overwhelmingly consistent evidence from observational studies. **C:** Observational studies (case control and cohort design). **D:** Expert opinion, case reports, reasoning from principles. **X:** Exceptional situations where validating studies cannot be performed and there is a clear preponderance of benefit or harm.

System for Rating Clinical Recommendations' Strength

Any combination of classification of recommendation and level of evidence is possible. A recommendation can be Class I, based entirely on expert opinion (level C), or Class IIB, with level A evidence if based on multiple RCTs with divergent conclusions.

Class I: Conditions for which there is evidence and/or general agreement that a given procedure or treatment is useful and effective. Class 1 statements may read: should, is recommended, is indicated, or is useful/effective/beneficial.

Class II: Conditions for which there is conflicting evidence and/or a divergence of opinion about the usefulness/efficacy of a procedure or treatment.

    Class IIa: Weight of evidence/opinion is in favor of usefulness/efficacy. Class IIa statements may read: is reasonable, can be useful/effective/beneficial, is probably recommended, is probably indicated.

    Class IIb: Usefulness/efficacy is less well established by evidence/opinion. Class IIb statements may read: may/might be considered, may/might be reasonable, usefulness/effectiveness is unknown/unclear/uncertain/not well established.

Class III: Conditions for which there is evidence and/or general agreement that the procedure/treatment is not useful/effective and in some cases may be harmful. Class III statements may read: is not recommended, is not indicated, should not, is not useful/effective/beneficial, may be harmful.

Strong recommendation: The benefits of the recommended approach clearly exceed the harms (or in the case of a negative recommendation, the harms clearly exceed the benefits) and the quality of the evidence is either excellent or impossible to obtain (A, sometimes B, or X).

Recommendation: The benefits exceed the harms or vice versa, but the quality of evidence is not as strong (sometimes B, C, or X).

Option: The evidence quality that exists is suspect or not that well-designed; well-conducted studies have demonstrated little clear advantage of one approach versus another (A, B, C, or D).

No recommendation: There is both lack of pertinent evidence and an unclear balance between benefits and harms (D).

continued

TABLE D-1 Continued

System	Focus/ Audience	Systems for Rating Evidence Quality
American Academy of Neurology (AAN) (2004)	**Focus:** Screening, diagnosis, prognosis, and therapy of neurologic disorders **Audiences:** Neurologists, patients, payers, federal agencies, other healthcare providers, and clinical researchers	Similar ratings systems exist for diagnostic, prognostic, and screening interventions. Therapeutic interventions is one example: **Class I:** Prospective, RCT with masked outcome assessment, in a representative population. The following are required: (a) primary outcome(s) clearly defined, (b) exclusion/inclusion criteria clearly defined, (c) adequate accounting for dropouts and crossovers with numbers sufficiently low to have minimal potential for bias, (d) relevant baseline characteristics are presented and substantially equivalent among treatment groups or there is appropriate statistical adjustment for differences. **Class II:** Prospective matched group cohort study in a representative population with masked outcome assessment that meets a through d above *or* an RCT in a representative population that lacks one criteria in a through d. **Class III:** All other controlled trials (including well-defined natural history controls or patients serving as own controls) in a representative population, where outcome is independently assessed, or independently derived by objective outcome measurement. **Class IV:** Evidence from uncontrolled studies, case series, case reports, or expert opinion.

System for Rating Clinical Recommendations' Strength

A: Established as effective, ineffective, or harmful (or established as useful/predictive or not useful/predictive) for the given condition in the specified population.
Recommendation: Should be done or should not be done.
Translation of evidence to recommendation: Requires at least two consistent Class I studies.

B: Probably effective, ineffective, or harmful (or probably useful/predictive or not useful/predictive) for the given condition in the specified population.
Recommendation: Should be considered or should not be considered.
Translation of evidence to recommendation: Requires at least one Class I study or two consistent Class II studies.

C: Possibly effective, ineffective, or harmful (or possibly useful/predictive or not useful/predictive) for the given condition in the specified population.
Recommendation: May be considered or may not be considered.
Translation of evidence to recommendation: Level C rating requires at least one Class II study or two consistent Class III studies.

B: Data inadequate or conflicting. Given current knowledge, treatment (test, predictor) is unproven.
Recommendation: None.
Translation of evidence to recommendation: Studies not meeting criteria for Class I–Class III.

continued

TABLE D-1 Continued

System	Focus/ Audience	Systems for Rating Evidence Quality
American College of Chest Physicians (ACCP) (2009)	**Focus:** Diagnosis and management of chest disease **Audience:** Chest physicians	**High:** RCTs without important limitations or overwhelming evidence from observational studies. **Moderate:** RCTs with important limitations (inconsistent results, methodologic flaws, indirect, or imprecise) or exceptionally strong evidence from observational studies. **Low:** Observational studies or case series.
National Comprehensive Cancer Network (NCCN) (2008)	**Focus:** Prevention, diagnosis, and therapy related to cancer **Audience:** Oncologists and other healthcare providers	**High:** High-powered randomized clinical trials or meta-analysis. **Lower:** Runs the gamut from phase II to large cohort studies to case series to individual practitioner experience.

System for Rating Clinical Recommendations' Strength

1A: Strong recommendation. High level of evidence. Benefits outweigh the risks/burdens, or the risks/burdens outweigh the benefits.

1B: Strong recommendation. Moderate evidence. Benefits outweigh the risks/burdens, or the risks/burdens outweigh the benefits.

1C: Strong recommendation. Low or very low evidence. Benefits outweigh the risks/burdens, or the risks/burdens outweigh the benefits.

2A: Weak recommendation. High evidence, and the risks/burdens are evenly balanced with the benefits.

2B: Weak recommendation. Moderate evidence, and the risks/burdens are evenly balanced with the benefits.

2C: Weak recommendation. Low or very low evidence, and the risks/burdens are evenly balanced with the benefits. Or the balance of benefits to risks and burdens is uncertain.

Category 1: The recommendation is based on high-level evidence (e.g., randomized controlled trials), and there is uniform NCCN consensus.

Category 2A: The recommendation is based on lower level evidence and there is uniform NCCN consensus.

Category 2B: The recommendation is based on lower level evidence and there is non-uniform NCCN consensus (but no major disagreement).

Category 3: The recommendation is based on any level of evidence, but reflects major disagreement.

continued

TABLE D-1 Continued

System	Focus/ Audience	Systems for Rating Evidence Quality
Infectious Diseases Society of America (2001)	**Focus:** Healthcare interventions for infectious diseases **Audience:** Infectious disease clinicians	**I:** Evidence from >1 properly randomized, controlled trial. **II:** Evidence from >1 well-designed clinical trial, without randomization; from cohort or case-controlled analytic studies (preferably from >1 center); from multiple time-series; or from dramatic results from uncontrolled experiments. **III:** Evidence from opinions of respected authorities, based on clinical experience, descriptive studies, or reports of expert committees.

[a] Homogeneity refers to an SR that is free of worrisome variations (heterogeneity) in the directions and degrees of results between individual studies.

[b] Met when all patients died before the Rx became available, but some now survive on it, or when some patients died before the Rx became available, but none now die on it.

[c] A member of CEBM stated that this ranking requires further analysis, as well as more detailed explanation of what is meant by ecological and outcomes research.

[d] Poor-quality prognostic cohort study refers to one in which sampling is biased in favor of patients who already had the target outcome, or the measurement of outcomes is accomplished in < 80 percent of study patients, or outcomes were determined in an unblinded, non-objective way, or there is no correction for confounding errors.

[e] Extrapolations are where data are used in a situation that has potentially clinically important differences than the original study situation.

System for Rating Clinical Recommendations' Strength

A: Good evidence to support a recommendation for use.

B: Moderate evidence to support a recommendation for use.

C: Poor evidence to support a recommendation for use.

[f] Clinical decision rules (CDRs) are tools designed to help clinicians make bedside diagnostic and therapeutic decisions. The development of a CDR involves three stages: derivation, validation, and implementation.

[g] Patient-oriented evidence measures outcomes that matter to patients: morbidity, mortality, symptom improvement, cost reduction, and quality of life. Disease-oriented evidence measures intermediate, physiologic, or surrogate end points that may or may not reflect improvements in patient outcomes (e.g., blood pressure, blood chemistry, physiologic function, pathologic findings).

SOURCES: AAN (2004); ACCF/AHA (2009); ACCP (2009); CEBM (2009); Ebell et al. (2004); GRADE Working Group (2009); ICSI (2003); Kish (2001); NCCN (2008); NZGG (2007); SIGN (2009); Steering Committee on Quality Improvement Management (2004); Tobe et al. (2007); USPSTF (2008).

REFERENCES

AAN (American Academy of Neurology). 2004. Clinical practice guidelines process manual. http://www.aan.com/globals/axon/assets/3749.pdf (accessed July 28, 2009).

ACCF/AHA (American College of Cardiology Foundation/American Heart Association). 2009. Methodology manual for ACCF/AHA guideline writing committees. http://www.americanheart.org/downloadable/heart/12378388766452009Met hodologyManualACCF_AHAGuidelineWritingCommittees.pdf (accessed July 29, 2009).

ACCP (American College of Chest Physicians). 2009. The ACCP grading system for guideline recommendations. http://www.chestnet.org/education/hsp/grading System.php (accessed July 28, 2009).

CEBM (Centre for Evidence-Based Medicine). 2009. Oxford Centre for Evidence-based Medicine—Levels of Evidence (March 2009). http://www.cebm.net/index.aspx?o=1025 (accessed July 28, 2009).

Ebell, M. H., J. Siwek, B. D. Weiss, S. H. Woolf, J. Susman, B. Ewigman, and M. Bowman. 2004. Strength of recommendation taxonomy (SORT): A patient-centered approach to grading evidence in medical literature. *American Family Physician* 69(3):548–556.

GRADE Working Group (Grading of Recommendations Assessment, Development, and Evaluation Working Group). 2009. Grading the quality of evidence and the strength of recommendations http://www.gradeworkinggroup.org/intro.htm (accessed July 20, 2009).

ICSI (Institute for Clinical Systems Improvement). 2003. Evidence grading system. http://www.icsi.org/evidence_grading_system_6/evidence_grading_system_ pdf_.html (accessed September 8, 2009).

Kish, M. A. 2001. Guide to development of practice guidelines. *Clinical Infectious Diseases* 32(6):851–854.

NCCN (National Comprehensive Cancer Network). 2008. About the NCCN clinical practice guidelines in oncology. http://www.nccn.org/professionals/physician_ gls/about.asp (accessed September 8, 2009).

NZGG (New Zealand Guidelines Group). 2007. Handbook for the preparation of explicit evidence-based clinical practice guidelines. http://www.nzgg.org.nz/download/files/nzgg_guideline_handbook.pdf (accessed September 4, 2009).

SIGN (Scottish Intercollegiate Guidelines Network). 2009. SIGN 50: A guideline developer's handbook http://www.sign.ac.uk/guidelines/fulltext/50/index.html (accessed July 20, 2009).

Steering Committee on Quality Improvement Management. 2004. Classifying recommendations for clinical practice guidelines. *Pediatrics* 114(3):874–877.

Tobe, S. W., R. M. Touyz, and N. R. C. Campbell. 2007. The Canadian Hypertension Education Program—a unique Canadian knowledge translation program. *Canadian Journal of Cardiology* 23(7):551–555.

USPSTF (U.S. Preventive Services Task Force). 2008. Grade definitions. http://www.ahrq.gov/clinic/uspstf/grades.htm (accessed July 28, 2009).

Appendix E

Literature Search Strategy: Clinical Practice Guidelines

SEARCH CONTENT

1. OVID Databases:
   a. Ovid MEDLINE® In-process and Other Non-indexed Citations and Ovid MEDLINE® (1950–Present): The U.S. National Library of Medicine's® bibliographic database providing information on medicine, nursing , dentistry, veterinary medicine, allied health, and preclinical sciences.
   b. EMBASE (1988–September 2009): A biomedical database produced by Elsevier. EMBASE covers nearly 5,000 active journals, of which nearly 2,000 are unique compared with MEDLINE.
   c. PsycINFO (1987–September 2009): A database containing a wide variety of scholarly publications in the behavioral and social sciences.
   d. Global Health (1973–2009): An abstracting and indexing database dedicated to public health research and practice.

2. Web of Science (1900–2009): Current and retrospective coverage in the sciences, social sciences, arts, and humanities. Its content covers more than 10,000 of the highest impact journals worldwide, including Open Access journals, and over 110,000 conference proceedings.

3. Electronic Tables of Contents:
   a. E-mail alerts via LexisNexis and OVID of the following pub-
      lications' tables of contents: EPC reports, *JAMA, NEJM, J of
      Clin Epi, BMJ, Health Affairs, Health Qual Life Out, Med Care,
      Milbank Q, Med Decis Making, Health Serv Res, Eval Health
      Prof, Qual Saf Health Care, Med Care Res Rev, J Health Econ,
      Health Econ, Health Policy Plan, J of Health Polit Polic, Health
      Policy, J of Public Health Pol, Implementation Science.*

4. Grey Literature (conference proceedings, PowerPoint presentations, unpublished manuscripts):
   a. NTIS (1964–present): A resource for accessing the latest re-
      search sponsored by the United States and select foreign
      governments.
   b. New York Academy of Medicine.
   c. GIN Database.
   d. Government clinical practice guideline development groups:
      AHRQ, NICE, SIGN, NZGG, GAC.
   e. Search websites of AGREE, GRADE, AHIP, BCBS Tec, Kaiser
      Permanente, KFF, RWJF.

SEARCH PROCESS

1. Search each database uniquely.
2. Limit to English and human studies.
3. Search clinical practice guideline or practice guideline in the
   subject heading.
4. Search the following in the title or abstract: consensus development or decision making, development, evaluation, implementation, comorbidities, heterogeneity, policy or law or legal,
   implications, tool or taxonomy, reimbursement, measurement,
   performance or performance measures, consumer or public,
   grading or rating, issues or concerns, methods, quality, electronic medical record (EMR) or computer decision support system (CDSS).
5. Two independent reviewers track subject headings and key
   terms in key articles and use to further electronic search.
6. Two independent reviewers screen article abstracts and full
   articles to determine if they fit the committee's charge.
7. Handsearch cited references within key identified literature.
8. Manage references in EndNote.

Appendix F

Committee Biographies

Sheldon Greenfield, M.D. (*Chair*), an internationally recognized leader in quality of care and health services research, is the Donald Bren Professor of Medicine and Executive Codirector of the Health Policy Research Institute at the University of California–Irvine. Dr. Greenfield's research has focused on primary care outcomes, quality of chronic disease care, patient participation in care, and assessment of comorbidity. He was the 1995 recipient of the PEW Health Professions Commission Award for lifetime achievement in Primary Care Research. Dr. Greenfield is a recipient of the Glaser Award of the Society of General Internal Medicine and the 1999 Novartis Global Outcomes Leadership Award. Dr. Greenfield is the 2006 recipient of the Founders Award by the American College of Medical Quality. Dr Greenfield was elected to the Institute of Medicine (IOM) in 1996. He chaired the IOM Committee on Guidance for Designing a National Health Care Disparities Report, and chaired the IOM cancer survivorship report. He was chair of the National Diabetes Quality Improvement Alliance. He was also cochair of the IOM Committee on Initial National Priorities for Comparative Effectiveness Research. His current research focus is on performance assessment at the individual physician level, heterogeneity of treatment effects, and quality of chronic disease care for ethnic and racial minorities. He received his undergraduate degree from Harvard College and his M.D. from the University of Cincinnati College of Medicine.

Earl P. Steinberg, M.D., M.P.P. (*Vice Chair*), is senior vice president for Integrated Health Strategy and Evaluation at WellPoint, Inc., and president and chief executive officer CEO of Resolution Health, Inc., a wholly owned subsidiary of WellPoint Inc. He is a nationally recognized expert in evaluation and improvement of the quality and efficiency of health care. He has had considerable experience in development of evidence-based clinical practice guidelines and of performance measures based on them, as well as with interventions to increase compliance with them. At the IOM, Dr. Steinberg served on the Committee on Medicare Payment Methodology for Clinical Laboratory Services and the Evaluation Panel of the Council on Health Care Technology. Prior to joining Resolution Health, Dr. Steinberg was vice president of Covance Health Economics and Outcomes Services, Inc., where he was also codirector of the Outcomes Studies Group and director of the Quality Assessment and Improvement Systems Division. Dr. Steinberg spent 12 years as a full-time faculty member at Johns Hopkins University, where he was a professor of medicine, a professor of health policy and management, and the founder and director of the Johns Hopkins Program for Medical Technology and Practice Assessment. Dr. Steinberg has spent many years on the Blue Cross Blue Shield Association's National Medical Advisory Panel. Dr. Steinberg received his A.B. from Harvard College, his M.D. from Harvard Medical School, and his M.P.P. from the Kennedy School of Government at Harvard. He performed his residency training in internal medicine at the Massachusetts General Hospital.

Andrew Auerbach, M.D., M.P.H., is associate professor of medicine in residence at the University of California–San Francisco (UCSF) and a clinician–researcher in the Division of Hospital Medicine. He joined the faculty at UCSF as the nation's first hospitalist clinician–researcher in 1998. Dr. Auerbach retains an active clinical practice as a hospitalist—both as a ward attending and as an attending on the medical consultation service. In addition to leading clinical practice standardization and order-entry projects at UCSF, his research there has focused primarily on assessments of patient outcomes in different systems of care, with a special interest in the hospitalist model. Additionally he has concentrated on novel approaches to clinical practice translation through enhanced performance measurement. He did his medical residency training at Yale-New Haven Hospital, and a Fellowship in General Internal Medicine at Harvard and Beth Israel Deaconess Medical Center.

Jerome Avorn, M.D., is a professor of medicine at Harvard Medical School and chief of the Division of Pharmacoepidemiology and

Pharmacoeconomics at Brigham and Women's Hospital. Previously, Dr. Avorn was a member of the IOM Committee on Health Promotion and Disability Prevention for the "Second Fifty." An internist, geriatrician, and pharmacoepidemiologist, his research centers on medication use, with particular reference to elderly patients and chronic disease. Topics of particular interest include drug approval; transparency; scientific, policy, and social determinants of physician prescribing practices; efficacy and effectiveness of specific medications; compliance by patients with prescribed regimens; methods to improve the appropriateness of drug prescribing and drug taking; quantification of risks and benefits of drugs; and pharmaceutical cost-effectiveness analysis. The research unit Dr. Avorn founded includes faculty representing the disciplines of epidemiology, internal medicine, health services research and policy, social science, and biostatistics. Dr. Avorn has served on several national and international panels as an expert on the determinants and outcomes of medication use. He is a past president of the International Society for Pharmaco-Epidemiology. He is author or coauthor of more than 250 papers in the medical literature on medication use and its outcomes and of the book, *Powerful Medicines: The Benefits, Risks, and Costs of Prescription Drugs* (Knopf, 2004), now in its 11th printing. He attended Columbia College and Harvard Medical School, and completed a residency in Internal Medicine at the Beth Israel Hospital in Boston.

Robert S. Galvin, M.D., M.B.A., is chief executive officer of Equity Healthcare (EH), which oversees the management of health care for firms owned by private equity companies. The focus is on using purchasing power to create innovative ways to achieve higher value in health care through improved population health, clinical quality, and delivery system reforms. EH encompasses more than 30 companies with healthcare spending exceeding $2 billion annually. Before joining Blackstone, Dr. Galvin was executive director of health services and chief medical officer for General Electric (GE) for 15 years. At GE he was in charge of the design and the financial and clinical performance of GE's health programs. He was also responsible for health policy strategies affecting employees. Dr. Galvin is a nationally recognized leader in the areas of market-based health policy and financing, quality measurement, and payment reform. His work has been widely published in the *New England Journal of Medicine* and *Health Affairs*. He was a cofounder of the Leapfrog Group and founder of Bridges to Excellence, two innovative nonprofits that have helped drive the quality agenda. Dr. Galvin is on the IOM Board on Health Care Services and has served on numerous IOM committees. He is on the Board of Directors of the National Quality Forum. He is a member of the National Advisory Council for the Agency for Healthcare Research and Quality (AHRQ) and is a former member of the Defense Health Board. Dr. Galvin is also an adjunct professor of medicine and health policy at Yale. His work has received awards from the National Business Group on Health, the Healthcare Financial Management Association, and the National Coalition for Cancer Survivorship. He is a fellow of the American College of Physicians.

Raymond Gibbons, M.D., is the Arthur M. and Gladys D. Gray Professor of Medicine at the Mayo Clinic. Dr. Gibbons' research interests include coronary disease, myocardial infarct quantitation, and cardiac imaging. He was president of the American Heart Association (AHA) from 2006 to 2007. He served previously as chair of the American College of Cardiology/AHA Task Force on Practice Guidelines, chair of two ACC/AHA guideline writing committees (stable angina and exercise testing), and chair of the Committee on Scientific Sessions of the AHA. After graduate work in Mathematics at Oxford and Biomedical Engineering at the Johns Hopkins University, he completed his M.D. at Harvard Medical School, where he was a member of the Harvard–Massachusetts Institute of Technology (MIT) Program in Health Sciences and Technology. He then completed a residency in Internal Medicine at Massachusetts General Hospital and a Cardiology Fellowship at Duke University Medical Center.

Joseph Lau, M.D., is professor of medicine, professor of clinical and translational science (Sackler School for Graduate Biomedical Sciences), and adjunct professor (Friedman School for Nutrition Sciences and Policy) at Tufts University. He directs the Tufts Evidence-based Practice Center (EPC), one of 14 AHRQ-designated evidence-based practice centers. Dr. Lau also directed the Boston Branch of the U.S. Cochrane Center (1996–2007) and the evidence review team of the National Kidney Foundation's clinical practice guidelines program (2000–2009). He has published more than 200 journal articles and book chapters on applications and methodologies of systematic review and meta-analysis, along with more than 50 evidence reports and technology assessments. He has served on a Food and Drug Administration advisory panel, an IOM committee (Framework for Evaluating the Safety of Dietary Supplements), and as a drafting expert on an FAO/WHO workgroup. He is on the editorial boards of the *European Journal of Clinical Investigation, Journal* *of Research Synthesis Methods, Journal of Nutrition,* and *BMC Medical Research Methodology.* He is a member of the Association of American Physicians. Dr. Lau received his M.D. from the Tufts University School of Medicine.

Monica Morrow, M.D., is chief of the Breast Service in the Department of Surgery and the Anne Burnett Windfohr Chair of Clinical Oncology at Memorial Sloan-Kettering Cancer Center and a professor of surgery at Weill Medical College of Cornell University. At the IOM, she was a member of the Committee on Cancer Survivorship: Improving Care and Quality of Life After Treatment, the National Cancer Policy Board, and the Committee to Conduct a Workshop on the Development of a Research Agenda Concerning Medical Diagnosis and Treatment of Breast Cancer. Her current research interest is focused on how treatment choices for breast cancer surgery are made. She is the surgical editor of the textbook *Diseases of the Breast* and a coauthor of *Breast Cancer for Dummies.* Dr. Morrow cochaired the joint committee of the American College of Surgeons, American College of Radiology, and College of American Pathologists on Standards for Breast Conserving Therapy for Invasive Breast Cancer and for Ductal Carcinoma In Situ in 2002 and 2007. She is currently serving as secretary of the Society for Surgical Oncology. She received her M.D. from Jefferson Medical College in Philadelphia.

Cynthia Mulrow, M.D., M.Sc., is clinical professor of medicine at the University of Texas Health Science Center at San Antonio and the senior deputy editor of the *Annals of Internal Medicine.* She was previously director of the San Antonio VA Cochrane Center, program director of the Robert Wood Johnson Foundation's Generalists Physician Scholars Program, and director of the San Antonio Evidence-based Practice Center. Dr. Mulrow has served on the editorial boards of the *British Medical Journal, American Journal of Medicine, ACP Journal Club,* and *Clinical Evidence-based Therapeutics Compendium.* She is a member of the IOM and serves on the IOM Board on Health Care Services. She was a member of the IOM Subcommittee on the Health Outcomes of the Uninsured. She was also a member of the U.S. Preventive Services Task Force and has served on guideline development panels for RAND and AHRQ. Dr. Mulrow's expertise is in clinical methodology, information synthesis, systematic reviews, and clinical guidelines. She participates in multiple groups that develop reporting standards for medical research, including CONSORT (reporting standards for trials), PRISMA (reporting standards for systematic reviews), and STROBE (reporting standards for observational studies).

Arnold J. Rosoff, J.D., is a professor of legal studies and business ethics and a professor of healthcare management at the Wharton School of the University of Pennsylvania (Penn) as well as a Senior Fellow at Penn's Leonard Davis Institute of Health Economics. His research and writing have covered a diverse range of subjects in health law and policy, including legal, regulatory, and business aspects of health care; legal implications of evidence-based medicine (i.e., the law's recognition and treatment of clinical practice guidelines, or CPGs); ethical issues in public health practice; legal and regulatory controls on healthcare cost and quality; patients' rights, especially "informed consent" issues; pharmacy benefits management; private and governmental financing of health care, including health maintenance organizations; antitrust issues in health care; and comparative healthcare systems. His recent research has focused on U.S. attempts to achieve universal health care (UHC); analysis of GINA, the *Genetic Information Non-Discrimination Act of 2008*; implications of consumer-driven health care; and applications of information technology to healthcare delivery and financing. He is currently writing a comparative study of the path that five nations—Argentina, France, Italy, Japan, and Singapore—took to reach their national commitment to UHC, analyzing how their experiences may be useful to U.S. efforts to achieve UHC. Professor Rosoff's most direct connection with this committee's subject matter is the research and writing he has done on the promotion of evidence-based medicine and its implementation through CPGs and computerized clinical decision support systems. Professor Rosoff has an undergraduate degree in Economics from Penn and a J.D. from Columbia University.

John Santa, M.D., M.P.H., is director of the Consumer Reports Health Ratings Center. The Center provides unbiased analyses and ratings to help consumers make informed healthcare decisions. Objective, up-to-date comparisons of health services, drugs, devices, and consumer experiences from credible internal and external testing sources are used. Dr. Santa was the administrator of the Office of Oregon Health Policy and Research from 2000 to 2003, focusing on evidence-based approaches to treatments and prescription drugs. He previously worked in medical leadership positions for hospitals, physician groups, and health insurers. In each position he focused on clinical guidelines, quality improvement, and performance. Dr. Santa has taught in multiple environments, including medical school, residency training, and graduate courses, most recently serving as an associate professor at Oregon Health & Science University and

Portland State University. He has practiced primary care internal medicine in solo, group, and institutional settings, most recently at the Portland VA.

Richard Shiffman, M.D., MCIS, is professor of pediatrics and associate director of the Center for Medical Informatics at Yale School of Medicine. He is a Fellow of the American College of Medical Informatics and the American Academy of Pediatrics. Dr. Shiffman has served on several guideline development panels for national professional societies and on the American Academy of Pediatrics Steering Committee on Quality Improvement and Management. He was also a member of the Board of the Guidelines International Network. Dr. Shiffman convened the Conference on Guideline Standardization in 2002 and leads the group that developed the Guideline Elements Model, a standard for electronic representation of guideline documents. Currently, he leads the GLIDES Project, an AHRQ-sponsored initiative to define best practices for transforming guidelines into clinical decision support. Dr. Shiffman served his pediatric residency at Children's Hospital of Philadelphia and the Riley Children's Hospital in Indianapolis. He was Chief Resident in Pediatrics at the University of Colorado Medical Center and completed a Fellowship there in Developmental Pediatrics. Dr. Shiffman practiced primary care pediatrics in Colorado for 12 years. He earned a Master's in Computer Information Systems from the University of Denver. He completed a Fellowship in Medical Informatics in the Harvard–MIT program before joining the faculty at Yale.

Wally Renee Smith, M.D., is a general internist, professor of internal medicine, and chair of the Division of Quality Health Care at Virginia Commonwealth University (VCU). He is also scientific director of the VCU Center on Health Disparities and vice president of the Foundation for Integrity and Responsibility in Medicine. Dr. Smith was an inaugural Robert Wood Johnson Generalist Physician Faculty Scholar. He has been on the editorial boards of the journals *Medical Decision Making* and the *Journal of Continuing Education in the Health Professions.* He is past North American editor of *Clinical Governance,* an international journal, and past deputy editor of the *Journal of General Internal Medicine.* He has served on study sections or expert leadership panels for the National Institutes of Health (NIH), AHRQ, National Library of Medicine, Veterans Administration Health Services Research and Development Program, and the Health Resources and Services Administration. He is past secretary of the Society of General Internal Medicine and past Trustee for the Society for Medical Decision Making. He has authored more than 70 peer-reviewed publications and 40 externally funded grants or contracts. He is an expert in disparities issues in clinical and health services, clinical epidemiology, and medical decision making.

Walter F. Stewart, Ph.D., M.P.H., is associate chief research officer for the Geisinger Health System and director of the Center for Health Research. The Center has a strong focus on health services research and the use of information technology in reengineering care processes, as well as other areas of emphasis, including comparative effectiveness studies, population-level validation of biomarkers for clinical decision making, and formalizing system-level processes for translating research to practice. Prior to taking his position at Geisinger in 2003, Dr. Stewart started IMR, a privately held clinical trials and survey research company. The company developed novel approaches to population-based clinical trials that accelerated Phase III time lines. IMR was acquired in 1998 by AdvancePCS, where Dr. Stewart was vice president of Research and Development and director of the Center for Work and Health from 1998 to 2002. The latter focused on employer direct and indirect costs from illness and development of tools to measure lost productivity. Between 1983 and 1995, Dr. Stewart was a full-time faculty member of the Johns Hopkins Bloomberg School of Public Health, where he maintains an adjunct professor position. Since his tenure at Hopkins, Dr. Stewart has studied the epidemiology of common chronic episodic conditions (e.g., migraine, bladder control, gastrointestinal disorders), the work impact of these conditions, and the progressive central nervous system disorders. He has authored more than 240 journal articles and book chapters on these and other subjects. Dr. Stewart earned his Ph.D. in Epidemiology from Johns Hopkins University, an M.P.H. from the University of California–Los Angeles, and a Bachelor's Degree in Psychobiology from the University of California–Riverside.

Ellen Stovall is a 39-year survivor of three diagnoses of cancer. Following 18 years as CEO of the National Coalition for Cancer Survivorship (NCCS), she stepped down from that position and currently serves as the NCCS senior health policy advisor. Ms. Stovall has served on a number of IOM committees and was vice chair of the IOM's National Cancer Policy Board as well as vice chair of its Committee on Cancer Survivorship. In that role, Ms. Stovall coedited the IOM report titled *From Cancer Patient to Cancer Survivor: Lost in Transition*. She was also a member of the IOM National Cancer Policy

Forum. In addition, Ms. Stovall served as vice chair of the Robert Wood Johnson Foundation's National Advisory Committee for Pursuing Perfection: Raising the Bar for Health Care Performance. She also served on the Board of Directors of the National Committee for Quality Assurance and the Leapfrog Group. In an appointment she received from President Bill Clinton, Ms. Stovall was a member of the National Cancer Institute's National Cancer Advisory Board, an appointment she received from President Bill Clinton. Ms. Stovall is a founder and, along with Dr. Patricia Ganz, cochairs the Cancer Quality Alliance (CQA)—an alliance formed in 2005 to promote collaboration among stakeholders who are committed to cancer quality improvement. CQA activities include fostering the rapid development and implementation of measures appropriate for quality improvement and accountability; enhancing mechanisms for data collection; promoting development and adoption of oncology electronic medical records; and endorsing a blueprint for optimal cancer care. Recognizing a need for the voice of cancer survivors to be heard during the national debate over healthcare reform, the Cancer Leadership Council was convened in 1993 under her direction. Ms. Stovall currently serves as cochair with Dr. George Isham of the National Quality Forum's Measures Prioritization Committee, and is a member of the IOM Committee on Standards for Developing Trustworthy Clinical Practice Guidelines.

Brian L. Strom, M.D., M.P.H., holds numerous leadership positions at the University of Pennsylvania. He is George S. Pepper Professor of Public Health and Preventive Medicine, founding chair and professor of biostatistics & epidemiology, professor of medicine, professor of pharmacology, founding director of the Center for Clinical Epidemiology & Biostatistics, founding director of the Graduate Group in Epidemiology & Biostatistics, vice dean for Institutional Affairs School of Medicine, and senior advisor to the Provost for Global Health Initiatives. He is a member of the IOM and chair of the IOM Committee to Assess the Safety and Efficacy of the Anthrax Vaccine and the Committee on the Smallpox Vaccination Program Implementation, He is also a member of the Committee to Review the CDC (Centers for Disease Control and Prevention) Anthrax Vaccine Safety and Efficacy Research Program and the Committee to Review the NIOSH (National Institute for Institutional Safety and Health) Traumatic Injury Research Program. Internationally known for multiple areas of clinical epidemiology, Dr. Strom's major career interest is pharmacoepidemiology, specifically looking at adverse drug reactions and medical errors. He is editor of the field's major text (now going into its fifth edition), was president of the International Society of Pharmacoepidemiology (ISPE), and is now editor in chief for *Pharmacoepidemiology and Drug Safety*, ISPE's official journal. He received his M.D. from Johns Hopkins University School of Medicine and his M.P.H. from the University of California–Berkeley.

Marita G. Titler, Ph.D., R.N., FAAN, is a professor and associate dean of Clinical Scholarship & Practice Development and the Rhetaugh G. Dumas Endowed Chair at the University of Michigan School of Nursing. At the IOM, she was a member of the Forum on the Science of Health Care Quality Improvement and Implementation. Her experience includes serving as director of the Translation Core of the $2.34 million federally funded Gerontological Nursing Interventions Research Center and the Institute of Translational Practice on the $3.49 million Department of Veterans Affairs Center of Excellence and the Implementation of Innovative Strategies in Practice (CRIISP) at the University of Iowa. She served as Principal Investigator and completed a $1.5 million AHRQ grant on Evidence-Based Practice: From Book to Bedside, competing continuation From Book to Bedside: Promoting and Sustaining EBPs in the Elders, a $1.3 million NINR grant on Nursing Interventions & Outcomes in 3 Older Populations, and the Robert Wood Johnson Foundation INQRI grant on Impact of System-Centered Factors, and Processes of Nursing Care on Fall Prevalence and Injuries from Falls. She is currently Principal Investigator on the Robert Wood Johnson Foundation INQRI grant Moving Beyond Fall Risk Scores: Implementing and Evaluating the Impact of an Evidence-Based "Targeted Risk Factor Fall Prevention Bundle"; Co-Principal Investigator on the $2.8 million National Cancer Institute Grant on Cancer Pain in Elders: Promoting EBPs in Hospices; Investigator on AHRQ R03, Call Light Responsiveness and Effect on Inpatient Falls and Patient Satisfaction; Co-Investigator on an NIH R41 Advancing Patient Call Light Systems to Achieve Better Outcomes; Co-Investigator on a Department of Health and Human Services, NIH U01, Dissemination of Tobacco Tactics versus 1-800-QUIT-NOW for Hospitalized Smokers; Co-Investigator on the Department of Defense grant Assessing the Effect of a Handheld Decision-Support Device for Reducing Medication Errors; and Co-Investigator on the University of Michigan Clinical and Translational Science Award for the Michigan Institute of Clinical and Health Research.